I0462081

THE POLITICS OF DRESS
IN SOMALI CULTURE

African Expressive Cultures

Patrick McNaughton, editor

Associate editors

Catherine M. Cole
Barbara G. Hoffman
Eileen Julien
Kassim Koné
D. A. Masolo
Elisha Renne
Zoë Strother

The Politics of Dress
in Somali Culture

Heather Marie Akou

Indiana University Press · *Bloomington & Indianapolis*

This book is a publication of

Indiana University Press
601 North Morton Street
Bloomington, Indiana 47404-3797 USA

www.iupress.indiana.edu

Telephone orders   800-842-6796
Fax orders   812-855-7931
Orders by e-mail   iuporder@indiana.edu

© 2011 by Heather M. Akou
All rights reserved

No part of this book may be reproduced
or utilized in any form or by any means,
electronic or mechanical, including
photocopying and recording, or by
any information storage and retrieval
system, without permission in writing
from the publisher. The Association
of American University Presses'
Resolution on Permissions constitutes
the only exception to this prohibition.

♾ The paper used in this publication
meets the minimum requirements of
the American National Standard for
Information Sciences—Permanence
of Paper for Printed Library
Materials, ANSI Z39.48-1992.

Manufactured in the United
States of America

Library of Congress Cataloging-
in-Publication Data

Akou, Heather Marie.
  The politics of dress in Somali
culture / Heather Marie Akou.
    p. cm.
  Includes bibliographical
references and index.
  ISBN 978-0-253-35629-1 (cl. : alk.
paper) — ISBN 978-0-253-22313-5 (pbk.
: alk. paper) 1. Clothing and dress—
Somalia. 2. Clothing and dress—Political
aspects—Somalia. 3. Somalia—
Social life and customs. I. Title.
  GT1589.S63A56 2011
  391.0096773—dc22

                        2010050627

1 2 3 4 5   16 15 14 13 12 11

To all of my children,
Jamilah, Jibril, and Abdul-Khaliq

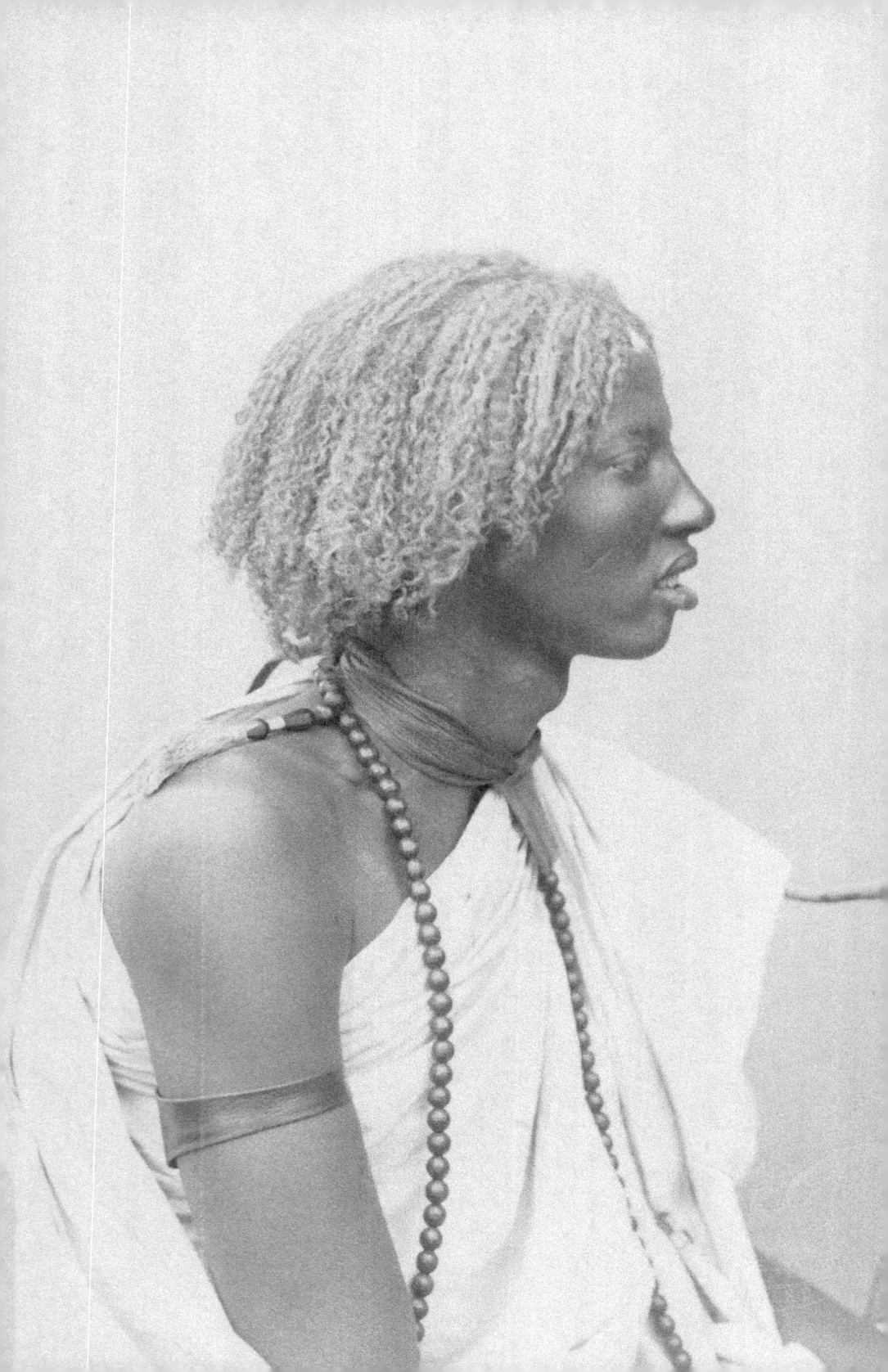

Contents

Illustrations follow pages 49 and 117.

Acknowledgments

During the decade I spent doing research on Somali dress and then publishing my work (including this book), I was blessed to be supported by many fine people. First and foremost, I would like to thank my friend and colleague, Dr. Theresa Winge, who not only gave me valuable feedback from the very beginning, but shared her time, her home, and her wicked sense of humor, and gave me her shoulder to cry on when I needed it. I really cannot thank her enough.

My mentor, Dr. Joanne Eicher, is the person who fanned the sparks of my initial interest in Somali dress. It was an honor to work with her at the end of her very illustrious career at the University of Minnesota. She gave me space to develop my ideas, but was always there to support me when I needed help. I would also like to thank Dr. Catherine (Kate) Daly, who started working with Somali women in Minnesota not long after I did. At a time when there was no other person in the world doing research on Somali dress, it was invaluable having a more experienced scholar to discuss my ideas with.

At Indiana University, my colleagues in African Studies have been a true pleasure to work with. Specifically, I would like to thank a few of my informal mentors—A. B. Assensoh, John Hanson, Beverly Stoelje, and Maria Grosz-Ngate—who took time out of their busy schedules to help me navigate through the process of tenure and securing a book contract. John Johnson shared some of his experiences doing field research in Somalia in the 1960s and '70s; I hope he enjoyed our conversations as much as I did! I would also like to thank my contemporaries in African Studies, Beth Buggenhagen,

Lauren MacLean, Michelle Moyd, and Marissa Moorman, for their unfailing support. I could not have asked for a more intelligent and enjoyable group of colleagues.

The members of my writing group, Kalpana Shankar and Barbara Andrews, were truly fantastic as well. This book would not be the same without them! They believed in me, but also pushed me to dig deeper, as did Mara Margolis, who introduced me to them. Other fine scholars who have critiqued my research and publications on Somali dress over the years include Marilyn DeLong, Rose Brewer, Jean Allman, Suzanne Gott, Doran Ross, Beverly Gordon, Karen Tranberg-Hanson, Sally Helvenston-Gray, and Helen Bradley-Foster as well as numerous anonymous reviewers (including the reviewers for this book). Ladan Affi and Abdi Kusow were very encouraging in the early stages of my research and helped me gain valuable insight into the lives of Somalis in North America.

This book would not have been possible without the support of my editor, Dee Mortensen, and Indiana University Press. I would also like to thank my copy editor, Emma Young, for her excellent suggestions. It has been an honor to work with such respectful and distinguished professionals.

Finally, I would like to thank my family, including my parents, my husband, and especially my children. More than anyone else, they have shaped me into the person I am today. The laughter and hugs of my daughter, Jamilah, and my son, Khaliq, have sustained me through even the most difficult circumstances. This book is dedicated to them as well as to Jibril, the precious child and sibling we lost along the way.

Timeline of Events

1st century AD*	*The Periplus of the Erythrean Sea* describes trade between the Greco-Egyptian Empire and Somali territory.
1st–8th centuries	Declining influence of Egypt; growth of the Roman Empire; trade along the Red Sea and southern Arabia controlled by the Axumites.
8th century	Early migrations to Somali territory from the Middle East.
739	Exiled Shi'ites from Oman settle in Somali territory.
10th century	Exiles from present-day Saudi Arabia, Iran, Iraq, Yemen, and South Asia settle along the Benadir coast, intermarrying with the local population and founding or building up several urban areas.
1331	Ibn Battuta visits Mogadishu; notes that the Sultan is a non-Arab who speaks Arabic.
1280–1368	Emperors of the Chinese Yuan dynasty encourage traders to sail directly to the Horn of Africa.
Late 1400s	Portuguese explorer Vasco da Gama "discovers" Horn of Africa.
Early 1500s	Cities along the Somali coastlines are attacked and looted as the Portuguese try to gain control over Indian Ocean trade.
1670s	The northern coast of Somali territory becomes a peripheral part of the Turkish Ottoman Empire.
mid-1700s	Emergence of the Geledi Sultanate in southern Somali territory; cities along the Benadir coast decline as power shifts to the interior.

*All dates are AD.

early 1800s   Swahili Arabs take control over trade along the east coast of Africa; beginning of European exploration in the Horn of Africa.

1832   Sultan of Oman builds a palace on the island of Zanzibar.

1839   British take control over the port of Aden in present-day Yemen.

mid-1800s   Sultan of Oman builds fortifications for trade and the collection of taxes in Mogadishu, Marka, Brava, Kismayo, and Warsheikh.

1854   Richard Burton travels through northern Somali territory disguised as an Arab merchant.

1860s   The British navy begins disrupting the slave trade in East Africa; height of the slave trade along the Benadir coast.

1869   Suez Canal opens; trade along the Red Sea expands rapidly.

1884   First treaties signed between Somali clans and Europeans.

1887   Ethiopia takes control over Harar and the *Haud* (grasslands) region.

1889   Italian Somaliland founded when control over the Benadir coastal cities is transferred from the island of Zanzibar to Italy.

1891   British Somaliland founded in northern Somali territory; other areas become part of French Somaliland (now Djibouti) and British East Africa (now Kenya).

1897   Great Britain, Italy, France, Germany, Ethiopia, and Zanzibar sign treaties establishing fixed national borders in the Horn of Africa.

1900   Start of the "dervish wars" between the armies of Ethiopia, British Somaliland, and the Somali leader Sayyid Mohammed Abdulle Hassan.

1903   Final enforcement of ban on slave trading in Italian Somaliland.

1920s and 1930s   The fascist government of Italian Somaliland takes over land for banana, coffee, peanut, sesame, rice, and cotton plantations in the region between the Juba and Shabelle rivers; thousands of Somalis (particularly former slaves) are exploited as forced laborers.

1949   British and Italian Somaliland are combined into a trusteeship of the United Nations.

1954   First municipal elections; national flag adopted.

1960   Somalia becomes an independent nation.

1963   Somali Airlines partners with the Italian airline Alitalia.

1965   Siad Barre appointed commander-in-chief of the National Army.

1969   Second president assassinated; Siad Barre emerges as a new leader and dedicates the country to Scientific Socialism.

1970s and 80s   Somalis work as migrant laborers in the oil-rich Persian Gulf states.

1972   Somali becomes a written language; start of a widespread literacy campaign financed by the government.

1974   As part of the Cold War, Somalia signs a treaty with the Soviet Union in exchange for money, weapons, and advisors.

      Somalia joins the League of Arab States.

mid-1970s   Islamist organization al-Itihaad al-Islamiya is formed.

1976   Formation of the Somali Revolutionary Socialist Party (SRSP); out of 20,000 members, 60% are women.

1977   Haile Selassie is overthrown and replaced by Mengistu Haile Mariam in Ethiopia; Ethiopia becomes a Marxist country.

      Somalia invades Ethiopia in an effort to take over the Ogaden; Soviet Union withdraws support and the movement is defeated.

1979   The Iranian Revolution brings an Islamist government to power; enthusiasm for Islamism spreads throughout the Islamic world.

      The Somali Salvation Democratic Front (SSDF) is formed from a base in Ethiopia.

1981   The Somali National Movement (SNM) is formed in London.

1986   Siad Barre is involved in a severe car accident and is airlifted to a hospital in Saudi Arabia; in an act of defiance, the SNM begins stamping Somalia's currency with its own symbol.

1988   The government signs a peace treaty with Ethiopia; SNM rebels are forced to re-enter the country; rebels occupy Hargeisa and the city is bombed by government-controlled forces, killing more than 10,000 people.

1989   The opposition group United Somali Congress (USC) is formed with the intention of uniting all rebels to overthrow Siad Barre.

1990   USC splits into factions over a leadership disagreement; factions begin shelling each other and the city of Mogadishu.

1991   Siad Barre is forced to leave Mogadishu; the central government of Somalia collapses; massive numbers of Somalis are killed in the fighting or die from starvation; refugee camps are established in other parts of East Africa; Kenya takes in 400,000 Somalis.

1992   Siad Barre is forced out of Somalia altogether; beginning of U.S. humanitarian mission "Operation Restore Hope."

1993   Eighteen U.S. soldiers are killed and their bodies dragged through the streets of Mogadishu; public opinion turns against the mission.

1994   In March, the last U.S. troops pull out of Somalia.

1995   Siad Barre dies in exile in Nigeria.

mid-1990s   Beginning of large-scale Somali migration to the United States.

2000   The first Somali mall, Suuqa Karmel, opens in Minneapolis.

2001   A second Somali mall, the African International Marketplace, opens in Saint Paul; Mahamoud Wardere runs for mayor of Minneapolis; September 11 destruction of the World Trade Center towers in New York City; Somalia declared a "harbor for terrorists" by the U.S. government.

2002   As part of the U.S. War on Terrorism, some Somali businesses are shut down (including al-Barakaat, used to send money to relatives in East Africa); all male Somalis who are not citizens are forced to register with Immigration and Naturalization Services, resulting in a number of deportations.

2004   The African International Market closes, but a much larger Somali mall opens in South Minneapolis.

2006   Senator Barack Obama is photographed in northern Kenya wearing Somali dress.

2008   Stories circulate in the media about piracy off the coast of Somalia and young Somali men leaving the United States to train for armed jihadist movements in Somalia.

THE POLITICS OF DRESS
IN SOMALI CULTURE

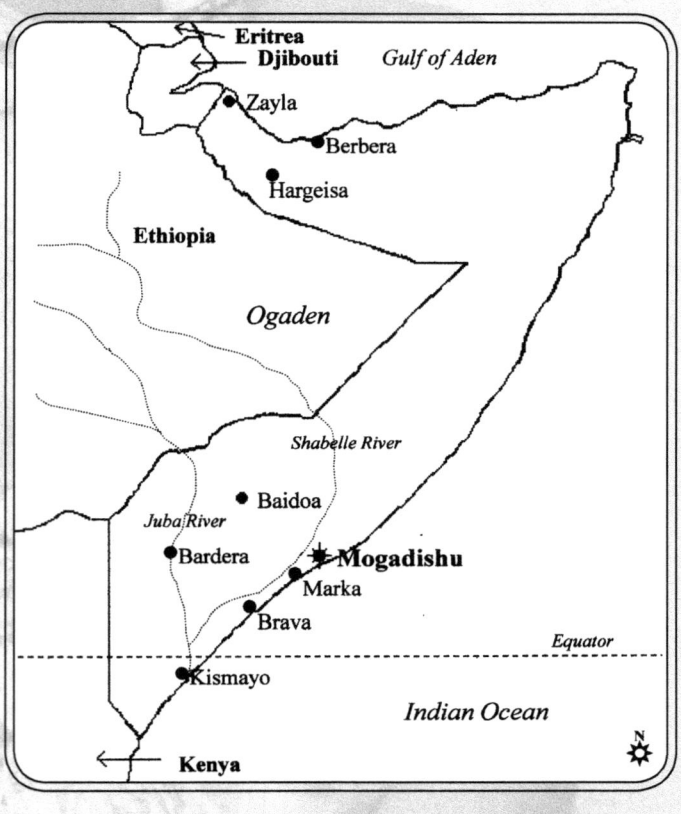

The Political Symbolism of Dress

Oh my god what is the world coming to?! Sen. Barack Obama has shocked
the world by daring to dress in traditional African clothes, and wear a Turban too! To many this will look 'Muslim' and of course we all know
that's officially A Bad Thing. How can he be President now . . . ?

—*pickledpolitics.com, February 25, 2008*

In September 2006—five months before he announced his candidacy for
President of the United States—Senator Barack Obama went on a diplomatic
tour of Africa. One stop included the city of Dire Dawa in southeastern Ethiopia, which had recently been hit by a flash flood that "killed more than 600
people and displaced tens of thousands."[1] U.S. naval engineers working under
the Combined Joint Task Force, an anti-terrorism group, had erected tents
to shelter people affected by the flood, including many Somalis.[2] The most
notable stop on Obama's tour, however, was Kenya—the birthplace of his
father and a strategic location in the U.S.-led "War on Terrorism." In honor of
his visit to the northeast province of Wajir (an area near Somalia with a high
concentration of Somalis), elders dressed him in a traditional Somali outfit
consisting of several pieces of white fabric—one piece wrapped around his
lower body (like a sarong), a second piece wrapped in an X across his chest,
and a third piece wrapped around his head as a turban. A photographer captured Obama wearing this ensemble over his own khakis and polo shirt. This
wrapped style of dress dates back to the nineteenth century and conveys a
strong sense of Somali nomadic identity, connected with Islamic and anti-

FACING PAGE The Horn of Africa; Somali territory historically included present-day
Somalia, northeastern Kenya, southern Djibouti, and southeastern Ethiopia.

1

colonial symbolism. Other dignitaries visiting the region—including several Kenyan presidents and a representative of the British monarchy—have been dressed in the same, now ceremonial, style.[3]

During Obama's campaign for U.S. president, this photograph of him in Somali dress—which had been displayed on the East Africa–based media website www.geeskaafrika.com for months—was held up by some as "proof" that Obama was indeed Muslim (despite his statements to the contrary) and a "non-citizen" with connections to terrorist organizations. Obama's campaign manager, David Plouffe, accused rivals working for the campaign of then Senator Hillary Clinton of releasing the photograph, calling it a "disturbing pattern" of dirty tricks and "the most shameful, offensive fear-mongering we've seen from either party in this election."[4] Regardless of the story behind it (which most Americans were probably not aware of) this photograph was widely circulated through television and the Internet, becoming an important visual symbol in the 2008 U.S. presidential election.

Clearly, many Americans were willing to believe that Barack Hussein Obama was hiding the truth about his religious background, but why did they read the outfit in the photograph as Muslim? Alec Rawls, author of the blog *Error Theory* argued, "There really isn't much excuse for reporters not knowing that this is symbolically Muslim attire." The key piece of information, according to Rawls, was the turban—a garment worn by members of Al-Qaeda in anti-American propaganda videos. Ignoring the fact that turbans are worn by hundreds of thousands of men around the world (including non-Muslim Sikhs and Hindus), this perspective reduces the turban to a symbol of "Muslim" and by extension "terrorist" identity.[5] The complicated history behind this outfit and the intentions of the Somali elders who dressed Obama were barely considered; American viewers merely looked at the turban and read their own meanings into it.

Why so much fuss about a piece of clothing? This high-profile case is one clear example of a process that occurs constantly even in everyday life—the politicizing of dress, the body, and appearance. In *The Empire of Things,* Fred Myers observed that "cultural objects externalize values and meanings embedded in social processes, making them available, visible, or negotiable for further action by subjects."[6] Using dress, identities like "Somali" and "American" can be embodied and played out, making these abstract concepts available for critique and refinement. A nation cannot be seen or felt, but it can be expressed through the body; shouldn't a candidate for president of the United

States look "American"? Even ordinary people are often expected to fit the mold.[7] Hair-straightening was a nearly universal practice among African Americans until the civil rights movement. Conversely, whites with dreadlocks have often endured criticism for deviating from the norm.[8] Whether or not a person intends for his or her own dress to be viewed as a political symbol, the perspective of the viewer is also important—sometimes more important—in the creation of meaning surrounding an item of dress. The Somali men who dressed Obama had one set of meanings in mind (to dignify him as an honorary nomad and warrior), but many non-Somali viewers had a completely different interpretation.

An Introduction to the Somali People

This book is about a complicated set of issues involving politics, refugees, globalization, gender, and Islam as a global political/religious system that both unites and separates, much like the Cold War created a gulf between the West and Communist countries. Somalis—as much as they have fought for survival and tried to determine their own fate—have often been like passengers in a small boat adrift in a stormy sea. In a little over two hundred years—the span of time that is necessary to understand the history and meaning of the outfit given to Obama—Somalis have gone from herding camels to hijacking supertankers with grenade launchers. If the "discovery" of this photograph had occurred several months later—during the height of the "Somali pirate" story—Americans might have been more interested in the Somali connection. For the most part, when Somalia has been featured in the American media the images have been distinctly unflattering—the site of *Black Hawk Down* (a book that was turned into a movie and later a popular video game), a "harbor for terrorists," part of the "War on Terrorism," a failed state, a training ground for jihadists, and now the home of modern-day pirates "living the high life" on ransom money while millions of people in the Horn of Africa suffer from drought and endemic violence.[9] Looking through the lens of dress, this book tells a parallel but somewhat different story—one of succeeding generations of Somalis using material culture to navigate through complicated social changes. Most Somalis are not pirates, just trying to live a dignified life filled with friends and family and all of the things that are important to most ordinary people. Although the act of dressing is both ordinary and very personal, dress nonetheless communicates in ways that are very public and political. These symbols can and should be analyzed to gain a greater understanding of Somali culture and politics beyond the limited depictions offered by the mass media.

When I moved to Minnesota in 1994 to attend college, Somalis were just starting to arrive from the refugee camps in East Africa. I remember seeing them as I rode the bus through downtown Minneapolis. From the women's clothing I could tell they were Muslims; from the color of their skin and their language I could tell they were Africans (not African Americans), but who were they? I really had no idea. Their clothing was unlike anything I had seen during my college semester abroad in Mali (in West Africa). By the time I started graduate school at the University of Minnesota I knew they were Somalis. When I decided to focus my research on Somali dress, I discovered that there hadn't been a systematic study since the late 1800s.[10] In fact, there was nothing really spectacular that would have attracted most researchers interested in dress—no embroidery, no printing, no complicated weaving. Even before European colonization much of their clothing and jewelry had been imported. Why study Somali nomadic dress that is simply made of plain, white, American-made factory cloth?

From my perspective, Somali dress is a fascinating case study in globalization. Somalis were far ahead of their time when it comes to borrowing items of dress from other cultures, combining them in new ways (a practice that postmodern writers call *bricolage*) and making them an integral part of their own culture. I was also impressed by the layers of religious and political symbolism in Somali dress. Some people would tell me that being covered head-to-toe was "religiously mandated" or even "traditional," but others would scoff and tell me about the dangers of "Arabization" and dressing like non-Somalis. Everybody had a strong opinion! Educating myself about the history of Somalia and Somali dress was the only way to unravel this ball of contradictions. The more I learned the more interested I became.

Somalia was a nation named after the Somali people, created by joining the colonies of British and Italian Somaliland. Although there has been debate over who exactly the "Somalis" are and where they came from,[11] two things are clear. First, the nation of Somalia included both Somalis and a fair number of people who were non-Somali or partly Somali—the descendants of settlers from the Middle East and South Asia, slaves from Central Africa, European expatriates, and the *Saab*, a caste of artisans who might have been the original inhabitants of that territory. Second, as a result of colonization, the Somali people were artificially separated into what are now four different nations: southern Djibouti, southeastern Ethiopia, Somalia, and northeastern Kenya (see map). Therefore, in this book I use the term "Somali" instead of "Somalian," since the latter term refers only to the citizens of Somalia.

Somali territory occupies a large portion of the Horn of Africa, the pointed section of East Africa that extends out into the Indian Ocean. Much of this area is a desert, although there is an agricultural area in southern Somalia fed by two rivers as well as an important grasslands region called the *Haud*, which is now in Ethiopia. Since the northern edge of Somali territory is less than 100 miles from the Arabian Peninsula, Somalis have a long history of connections with the Middle East and were very early adopters of Islam. This is a point of pride for many Somalis, albeit one that comes with baggage; many are just as concerned as Americans about the rise of Islamic fundamentalism in East Africa—its strict interpretations of the religion conflict with many aspects of traditional Somali history and culture.

Since the start of the civil war in the late 1980s and the total collapse of the government in 1991, the Somali people have been dispersed all over the world. Some of the largest refugee communities outside of East Africa are in Italy and the United Kingdom (the former colonial powers), but there are also sizable numbers of Somalis in Canada, the United States, South Africa, Australia, and the Middle East. In the Netherlands, a Somali woman (Ayaan Hirsi Ali) was elected to Parliament. In the United States, the highest concentrations of Somalis are found in Minnesota, followed by Columbus, Ohio; Seattle, Washington; and Phoenix, Arizona. This is due in part to immigration policies, but also to the Somali nomadic practice of "scouting" new locations to live: instead of looking for pastures, refugees have been looking for housing, jobs, and low crime rates. In spite of the freezing cold winters followed by intense, humid summers, Minnesota was attractive to Somalis looking for friends and family, a good public education system, jobs, and the availability of goods such as *halal* meat (essentially, a Muslim version of kosher, "permitted" meat where the animals are ritually slaughtered) and clothing imported from East Africa. From this point of view, Minnesota offered virtually everything a refugee might hope to obtain in lieu of returning home.

Without their own functioning government Somalis are extremely vulnerable to the winds of political, economic, and cultural change happening in other parts of the world. Because of this, Somalis must carefully consider the images they project through their dress. Should Somalis wear Islamic dress and align themselves more closely with the Islamic world? This path might offer personal satisfaction and hope for positive change in Somalia, but it also puts many refugees in conflict with the societies in which they have resettled. The constitution of the United States, for instance, is designed to protect freedom of religious expression, but in schools and workplaces many Somali refugees feel intense pressure to learn English and wear Western styles of dress. For men, this is typically not a very difficult choice; pants and shirts had been the dominant form of dress for men in Somalia for several decades. The same is not true for Somali women, who bear the major burden of keeping their families and culture intact through cues such as language, ritual, and dress. Choosing what to wear in the United States involves a complex intercultural negotiation.

Uncovering Clues about Somali Dress

Studying Somali dress under these conditions has been captivating, but also extremely challenging. Museums and libraries in Somalia were destroyed by the civil war. Although there are some collections of material objects in Europe and North America that are useful for understanding dress in the nineteenth and early twentieth centuries, more contemporary objects and images are difficult to come by.[12] Fieldwork in Somalia—particularly southern Somalia where the fighting has been heaviest—is nearly impossible. Speaking with refugees, I quickly realized that many were preoccupied with the day-to-day challenges of trying to make a new life. One middle-aged woman I met at a public forum on employment issues had earned an engineering degree in Somalia and worked for the United Nations. In the United States, however, she found it nearly impossible to obtain any kind of job since her first language was not English and employers would not recognize the degrees she had earned in Somalia. Teachers and doctors had found themselves working as cab drivers and parking lot attendants just to support their families. An American colleague in Minnesota who was interviewing Somali women about dress and employment issues found that many were suffering not just from a lack of employment but from post-traumatic stress after being raped or witnessing the murder of family members.[13] Being a non-native speaker with no family ties to Somalis, I was not exactly welcomed with open arms. Perhaps if I had converted to Islam while I still lived in Minnesota I would have found more common ground (I did later convert, but not until March 2007, almost three years after leaving Minnesota). After the events of September 11, 2001, and the backlash that followed, many refugees seemed suspicious of my motives for doing "research." How could they be sure I wasn't working for the FBI? Terrifying experiences with the government of Somalia had quickly turned into fears about the motivations of the U.S. government.

Because of these challenges I had to be very creative in my search for information about Somali dress. Although I spent a lot of time at the Somali malls buying garments and talking to merchants, I also took tie-dye lessons from an elder Somali woman (it turned out that she had been taught by an American, perhaps someone from the Peace Corps), attended community and university seminars on issues pertaining to immigration in Minnesota, did archival research at the Smithsonian and the Library of Congress, and bought objects with images of dress such as postcards, stamps, and currency on the Internet. Living in Saint Paul I encountered Somalis on an almost daily basis. In the process of collecting data I built a binder with hundreds of images. It was exciting to show this to Somalis who had never been in Somalia or left as children, since many had never seen these kinds of artifacts and archival images before. This research began in 2000, with the most intense activity occurring in 2003. I also continued to add more data and analysis after I completed my graduate degrees, based on valuable feedback from numerous readers.

One concept that helped to guide and expand my research was the definition of "dress" as set forth by Joanne Eicher in the *Routledge International Encyclopedia of Women*:

> Dress is a system of nonverbal communication that enhances human beings' interaction as they move in space and time. As a coded sensory system, dressing the body occurs when human beings modify their bodies visually or through other sensory measures by manipulating color, texture, scent, sound, and taste or by supplementing their bodies with articles of clothing, accessories, and jewelry.[14]

Although objects like clothing and jewelry can be seen, certain parts of Somali dress appeal to the other senses. Frankincense, for example, has been collected in Somali territory for centuries and is still in use today. When chewed it becomes a breath freshener; when burned the smoke is used to change the scent of the body, clothing, and interior spaces. Hairstyles are not "clothing," but they are part of dress. Somalis have a rich history of age-

and gender-based practices of bleaching, dyeing, straightening, braiding, and shaving their hair into various shapes. Some other important aspects of traditional Somali dress, such as amulets, sandals, weapons, shields, and even circumcision (a very controversial body modification) also fall outside the bounds of "clothing," but can be analyzed for their cultural and political symbolism.[15] This broad definition led me to a much richer understanding of Somali aesthetics surrounding the body.

Why Study Dress?

Not surprisingly—for a "failed state" that has been in dramatic politic turmoil for more than two decades—much of the literature about Somalia concerns politics. What went wrong? Why did the government break down? What can be done to rebuild the nation and provide a safe place for Somalis to live? Much of this discussion revolves around clans, colonization, and the dictatorship of Siad Barre. To be sure, these are critical elements of Somali history and politics. Even so, there are other important aspects that are not as frequently discussed: slave trading and the presence of slaves; Somalia's relationship to the Arab League; competing forms of Islam; the lives of women; and the valorization of nomadic culture over other lifestyles (urban, farming, fishing, artisanal production, etc.). In much of this literature there is very little sense of Somali material culture and almost no sense of dress.

The last (and really only) recent book that touched on elements of Somali dress, *Somalia in Word and Image,* by Katheryne S. Loughran et al., was published in 1986 in conjunction with an exhibit at Indiana University. The goal of the authors was to connect Somali material culture with a much larger body of literature on oral poetry, juxtaposing poems with photographs of objects such as jewelry, wood carvings, and baskets. Although they included some images of "Benadir" weaving, named after the coastal Benadir region of Somalia, there was very little information about who the cloth was intended for and how it was worn. This book picks up where *Somalia in Word and Image* left off. Perhaps more importantly, it also connects Somali material culture to politics: how political trends have been displayed and constructed through Somali dress. This is a radical departure from any other book about Somali history and culture.

This connection should not be a surprise to other scholars interested in material culture, such as anthropologists, historians, and art historians. A

growing body of literature explores the role of dress in politics (both historical and contemporary) all over the world: comparatively, as well as in Europe,
Asia, Africa, and the Americas.[16] It is important to note that these books have
been written by scholars in the humanities, not political scientists. Although
in many ways this gap is understandable, I believe both groups have much
to share and learn from one another. It would not be reasonable for me to
ignore the scholarship on politics in Somalia, but I am troubled at how often
this literature leaves women and other minorities out of the picture. How can
Somalis possibly expect to establish a new, functioning government if more
than half the population is ignored? These other voices must be sought out.

Dress is one place where the voices of women can be heard. Historically,
Somali women have not been allowed to play a direct role in politics, but
that does not mean that they are disinterested or disengaged. From what I
have seen, Somali women are the heroes of their culture. They are the ones
who bear the children and do much of the work to keep them housed, fed,
and clothed. They are not waiting for the government to do something; they
have already taken action. When a mother dresses herself or her child she
is making a statement: what kind of life does she want her child to lead? In
Minnesota I have seen girls as young as three years old wearing *hijab*—a dramatic statement about the role of Islam in Somali culture, but also one that
makes some people (both Somalis and non-Somalis) very uncomfortable.
We should explore this discomfort instead of dismissing it. Dress is much
more than "just clothing." Although there are some styles of dress where a
culture or philosophy is formed and then a style of dress is chosen to signify
it—military uniforms are a good example—more frequently people use dress
to build something that only partially exists. We "dress the part" in hopes of
becoming what we desire (whether consciously or not) and "vote" with the
clothes on our backs.

Dress, as a basic necessity of life, offers many opportunities for individuals to build a sense of community through modifying and/or supple-
menting their bodies. Although there are other items of material culture that
can "foster national belonging and a sense of identification,"[17] such as flags,
monuments, and architecture, in many cases people (especially women) have
little personal connection to these objects. As an extension of the body, dress
can "speak" much more loudly and continuously. Introducing the anthology
Fashioning Africa: Power and the Politics of Dress, Jean Allman argued that
dress can be "an incisive political language capable of unifying, differentiat-

ing, challenging, contesting, and dominating."[18] Although not everyone in a society is equally aware of the symbolism of dress or interested in engaging with it, the very act of dressing is a universal part of human experience. Access to certain items may differ by social and economic status, but nobody is completely denied access to the symbolic language of dress. In *Clothing and Difference,* Hildi Hendrickson remarked that in comparison to "depersonalized markers of European identity" (such as national flags), dress expresses the "intimate relation of the individual to the collectivity. . . . These bodily symbols are indices of individual commitment to shared social values, visions of the past, and images of the future."[19]

As this book examines the history and politics of Somali dress from precolonial times to the first decade of the twenty-first century, two important themes emerge: Somalis' long (often intense) history of involvement with the outside world, and growing tensions over the roles of men and women in Somali society. Although we should not idealize the lives of Somali women in precolonial times, it is striking how different dress is today. As the freedoms and satisfactions of nomadic life were replaced by the restrictions and fears of contemporary life, women's bodies gradually disappeared under layers of cloth (sometimes by choice, sometimes not). Exceptions in the 1960s and '70s were brief and highly controversial.

The next chapter establishes what dress was probably like in precolonial times. While men and women in cities along the coast wore clothing they obtained through trade with ships from Asia and the Middle East, many items of dress in rural areas were constructed out of local materials. Differences in dress between nomadic men and women were minimal, reflecting the equally important roles they played in society. Contacts with Europeans began as early as the 1400s with the arrival of Ibn Battuta and the first Portuguese explorers. In contrast to many other parts of Africa, European colonization lasted only a brief time (seventy years), so chapter 3 begins in the 1800s with increased European exploration and the British colonization of Aden, less than 100 miles off the coast of northern Somalia. In exchange for voluntary trade with Europeans (who were looking for livestock, ivory, and other valuable raw materials), Somalis received tremendous amounts of cotton cloth from as far away as India and the United States. This dynamic changed during colonization when dress was used as a visual tool of resistance.

Chapter 4 picks up at the end of World War II as colonization was winding down (British and Italian Somaliland were protectorates of the United

Nations for fifteen years before national independence). In rebuilding their nation, Somalis had an opportunity to reflect on their history and imagine a new future. Styles of dress grew to include European fashions, new forms of Islamic dress, and updated "traditional" styles using both locally made and imported fabrics. Denied access to many educational opportunities and jobs, Somali women were increasingly expected to dress "Somali" while men switched to pants, t-shirts, and three-piece business suits. These differences were increasingly politicized as the nation began to break down, leading to the total collapse of the government in January 1991. Chapter 5 considers how dress has changed even further as Somali refugees have settled in other parts of the world. In the conclusion, chapter 6, I take up some lingering questions. Considering the vast differences in lifestyle and dress between countries such as the United States, the Netherlands, Saudi Arabia, and Kenya, will the pieces of the puzzle ever be assembled into a clear picture of what it means to be "Somali"? What is the future of Somali culture and Somali dress? Given the ravages of colonialism, diaspora, and ongoing violence, what can researchers do to further understanding of Somali identities?

The Origins of Somali Dress—
Prehistory to 1800

The Somali are generally tall and well made, with a very
smooth, dark skin; their features express great intelligence
and animation, and are of a Grecian type, with thin lips
and aquiline noses; their hair is long and very thick.

—C. P. Rigby, 1867

In the nineteenth century, European writers often compared Somali dress
to the clothing of the ancient Mediterranean, the *peplos* of Greece and toga
of Rome. Although there are some aesthetic similarities between these garments and Somali nomadic dress, all being wrapped garments as opposed
to pre-shaped,[1] this style of dress is much less ancient in the Horn of Africa.
Prior to the nineteenth century there were essentially two different ways
of life in Somali territory—urban and rural—and two major categories of
dress. Many urban dwellers were the descendents of settlers from the Middle
East who had built homes along the coast and sometimes intermarried with
Somalis; their dress consisted of styles from the Middle East and was often
made with imported materials. In rural areas, most people (with a few notable
exceptions) were nomads, making a living by traveling with their herds of
camels and sheep. Their animals provided milk and meat as well as leather for
clothing, shoes, amulets, and other accessories. Somalis wore clothing, but
it was crafted out of leather, not woven cloth like the toga. Other elements of
dress were produced using local materials such as frankincense, camel butter,
henna, stones, and shells. There were differences in dress between men and
women, but they were minimal. Men played a critical role in nomadic life
by scouting for water and pastures, taking care of the herds, and protecting

the household from raids and wild animals; women were equally essential, responsible for raising the children and baby animals, moving the household from place to place, making baskets to store provisions, and preparing food. Along with this responsibility came a great deal of autonomy and freedom of movement, which was reflected in their dress.

In the first half of this chapter I discuss early patterns of trade and settlement in Somali territory. This is important for understanding how wrapped garments made of woven (usually imported) cloth were incorporated so easily into Somali nomadic dress. The cloth for the outfit given to Senator Obama was probably not made by Somali artisans. In contrast to many styles of ethnic dress that feature elements like elaborate weaving, embroidery, or dyeing, the defining feature of Somali nomadic dress is the style of wrapping. In the second half of this chapter, I discuss what dress was probably like in Somali territory prior to the 1800s based on early written accounts from Europeans as well as speculation about what kinds of materials Somalis would have had access to during that time.

Cultures Crossing: Early Trade and Settlement

Since the Horn of Africa lies at a crossroads between the Red Sea and the Indian Ocean, Somalis have a very long history of contact with people from other cultures. One of the earliest written documents still in existence that describes Somali territory is *The Periplus of the Erythraean Sea,* a Greco-Egyptian shipping manual from the first century A D. Ports along the northwest coast of present-day Somalia were listed as providing "a great quantity of cinnamon . . . fragrant gums, spices, a little tortoise shell . . . frankincense . . . ivory and myrrh."[2] These products were in great demand in ancient Egypt, Greece, and Rome for use in religious rituals, cosmetics, ornaments, and the preparation of food. Although some of these products (such as cinnamon) came from farther away and were simply being relayed through the Horn of Africa by outsiders, Somali nomads also carried some goods (particularly frankincense) from the interior to the coastline in order to conduct trade. Unfortunately, the author of the *Periplus* did not describe the inhabitants of these areas or what kinds of imported materials they were seeking in exchange.

The Axumite Empire, based in present-day Ethiopia and Eritrea, was closely aligned with the Roman Empire and controlled much of the long-distance trade in the Horn of Africa. The Axumites also controlled the coastline on both sides of the Red Sea (including present-day Yemen, which is still a major center of international shipping) until they were pushed back into the interior of East Africa by the Islamic conquest of northeast Africa. By the seventh century A D, traders and religious exiles from present-day Syria, Lebanon, Oman, and Saudi Arabia were settling in the Horn of Africa. Because of this influence, Somalis were some of the earliest non-Arabs who converted to Islam. In many cases, Somalis intermarried with these settlers, who are credited with founding all the major coastal cities in Somalia. Like the Swahili coast (which includes the southernmost part of Somali territory), the Horn of Africa was a haven for waves of migrants from the Middle East and South Asia. In 975 A D, for example, a group of ships sailed from the Persian Gulf to East Africa, depositing settlers in present-day Somalia, Kenya, Tanzania, and the Comoros Islands. At Kilwa (an island off the coast of Tanzania) they persuaded native inhabitants to sell them the land "for as much cloth as would go round it." Gravestones, mosque inscriptions, and family documents in Somalia contain written records of these migrations.[3]

When Ibn Battuta visited Mogadishu in A D 1331, he noted that the Sultan of Mogadishu "is in origin from the Barbara [a non-Arab native], and his speech is Maqdishi [the language of Mogadishu], but he knows the Arabic tongue." He also recorded a thriving textile industry that was producing cloth "transported as far as Egypt and elsewhere."[4] It is unclear, however, exactly where this technology came from and who was doing the weaving. In his dissertation on "The Arab Factor in Somali History," Ali Abdirahman Hersi suggested that knowledge of weaving was introduced from Persia.[5] Another possible explanation, recorded by the National Museum of Somalia, is that "in Mogdisho [weaving] is remembered as being introduced by traders who went to India and learned their skills there."[6] In an article on the history of cotton in Ethiopia, G. Edward Nicholson argued that weaving throughout East Africa was heavily influenced by ancient technology coming from southwest Ethiopia.[7] Although it seems that cotton textiles were being made in Somali territory, the weavers may have originally been Abyssinian or Galla (Oromo) slaves. Somali women have a history of weaving baskets and mats out of grasses for domestic use, but unlike other pastoralists in North and West Africa, they do not have a history of using wool from their herds of sheep to weave cloth. In any case, as one European explorer observed in the late 1800s, the species of sheep favored by Somali nomads were "very excellent eating" but had "little or no wool" suitable for weaving.[8]

Sailors from present-day India were attracted to the east coast of Africa by opportunities for trade, which flourished as Arab and Persian settlers established towns and trading posts along the coastline. Parts of southern Somalia, including Mogadishu, Marka, Brava, and Kismayo, were considered Swahili, a coastal urban culture formed when settlers from the Middle East intermarried with local populations. To this day, Swahili is spoken by some Somalis in Africa and the diaspora. Although Arabs had been trading with the Chinese for hundreds of years, leaving deposits of Chinese coins and porcelain along the coasts of Arabia and East Africa, emperors of the Yuan dynasty (AD1280–1368) encouraged Chinese merchants to sail directly to the Horn of Africa. While they did not stay in the area, they did acquire livestock as well as luxury goods such as exotic animals, "frankincense, dragon's blood [a resin], aloes, tortoise-shell and ambergris [sperm whale oil]."[9]

Vasco da Gama was the first European to "discover" the Horn of Africa in the late 1400s. Zayla, in northwestern Somali territory, had become a thriving city serving as the main port of call for goods entering and leaving southeastern Ethiopia. The Portuguese explorer Almeida noted that along both sides of the Red Sea "Moors" (Arabs, Somalis, Beja, Harari) had complete control over long-distance trade.

> there is no Kingdom in which there are not some [Moors], and certain provinces are wholly populated with them. . . . They do not allow Christians to come to the sea ports, especially those of Arabia . . . and though the former do come to [Massawa, in present-day Eritrea], the Moors are better received and more welcome there, so that they are left in control of all the important trade of Ethiopia. The great and rich men of [Ethiopia] all have many of these Moors as their agents, and they carry gold to the sea for them and bring them silks and clothing.[10]

The Portuguese were looking for (and found) a sea route to Asia, but reports on the wealth of local traders attracted a great deal of attention; sailors attacked and looted many cities along the Horn of Africa including Zayla and Mogadishu.[11] Traveling along the eastern coast of Africa in the early 1500s, Duarte Barbosa noted that Brava (a coastal city not far from Mogadishu) was

> a place of trade, which has already been destroyed by the Portuguese, with great slaughter of the inhabitants, of whom many were made captives, and great riches in gold, silver, and other merchandise were taken here, and those who escaped fled into the country, and after the place was destroyed they returned to people it.[12]

While the Portuguese were never able to gain control over the local trade, political power gradually shifted to the interior where traders were relatively safe from interference. Nomadism became the dominant way of life, a trend that would have profound effects later on.

Nomads in the City: Leather, Hairdos, and the Making of Somali Dress

Although it is difficult to estimate the impact of early trade on Somali dress, residents of the coastal towns were noted for wearing jewelry, textiles, and clothing imported from India, North Africa, and the Middle East. When Ibn Battuta visited Mogadishu he observed that for Friday prayers the Sultan wore "a robe of green Jerusalem stuff and underneath it fine loose robes [from] Egypt. He was dressed in a wrapper of silk and [wore] a large turban." Battuta himself was given "a suit of their clothing—a silk wrapper to tie around the middle instead of trousers (which they do not know), an upper garment of Egyptian linen with markings, a lined gown of Jerusalem material, and an Egyptian turban with embroideries."[13] As discussed in the next chapter, photographs from the 1800s frequently showed judges (*qadi*), religious leaders (*imams, sheikhs*), and pilgrims returned from Mecca (*hajji*), wearing Arab styles of dress such as turbans, robes (*bisht*), and close-fitting caps (*kufi*). It seems likely that these items were also worn before the 1800s, since many mosques and Islamic courts were established in Somali territory long before the nineteenth century.

The dress of nomads, however, was very different, manufactured out of leather taken from their herds of animals, decorated with fringes, cowry shells, and leather appliqué.[14] By the nineteenth century this style of dress was rapidly disappearing, but it was observed by some of the early European explorers. In the 1860s, one British author noted,

> When the British first occupied Aden [in 1839], the dress of the Somali females usually consisted of goat skins tied over the left shoulder and hanging loosely in front; but they soon became ashamed of this primitive costume, and their dress now consists of a white or colored cotton cloth bound round the waist, with both ends fastened in a knot across the breast.[15]

At least for women, regardless of what these garments were made of (leather versus cotton cloth), the basic style remained the same: a piece of material knotted over the left shoulder that hung down and was wrapped around the

torso. Traveling through southern Somali territory in the mid-1800s, Georges
Révoil observed that this style of dress was relatively short and "generally
decorated with long fringes." Different versions of this garment were worn by
both sexes, called *kaïran* for men and *doù* for women.[16] During the same time
period in northern Somali territory, Richard Burton observed the process of
preparing leather for garments. He noted that the "[Somalis] macerate the
hide, dress, and stain it of a deep calf-skin colour with the bark of a tree called
Jirmah (mimosa), and [then] the leather is softened with the hand."[17] Later,
when cotton cloth became more widely available, pastoralists continued to
dye it with natural materials in shades of brown, red, and dull yellow. G. D.
Carleton mused that "A Somali family is a study in ochre with the exception
of the sheep. Men, women, children, camels, every article of furniture and
clothing is ochre colored, dark or light."[18]

Although many nomads, just like their urban counterparts, were Muslims (often blending Islamic and pre-Islamic practices), nomadic women
were not secluded; their clothing left their arms, shoulders, and lower legs
uncovered. Since women had responsibility for taking care of small children
as well as building, dismantling, and setting up shelter (*aqal*) whenever the
herd needed to move, it would have been impractical to stay "indoors" or wear
anything too restrictive.[19] Until the 1970s only the descendants of Arab and
Persian settlers living in urban areas were known for wearing Islamic head
coverings or observing *purdah* (seclusion). One aspect of dress that urban
and nomadic women shared, however, was the use of frankincense. Several
species of *boswellia* trees are native to both the Horn of Africa and the Arabian
Peninsula. Since ancient times, Somalis have been gathering frankincense in
the form of lumps of dried resin. It can be chewed as a breath freshener or
used as incense by adding a few pieces to a smoldering fire; the smoke changes
the scent of anything around the fire (such as clothing intentionally placed
near the smoke). In the 1870s a British explorer observed that the highest-
quality frankincense came from the Horn of Africa, but that Somalis would
even cross to the Arabian Peninsula in order to collect it for trade.[20]

Hairstyles were also an important part of Somali dress, since they indi-
cated age, gender, and marital status. Until circumcision at the age of six or
seven, children's hair would be shaved into patterns. One style, called the
"handle of Allah," consisting of a single tuft of hair on top of the head, might
be given to a child who was sick or dying in order that he or she could be
pulled into heaven. British anthropologist G. D. Carleton, working at the end
of the nineteenth century, described children's hairstyles as "a quaint-looking

fringe."[21] As girls advanced in age their hair would be allowed to grow longer. Around the time of puberty, a special hairstyle would signal that a girl was available for marriage; she would braid her long hair into hundreds of tiny cornrows from the top of her head to the base, leaving a "bushy halo" of unbraided hair around the neck (see figure 1). After being married, a woman would comb her hair out and shape it into two bundles at the nape of the neck, covering her hair with a thin head wrap called *shash* made of black- or indigo-dyed cloth. This practice was shared by women in other ethnic groups in the Horn of Africa include the Oromo, Saho, and Afar.[22]

Men's hairstyles were even more elaborate. Although one observer noted that an older man might shave his head and grow a small beard,[23] particularly if he had been fortunate enough to make the *Hajj* or pilgrimage to Mecca, photographs show that younger men frequently grew their hair to similar lengths as the women (see figure 2). Some of the early European explorers thought Somali men were wearing wigs. In the 1830s, Frederick Forbes wrote in his journal that "The wigs are made of black sheep skin with the wool dyed or burnt brown with lime & being neatly dressed & frizzled so as to resemble exactly an old fashioned barrister's wig."[24] In the 1860s, C. P. Rigby described how

> the men comb out their hair into little ringlets, having the appearance of a thick mop; they wear no head-dress and bestow much time and care in the arrangement of their luxuriant hair, and, in order not to derange it at night, they rest their head on a wood pillow scooped out to support the cheek. They also frequently change the colour of the hair by applying a preparation of quick lime. They also have a custom of shaving their own hair off, and substituting a large bushy sheep-skin wig dyed a bright red color.... Those who have slain an enemy in battle, wear an ostrich feather stuck upright in their hair.[25]

It is difficult to say whether some Somali men wore wigs or whether Europeans were simply confused by the appearance of their hair. Richard Burton, the most famous explorer to visit Somali territory, observed that men of courting age would shape their hair by oiling it with camel butter and then combing or teasing it out into styles that Burton likened to "a child's 'pudding,' an old bob-wig, a mop, a counsellor's peruke, or an old-fashioned coachman's wig."[26] The color and texture could be altered through a process of plastering the hair with mud, clay, ashes, and/or quicklime, allowing it to dry, and then shaking or combing it out. Perhaps seeing men with their hair still covered with mud or clay is what gave Europeans the impression that Somalis wore wigs. The "bright red color" that Rigby observed could be achieved by bleaching one's hair with lime and then dyeing it with henna. This was also good for hygienic purposes, since the mixture would kill lice.[27] Elaborate hairstyles could be maintained even at night by sleeping on a wooden headrest called a *barkin;* this kept the head elevated off the ground so the hair would not be flattened, but was also reputed to keep the user alert to attacks by lions and rival nomads. Headrests were highly personal, decorative objects that were often carved with intricate geometric designs along the curved sides.

The bodies of nomads were frequently marked with scars due to a medical treatment that involved searing the skin with a piece of heated metal or a burning twig.[28] In the description of his travels, French explorer Georges Révoil noted, "it is rare to meet a 'natural' whose body is not covered in a veritable tattooing of burns and scarifications."[29] Unlike many groups in West and Central Africa, however, there is no indication that Somalis engaged in scarification for ritual or decorative purposes. Rigby also observed that "Both sexes pay great attention to their teeth. The tooth-brush, consisting of a fibrous twig of a tree, is in constant use; and I have never seen any race of people possessing such white, regular, and perfect sets of teeth."[30] In addition to these body modifications, nomadic women made simple jewelry out of natural objects such as pieces of horn, wood, stones, copal, shells, fish bones, and hooves by piercing them and stringing them on thin strips of leather.[31] Among the Somali materials at the Smithsonian National Museum of Natural History is a string of beads made from *doum* nuts (the inner kernel of a fruit that grows on a particular species of palm tree in East Africa) which were pierced and decorated with lines of incised dots.

Other important aspects of nomadic dress—objects worn or carried on the body—included sandals, amulets, shields, and weapons. Many of these items were not made by nomads but by a caste of artisans called the *Saab,* considered subservient to the "noble" Somali clans.[32] This group included the *Boni* (who may have been the original inhabitants of the Horn of Africa before Somali territorial expansion) as well as some former slaves and Somalis who intermarried with the *Saab.* In many ways they were feared for their power and knowledge, but also reviled for working with "dirty" materials. Within the *Saab* there were also three major groups of artisans known as the *Midgan, Yebir,* and *Tomal.* The *Midgan* were responsible for performing circumcisions as well as crafting objects out of leather. Somali nomads would kill lions to protect their herds, but they were not hunters. Animals like the hippopotamus, rhinoceros, oryx, antelope, and ostrich were considered dirty and too spiritually dangerous to handle. The *Midgan,* however, did hunt animals like the rhinoceros, and thus were able to produce sandals (*kabo*) and shields (*gaashaan*) from very tough and long-lasting leather. Less durable items could be made from the hides of camels, sheep, goats, and cattle, sometimes by the nomads themselves.[33] The British explorer Ralph Drake-Brockman wrote that "as workers in leather [*Midgan*] methods are crude."[34] However, these pieces were solidly made for everyday, utilitarian purposes, not for artistic expression. The sandals consisted of many layers of leather (up to a thickness of one inch) that were punched with an awl and stitched together by hand, turning up and coming to a gentle point in front of the toes. To wear the sandals, there were strips of leather that went around the second toe, over the top of the foot, and around the back of the heel. For special occasions the sandals could be more elaborate. The Smithsonian National Museum of Natural History has a pair of sandals which the donor listed as being for a bridegroom; the edges were notched with tiny points (as if the layers of leather had been cut with pinking shears) and the insteps were painted with geometric designs. The Italian ethnographer, Nello Puccioni, observed that "The Somali ... does not always wear his sandals when he travels; when he is passing through an area that is sandy or covered with shifting clay, he prefers to take them off and walk barefoot." In such cases, a nomad might keep them handy by attaching them to the ends of a long strip of leather and draping the strip over one shoulder (allowing the weight of the sandals to keep the "sandal carrier" in place).[35]

Midgan leatherworkers also made shields out of wooden bases covered by leather. In the 1890s, Carleton described the appearance and use of this vital accessory.

> The shield is of oryx-antelope skin or (the best) rhinoceros hide. The middle of the back of the skin of a *male* oryx is alone accepted for a shield. A Somali tries to keep his shield white. The rhinoceros ones are the whitest, and are generally covered to preserve them from being soiled. A shield is carried, when in use, by a hide handle at the back, and held forward. It is carried on the arm when not in use; a string of three colored tassels hang from it.[36]

A shield might also be suspended from a strip of leather and hung between the shoulders when not in use.[37] Although made for utilitarian purposes, the shields were decorated with elaborate patterns of incised dots that formed rectangles, lines, and concentric circles. In addition, two shields in the collection of the Smithsonian National Museum of Natural History were painted on the back with red and black geometric designs; a form of art that ideally just the owner of the shield and his companions would have seen. These designs might have also had a spiritual or protective purpose. Other nomadic groups in Sudan, Djibouti, and Ethiopia used shields covered with leather, but they tended to be larger and lacking incised decorations.

The *Tomal,* descendants of nomads who had intermarried with the *Midgan,* were the blacksmiths of Somali territory, producing weapons as well as some types of jewelry out of iron and other metals. A simple piece of jewelry, for example, might consist of a twisted rod of metal wrapped around the bicep.[38] Although an Italian ethnographer, Vinigi Grottanelli, attributed all "rude" metal weapons to production by the *Tomal* and all finely crafted pieces to Arab artisans (imported or made by Arab artisans living in the Horn of Africa), the British explorer Drake-Brockman observed that the *Tomal* could easily and rapidly apply "neat ornamentation in brass wire on the shafts of the spears, and . . . elaborate white metal inlay on the handles of the bilawis [daggers]."[39] Rigby noted that from a young age all nomadic men carried at least one spear (sometimes a long one plus a "short light one for throwing"), a shield, a dagger, and "a bow with arrows poisoned with the juice of a tree called 'gergalla.'"[40] The longer spear, called *waran,* could also be used as a walking stick. The dagger (*bilawi* or *baydhabow*) was commonly tucked into a leather scabbard hidden at the waistline, which was also the case among many Arabs.[41] Although scholars do not often consider weapons as part of dress,[42] for Somali nomads these objects were literally carried or worn on the body every day.

The *Yebir,* also members of the *Saab* caste, were responsible for crafting amulets (*hardas*), prayer mats, and saddles, and for performing rituals designed to protect nomads from snakes and scorpions, illnesses, and harm during critical events such as marriage and childbirth. These were not strictly Islamic practices (even though the amulets often contained verses from the Qur'an), but came from a pre-Islamic belief system. Richard Burton compared the *Yebir* to the "Dushan" of southern Arabia, as jesters employed by local chiefs.[43] Fantastic stories existed about their powers. The first *Yebir* to hear of a marriage or birth of a child would collect a toll in exchange for an amulet; otherwise, the person who refused to pay would incur the "curse of

the *Yibir,* supposed to result in a violent death to the refusing party or defor-
mity in his child."[44] Drake-Brockman recorded "a common belief among the
Somalis that at death the Yebir disappears, and that no one has ever seen a
Yebir corpse."[45] J. W. C. Kirk observed that the *Yebir* and *Midgan* had their
own secret dialects that were "unknown to any Somali."[46] In the 1960s a
Peace Corps worker recorded the story of a woman in her village who had
been unlucky in life and paid a *Yebir* to make an amulet in hopes of protecting her unborn baby:

> When the Yibir medicine man came to the village, Chamis had to beg and
> beg [her husband] for the money to pay for an amulet to keep *jinn* [evil spir-
> its] away from the baby growing inside her body.... The Yibir laid a small
> stick along his outstretched arm to the tip of the little finger. He touched
> his chin to the stick and recited holy incantations from the Quran in favor
> of the child.... The Yibir medicine man inscribed the holy words from the
> Quran and other ritual signs on a bit of paper. He folded this into a piece
> of leather. Chamis tied this onto her arm to keep it close to the baby inside
> her body.... [After her son was born], she took the sacred amulet off of her
> arm and hung it around his little neck. Although she had been angry be-
> cause Ibrahim had given her only enough money to buy one small amulet,
> it looked enormous hanging on the baby's neck.... [When the baby died],
> he was wrapped in a white shroud, the color of death and mourning and
> buried with the amulet still covering his whole little belly.[47]

Adult men commonly wore amulets on a wide strip of leather that was tied
closely around the neck or a bicep (see figures 2 and 3). Women also wore
amulets, but were more likely to keep them concealed inside their clothing
at the waistline. For small children, who were "allowed to run naked," an
amulet might be the only type of body supplement worn on a daily basis.[48]

Echoes of Ancient Dress in Modern Times

Very few items of dress from this early time period have survived into the
twenty-first century. Even before Europeans colonized their territory, Somalis had replaced leather clothing with cotton. Eventually, they also discarded
leather sandals in favor of plastic; shields and spears were superseded by automatic weapons. Survivals include the use of frankincense and the head covering known as *shash,* although the fabric is now silk and the scarves are manufactured in India. (Also, all types of head coverings have taken on radical new

meanings, a theme I return to in chapters 4 and 5.) It is important, however, to realize two things. First, this early history represents a storehouse of ideas from Somali culture. Just because these body supplements and modifications have disappeared in the twenty-first century does not mean they can never be revived. After the collapse of the Soviet Union, for example, Lithuanians turned to pre-Soviet images, documents, and even archaeological finds to inspire new styles of ethnic and national dress.[49] Although contemporary Somali dress is heavily connected to styles in Europe, North America, and the Middle East, the political winds of change might someday bring a renewed interest in much older (more uniquely Somali) styles of dress. Second, the styles of dress that existed prior to the nineteenth century did establish some aesthetic preferences that are still in force today—colors, a few basic items (such as frankincense), and above all the acceptance of imported materials as part of Somali dress. The specific style of dress later given to Obama did not quite exist yet, but the nomadic way of life was already very strong.

CHAPTER 3

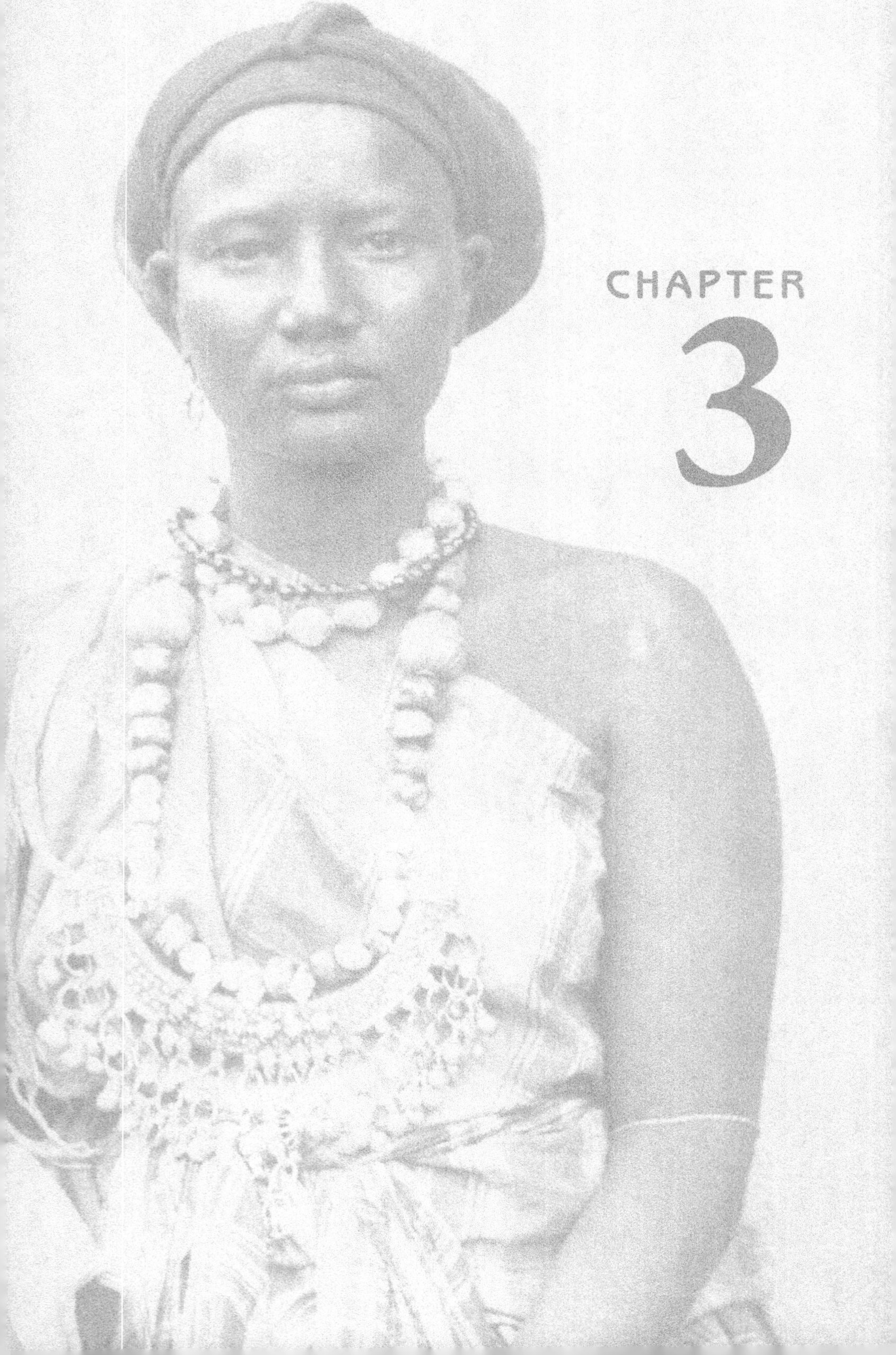

A Clash of Civilizations—1800 to 1945

> When abroad [the Somali] may array himself in European clothes . . .
> but when he returns to his country he will scornfully discard all the
> paraphernalia of European civilisation and dress himself
> once more in a tobe [wrap] of cotton cloth which he
> wears as proudly as the Roman wore his toga.
>
> —*Douglas Jardine, 1925*

Prior to the nineteenth century, Somalis were not in much direct contact with Europeans. By 1800, political power had shifted to the interior, but it began to shift back with changes in the Arab slave trade[1] and the opening of the Suez Canal in 1869. Suddenly, nomads had goods from the interior that Europeans were looking for: livestock to fuel their colonies in Africa and the Middle East as well as raw materials such as ostrich feathers, tortoise shell, ivory, and leather to supply factories back home. In exchange, Somalis received weapons, new types of jewelry, new foods such as spaghetti, and a great deal of cloth, which they began using in place of leather for their clothing. In the 1890s, G. D. Carleton observed that several types of currency were accepted in the Horn of Africa: Maria-Theresa thalers, American dollars, Indian rupees, and standardized lengths of unfinished cotton cloth, which were "often more acceptable" than coins.[2]

The invention of the steamship and establishment of regular service in the region brought new opportunities for Somalis to travel as sailors, laborers, pilgrims, and scholars. Many went to the Middle East, but some traveled as far as London and the United States. At the same time, increasing contact with Europeans (leading up to the colonization of East Africa) also drew Somalis into a growing "clash of civilizations" between Europe and the Islamic world. Dress during this time period reflected these tensions: Somalis wore *merikani* cloth manufactured in Britain and United States, but in a wrapped style more akin to historic forms of nomadic and Arab dress. European dress was accepted grudgingly and often rejected outright.

The Reign of Noble Nomadism

Well before the Treaty of Berlin (1885)—which divided almost the entire continent of Africa into French, British, Portuguese, Italian, German, Belgian, and Spanish colonies—there was the Ottoman Empire. At its height in the seventeenth century, the Empire included Egypt, northern Sudan, and both coasts along the Red Sea reaching down to the northern edge of Somali territory. However, since the Horn of Africa was on the periphery of the Ottoman Empire and long-distance communication was challenging, the Ottomans seem to have had little influence on Somali culture. For example, the fez (a brimless cap for men) was widely adopted in North Africa, but I have found no evidence that it was ever worn in Somali territory. Towns along the southern coast aligned with the Swahili and later the Omani Sultanate, but this too had only a limited influence (although a minority of Somalis still speak Swahili).

Until East Africa was colonized in the late nineteenth century, Somalis had almost total control over the interior. In fact, since Richard Burton's caravan was attacked outside the city of Zeyla and Burton himself nearly killed in 1855, Somali nomads had a reputation for being extremely fierce; very few European explorers dared to venture inland. Along the tip of the Horn of Africa (which is difficult to sail due to strong ocean currents), Somali nomads were known for attacking and usually killing the survivors of shipwrecks; their main source of wealth reportedly came from stripping survivors of their clothing and jewelry.[3]

The northern edge of Somali territory also has a very harsh climate, dominated by rocky hills 2,000–7,000 feet above sea level and a stretch of desert called the *Guban,* which receives less than four inches of rainfall per year. Somali nomads traveled regularly through this region, following a pattern of migration based on the seasons. At the beginning of the dry season, they would migrate to towns along the coastline to sell part of their livestock and then cluster around a series of deep wells. When the rainy season arrived, they would cross back through the hills and desert to reach a grassland in the interior called the *Haud,* which is now located in Ethiopia.[4] For several months they would graze their camels, sheep, and goats, raising the next generation of livestock and collecting other products such as frankincense that could be traded when the dry season returned.

Through this cycle of migration, nomads in the northern region were able to meet whatever material needs they could not satisfy on their own and keep a steady flow of goods moving between the interior and coastline. In a book on the political economy of the area, Abdi Samatar noted that nomads (pastoralists) were "far from being self-sufficient. Only the camel boys lived on milk alone for extended periods of time. The pastoral society bartered pastoral and wild products such as ghee, skins, gum, incense, ostrich feathers, ivory and livestock for grain and clothing."[5] Nomads were vital to the regional economy, since agriculture was virtually non-existent apart from a few isolated pockets in the higher elevations. On his journey through the interior from Zayla to the city of Harar, Richard Burton wondered how anyone could survive.

> [How the nomads] can exist here in the summer is a mystery. My arms were peeled even in the month of December; and my companions, panting with the heat, like the Atlantes of Herodotus, poured forth reproaches upon the rising sun. The townspeople, when forced to hurry across it in the hotter season, cover themselves during the day with Tobes wetted every half hour in sea water; yet they are sometimes killed by the fatal thirst which the [*Guban*] engenders. Even the Bedouins are now longing for rain; a few weeks' drought destroys half their herds.[6]

When the British colonized the port of Aden (in present-day Yemen) in 1839, Somali nomads were already well prepared to sell their livestock to the Europeans for milk and meat. Although the pace of trade undoubtedly increased, the seasonal cycle of trade was not new at all.

The southern part of Somali territory is also hot, being directly over the equator, but the terrain is flatter and there is more rainfall. Prior to European colonization, much of the southern region was controlled by a federation of noble Somali clans known as the Geledi Sultanate.[7] Based in Afgoy, approximately twenty miles north of Mogadishu, the sultanate held a firm grip on trade as well as an important agricultural area between the Juba and Shebelle rivers. Several of the older towns along the coast had dwindled significantly in size and prominence. According to Esmond B. Martin and T. C. I. Ryan,

Mogadishu, which had been a large and prosperous town of approximately 10,000 inhabitants at the time of the Portuguese conquest of East Africa in the sixteenth century had declined by 1811 to 150 to 200 houses, although at that time it was by far the most populous town on the Benadir coast. Brava had some one hundred houses, and Merca was of little significance; Kismayo did not exist at all.[8]

Thanks to these circumstances, nomadic culture had become dominant throughout Somali territory, both north and south. Although some of the more powerful nomadic families owned agricultural land, they considered farming to be an inferior way of life, relying on slaves to grow food and produce crops such as orchella weed (a dye plant), sesame seeds, and cotton for export to Europe.[9] Slaves captured from neighboring regions, particularly the Oromo, were also used as weavers, herdsmen, domestic servants, and concubines.

Although the Arab slave trade had already been going on for centuries, Somalis did not become regularly involved until the nineteenth century. In 1832, the Sultan of Oman built a palace on the island of Zanzibar to solidify his power over the east coast of Africa. Traders from Europe, the Middle East, and South Asia were looking for slaves (particularly as slave trading along the west coast of Africa was banned), but they were also looking for ivory. Somalis had some access to this material through contact with neighboring regions. Within forty years, the selling price of ivory had tripled, and in the mid-1800s, the Sultan built fortifications for trade and tax collection in the towns of Mogadishu, Marka, Brava, Kismayo, and Warsheikh.[10] Due to early and widespread conversion to Islam, Somalis were protected from being captured as slaves (since the Qur'an states that fellow believers cannot be owned), but some did participate in the trade as middlemen. For a short time, the southern coast of Somali territory (the Benadir region) served as an important transit point for slaves coming from Central Africa. Some slaves freed by the British were also absorbed into the Horn of Africa as forced laborers.[11]

Cloth is Wealth: How International Trade Changed Somali Dress Forever

While some aspects of Somali dress, such as hairstyles, amulets, leather sandals, and the use of incense, remained the same as they had been prior to European contact, other practices changed dramatically. Nomadic men used their earnings from trade to invest in livestock. Since Islamic law gave women the right to own and inherit property independently of their male relatives, they also invested; instead of animals, however, women typically chose jewelry—earrings, bracelets, anklets, rings, and necklaces—not just as protective amulets or decorative objects, but as a form of portable wealth. Brides were given jewelry to establish a certain amount of financial security; in difficult times such as droughts the pieces could be sold to buy food or livestock to keep the family going. This jewelry was made of silver, solid or repoussé (silver sheets with designs hammered into them from the back), and occasionally of gold; sometimes it contained other valuable materials including copal, amber, coral, carnelian, glass trade beads from the Italian cities of Venice and Trieste, trade beads from Bohemia (in the present-day Czech Republic), and silver coins such as Maria Theresa thalers. Jewish craftsmen living in Yemen and Oman made the highest-quality silver jewelry. It frequently had elaborate designs made with etching, filigree (minute strands of twisted silver wire), and granulation (small dots of silver solder applied in geometric and floral patterns). These forms of jewelry were not unique to Somalis but were traded to many parts of East and North Africa, Arabia, and southern Asia.[12]

One item of jewelry that *was* unique to Somali women was a large necklace called an *audulli* (see figure 4).[13] These pieces have several characteristic features: a very large, silver, crescent-shaped pendant with three or four loops at the top edge concealed by diamond-shaped decorations; dangling rows of tiny silver bells with one or more *xersi* (*hirz* in Arabic) in the shape of a box or cylinder holding verses from the Qur'an; and a chain strung with glass trade beads, silver repoussé beads, coral, and/or chunks of amber, long enough so the crescent-shaped pendant would lie at the chest or upper torso. The crescent shape was not a part of the typical repertoire for local metal workers or even silversmiths from the nearby areas that are now Yemen and Oman (they preferred to make cylinders and boxes). This might be why Italian scholar Alessandra Antinori identified the *audulli* as possibly coming from India.[14] Burton observed that "the Audulli or woman's necklace is [an] elaborate affair of amber, glass beads, generally colored, and coral: every matron who can afford it possesses at least one of these ornaments."[15] This would have represented a substantial financial investment. In addition, the *audulli* was often worn along with smaller, beaded necklaces and other types of armlets, cuffs, and bracelets. A *xersi* could also be worn as a pendant on a necklace with or without other beads.

European caravans often carried caches of glass beads, since they could be used "as presents, and to pay for trifling purchases"—however, there were frequent changes in the colors and styles that were in demand. Burton advised readers interested in exploring Somali territory that they should try to ascertain in advance "what may be the especial variety. Some [kinds of beads] are greedily sought for in one place, and in another place rejected with disdain."[16] In the 1880s, J. S. King observed that glass beads were also used by brides as hair ornaments.

> On the day fixed for the removal of the bride to her new home she is escorted to it from her father's house by a large party of young men and maidens, the latter dressed in their best clothes, and having their tightly-plaited and well-oiled hair tastefully decorated with cowries, colored beads, and flowers.[17]

In addition to silver and beads, explorers like George Révoil and Luigi Bricchetti observed women wearing strings of leather with a stone or a large shell used as a pendant.[18] Smaller cowry shells—which were obtained through trade from other parts of the Indian Ocean basin—were used as embellishments for wedding baskets, cushions, and hand-woven bags.

Men also wore ornaments, but these were usually for spiritual or decorative purposes and were not nearly as financially valuable. One popular ornament throughout East Africa for both men and women was a flat strip, rod, or twisted wire made of non-precious metal (copper, brass, or zinc) worn wrapped around the arm anywhere from the bicep to the wrist.[19] In some other nomadic cultures in East Africa women wore stacks of wire around their arms and lower legs, but after viewing hundreds of photographs from the nineteenth and early twentieth centuries I have not seen any evidence of this among Somalis.[20] In addition to small amulets made of leather or a larger square amulet strung on a thick band of leather called a *hardas* (see figures 2 and 3) some Somali men wore a choker called *makkawi* made from two chunks of amber strung on a band of leather (not to be confused with *macawis*, a wrapped garment).[21] Even more common was a *tusbah*, a strand of Islamic prayer beads that could be handled during times of stress as "worry beads" or used as a devotional tool to recite the ninety-nine names of God.

Although it is not technically a necklace, many photographs from the nineteenth and early twentieth centuries show Somali men wearing a *tusbah* around the neck. The beads could be made from found objects, including stones, seeds, or bits of wood, although more valuable versions were made of amber, copal, and carnelian. Drake-Brockman noted in 1912 that manufacturers in London and Hamburg were also compressing frankincense in order to produce imitation amber beads that were widely circulated throughout the Middle East as well as other parts of Africa.[22]

Although Somalis were handling ivory and transporting it to the coast, little made its way into their dress. Unlike people living in forested areas who were actually hunting elephants—the Mangbetu in present-day Congo, for example, wore ivory hairpins, bracelets, and anklets—for Somalis this material was not particularly meaningful. The few pieces of ivory jewelry that European explorers observed or collected in Somali territory were generally simple: cuffs or flat bangle bracelets decorated with incised lines and circles.[23]

During the nineteenth century most Somali nomads stopped wearing garments made of leather and replaced them with cotton cloth. In addition to the dominant *merikani* white cotton fabric that poured into Somali territory from India, Great Britain, and the United States as a result of trade with Arabs and Europeans, other plain and decorative textiles came to the region from Europe, India, Arabia, and Persia, as Richard Beachey describes:

> Cloth was brought inland by the ivory traders in immense quantity; it was of various kinds: *merikani,* a white inexpensive cotton—first introduced from America in the early nineteenth century; *kaniki,* a blue cotton cloth manufactured in Surat and Gujerat [India] especially for the East African market . . . and the more exotic cloths, *bandar, assilia, barsati,* and the much desired *dobwani* from Muscat [Oman]. There is a record of one caravan in the 1880s carrying 27,000 yards of *merikani* made up in loads of 30–40 yards each, and in addition, thousands of yards of other kinds of cloth.[24]

Quoting from a report by the British government, Luigi Bricchetti observed that from June to October of 1891, ports along the Benadir coast received more than three million yards of "American grey shirting," 840,000 yards of "American drill," more than 1.3 million yards of "European grey shirting," and 650,000 yards of Indian grey shirting. The value of these textiles was far greater than all other consumer imports combined. *Merikani* cloth, the largest single import, had become so popular that manufacturers in Bombay (under British control) were producing textiles labeled "Country American."[25]

At least in the southern parts of Somali territory, craftsmen—not nomads, but the descendants of Oromo and Abyssinian slaves—also produced a limited amount of cloth that came to be known as "Benadir cloth" using a mixture of locally grown cotton and imported threads woven on wide, Egyptian-style looms. Each piece was approximately thirty inches wide and four to five yards in length, enough for a complete garment. Weavers also used imported silk threads to create colorful borders on the edges of plain white garments, particularly for women.[26] Some of the finished cloth was exported to other countries, but much of it was consumed locally. Before Somalis established cotton plantations in the fertile Juba/Shebelle region (using slaves or forced labor) in order to sell it to Europeans, leather had been more common than cotton. The result of massive importation as well as increased domestic cotton production was that clothing made of leather became increasingly rare. In the 1960s, historian Virginia Luling was still able to photograph a young woman at a celebration wearing a leather cape decorated with fringes and cowry shells, but by then this style of dress was virtually nonexistent in everyday contexts. During his travels in the 1920s, Nello Puccioni recorded that leather clothing was "disappearing so rapidly that I had the greatest difficulty [acquiring an] example."[27]

Imported textiles were commonly sold in lengths of seven cubits, a measurement taken from the end of the elbow to the tip of the middle finger. In the territory controlled by the Geledi Sultanate, pieces of cloth cut to this length were accepted as currency.[28] It also happened to be the standard amount of cloth needed for an outfit. For a man's garment—called *tobe* (Arabic for "garment") or *maro* (Somali for "cloth")—the piece would be cut in half and stitched back together to form a large, square-shaped wrapper. This could be worn in several different ways depending on the activity and temperature. Drake-Brockman made one of the more detailed observations concerning how this garment was worn and how it could be rearranged.

> The method of wearing the "tobe" is as follows: Standing erect, one corner of the sheet is taken and thrown over the left shoulder, so that behind the corner reaches as far down as the waist; then as it hangs straight down in front it is passed round under the wearers right arm, then across his back and over the left shoulder, underneath the free end which is already lying there, and then round the body again over both shoulders, with its upper

> corner terminating over the left shoulder, and being brought forward and tucked in under the front piece; the arms are then both under the last roll of the "tobe," and can be raised at will without exposing the person . . . [29]

As an alternative, one shoulder could be left uncovered. This made the outfit cooler and gave that arm more freedom of movement. In cold weather (after sundown, for example), a loose edge might be draped over the head. To allow vigorous activity, the cloth could be wrapped just around the waist and lower body, securing it with a belt. Luling noted that in the south it was common for a man to wear a single piece of cloth, wrapping and rewrapping it in different ways; in the north it was more common for men to wear two separate pieces of cloth, one for the lower body and one for the upper.[30] In deserts, where the daytime is hot and the night is cold, wrappers have many practical advantages over tailored clothing since they can easily be adjusted to fit the changing temperatures. In many nomadic parts of Africa and the Middle East, wrapped forms of clothing have been common since ancient times.[31]

European explorers—who were virtually all men—also used the words *tobe* and *maro* when writing about Somali women's garments, but the construction was quite different. For a woman's garment, a length of cloth would not be cut in half, but simply wrapped around the body in its original, rectangular form. An additional small wrapper called a *futa,* made from approximately two yards of cloth, could be wrapped around the lower body as an undergarment or simple skirt. By the early 1900s, some women were making outfits by combining a *futa* with a blouse called *ambur.*[32] When worn around the upper body, the same piece of cloth was called a *garbasaar* (Somali for "shoulder cloth"). Short pieces were also used as baby carriers; a woman could keep her hands free by placing a child on her back, draping the cloth over both of them (leaving the child's head exposed), and then tying the corners in knots over her chest and waist.

The standard measure of cloth (seven cubits) was wrapped in a more complicated way to form a dress called a *guntiino* that covered both the lower and upper body. First, a woman would hold one corner of the cloth up to her nose and run her hand along the long edge until her fingers were extended; then she would grab the cloth at that point and tie it to the corner to form a loop. This loop would go over her head and under her right arm (so the cloth draped across her chest) leaving the knot sitting on her left shoulder. Then, the rest of the cloth could be pleated and wrapped around her upper torso until the short side of the rectangle hung vertically down in front of her left leg (a slender woman would need more pleating). Since the edge was simply tucked into the folds, this garment would have to be rewrapped throughout the day, although Virginia Luling observed that "with the right knack, it is remarkable how securely it holds, whatever strenuous jobs the wearer may be doing."[33] My personal experience suggests that this garment is easier to keep tucked in when it has a decorative border that makes the edge stiff. A longer wrapped garment, called *saddexqayd*, was similar to the *guntiino* but used up to twenty yards of cloth. Instead of tucking it in, all of this cloth was held in place with a handmade belt called *boqor*.[34] Several inches of excess cloth at the waist would be draped over the *boqor*, covering it up and accentuating the fullness of the hips.

Although nomads washed their clothes with water, frankincense, camel dung, and the juice of a root known to act as a bleaching agent,[35] undyed cotton cloth was difficult to keep clean. In some cases it was intentionally colored with natural dyes (yellow, brown, or dull red), which would have made it look more like leather. In the 1890s Harald Swayne observed that

> The [nomadic] men are nearly all dressed alike, in long "tobes" of white sheeting of different degrees of dirtiness, from brown to dazzling white; not a few of the tobes have been dipped in red clay and are of a bright burnt-sienna colour... the tobes are worn till they are brown and threadbare; but at the coast towns they are generally of dazzling whiteness.[36]

Since more colorful fabrics—imported or made by local weavers from imported threads—were not as common, they could be worn for special occasions or to indicate higher social status.

> Elders, horsemen, and those who wish to assume a little extra dignity, discard the common tobe and affect the *khalili*, a georgeous tartan arrangement in red, white, and blue, each colour being in two shades, with a narrow fringe of light yellow. On horseback it is a very becoming dress, and it is often affected by a favourite wife.[37]

The "tartan" cloth mentioned in this quote might have been Indian madras or even Benadir cloth.

Virtually every photograph taken in the nineteenth century by European explorers shows Somali nomads wearing some kind of wrapped cotton clothing. One exception to this was nomadic men who came into direct contact with Europeans. A photograph of Swayne's hunting party, for example, shows eight men wearing *maro* (wrapped in various ways) and two men wearing some kind of shirt with sleeves.[38] This could have been an Arab-style *kamiz* (an ankle-length tunic) or something Swayne gave the men to wear. A post-card of "Somali traders" from the early 1900s (see figure 5) shows two men wearing a mixture of Arab, European, and nomadic dress. One is wearing *saalwar* (drawstring pants that fit closely around the calves) along with a tunic and *maro* draped around his upper body. The other man is wearing a *kamiz*, some kind of vest (which appears to be embroidered), and a turban wrapped around his head and neck. Both are carrying walking sticks and wearing European-style, lace-up boots instead of locally crafted sandals.

In contrast, along the eastern coast of Africa from Mogadishu to south-ern Tanzania, men and women commonly wore Arab-style dress.[39] This re-flected their urban environment, Arab ancestry, and growing relationship with the Omani Sultanate. Garments for men included the *caftan, kamiz* (tunic), *bisht* (cloak), *kufi* (skull cap) and *imamad* (turban). Garments for women enveloped the whole body, leaving only the hands, feet, and face uncovered (in some cases, an additional garment called a *barakoa* was added to cover the lower half of the face). These styles were very different from the garments worn by nomads and would have been impractical for that way of life. Traveling through the area in the 1890s, abolitionist Luigi Bricchetti pho-tographed the "Sheriff of Brava" wearing a large turban made of striped cloth, an embroidered *kamiz*, a dark cloak (which is common even today in Arabia and North Africa), and a belt with a dagger (*bilawi*). An image of "Arabs in Marka" (see figure 6) shows a man wearing a *kufi, kamiz,* and a belt with a dagger; he is also holding what appears to be a rifle. The woman seated next to him is wearing a light-colored *garbasaar* with a darker decorative border and, curiously, instead of an Arab-style head covering, a head wrap with some kind of tie-dyed or printed pattern.[40]

Bricchetti also photographed an "Italian Sheikh" in the city of Brava wearing very similar clothing—a light-colored *kamiz*, dark cloak (with nar-row bands of light trim around the collar and hemline), a neatly wrapped turban, a decorative belt with a dagger, and leather sandals (which could have been made locally, but were not the same shape as nomadic sandals), holding a long sword in both hands across his lap. Although I have not been able to determine if this photograph was taken in costume or if this was an accepted form of dress for Europeans in the early days of Italian Somaliland, it is interesting to note that perhaps the boundaries between European and Somali dress had not yet crystallized. Toward the end of the colonial era,

Margaret Laurence recorded sharp differences in dress between Somalis and British officials.

> Somali men and women thronged indecisively around the edges of the square. . . . Their cotton robes were bright and stiff with newness. Here was the Qadi [judge] of Hargeisa, lean and hawk-nosed, resplendent in white burnoose and a black robe embroidered with spider-webs of gold. Here were the local elders with their beards freshly trimmed, arrayed in robes of scarlet, turquoise, royal blue. . . . The English were apart. They sat primly to one side, ourselves among them, behind a fence. Gloved and straw-hatted mothers hissed at their giggling young—*Behave yourself!* . . . The top officials emerged in the white uniform of the Colonial Service, and all the military men of any rank had medals sprouting like corsages from their out-puffed chests.[41]

The European Grip Tightens

By the 1860s, the British navy began making an effort to stop slave trading along the eastern coast of Africa. This did not completely halt the trade; instead, slaves captured from Central Africa were diverted from the island of Zanzibar or ports in present-day Kenya (Mombasa, Lamu, and Pate) to cities along the coast of southern Somalia. When control over the Benadir coast was ceded from Zanzibar to Italy (a sale fostered by the British Empire), Italian officials not only looked the other way on the slave trade but actually purchased slaves for themselves.[42] It was not until 1903 that slavery was outlawed and a ban on the slave trade was finally enforced.[43] By that time, tens of thousands of former slaves had been forced to settle in Somaliland, unable to return to their homelands. Once freed, many became farmers, struggling to claim whatever land they could. In urban areas, large numbers became domestic servants, factory workers, and dockhands. These former slaves represented a sizable underclass within Somali society—referred to as *habash, ooji,* or *addoon* (words meaning "slave") or *boon,* a reference to the native *Boni* who made up part of the *Saab* caste.

Another term used for these newcomers was *tiin jareer* meaning "hard hair."[44] This derogatory phrase was based on the physical appearance of the ex-slaves, whose tightly curled hair was not considered beautiful by Somali standards. The texture of most Somalis' hair was softer, allowing it to be combed, braided, and cut into what Richard Burton and Ralph Drake-Brockman called "fantastic shapes." Drake-Brockman observed, "The Somali is a great dandy, and is always admired by and is the envy of his friends if he possesses a well-kept chevelure [head of hair]."[45] The physical appearance of Somalis had been affected by intermarriage with Arabs and Persians as well as the Oromo, who have lighter skin, softer hair, and were historically considered very beautiful by Somali standards.[46] These preferences were in place long before slave trading ended in the early 1900s, but the importance of having "soft hair" was reinforced by comparisons to ex-slaves from Central and East Africa.

In the nineteenth century the British Empire also expanded rapidly to include parts of the Middle East, India, and Africa, including what is now northern Somalia and northeastern Kenya. After the invention of the steamship in 1822, the British government established a new intercontinental steamship service to connect the different colonies. This allowed administrators, soldiers, and their families to move relatively quickly between London and their posts, but it also created new opportunities for Somalis. Some traveled across the Red Sea and found employment in southern Arabia; others worked as sailors on British ships. In 1871, an unknown (probably American or British) traveler sent a postcard from the port of Aden noting,

> The Somali people are the (African?) work people . . . of S. Eastern Arabia. We (travelers to and from the East) see them only at the outgoing military station (Aden) of the Red Sea. They ply the boats to and from all anchored shipping—seem half fish half human. They are excellent divers and will pursue a copper far down and bring it to the water's surface . . .[47]

Although a small number of Somalis had been working as fishermen and pearl divers for several centuries, the expansion of trade along the Red Sea— particularly after the opening of the Suez Canal in 1869—increased demand for their products. Drake-Brockman noted that "the [pearl] divers are almost entirely engaged and financed by the merchants of Zeyla, who have the first call on their hauls, and who purchase the pearls, making very large profits as a rule."[48]

When ships were finally able to sail from the Mediterranean directly to the Red Sea, the Horn of Africa suddenly became a very strategic location for any European government trying to create an empire in Africa, acting as a vital transit point between the Red Sea and lucrative colonies in Central and southern Africa. In 1884, Somali clans signed their first treaties with British and Italian officials, giving them control over the coastline. Three years later, Ethiopia (which had become an independent nation in 1855 under Emperor

Tewodros II) seized control over the city of Harar and extended its borders into the *Haud*. This was highly disruptive to nomads in northern Somali territory, who suddenly found themselves having to cross borders to maintain their traditional way of life. In 1889, the colony of Italian Somaliland was carved out of what is now southern Somalia; two years later the northern region became the colony of British Somaliland. A smaller area in the southwest was incorporated into British East Africa (present-day Kenya), and the far north became part of French Somaliland (Djibouti). In this way, Somalis were split into five different countries.

In a move that would shift the balance of economic and political power away from the interior to the coastal areas, the British government granted some Somali men opportunities to attend universities in Cairo and London; the Italian government did likewise by sending students to Florence and Milan. This primarily benefited the families of young men in urban areas who had been educated in the Qur'anic schools and were well prepared for advanced study, particularly in Arabic-language institutions such as Al-Azhar University in Cairo. Pilgrims making the *Hajj* to Mecca found their own uses for the new steamship lines, fulfilling the ritual with less time and effort and sometimes staying for an advanced religious education. A small number of Somalis worked on British ships and even married British women, establishing expatriate communities in London and Liverpool.[49] Whether these changes were welcome or not, Somalis were getting a much broader sense of what it meant to be "Somali" not just in East Africa but in relationship to people in the Middle East, North Africa, and Europe, encountering all kinds of new behaviors, ideas, and styles of dress. I. M. Lewis has argued that these inter-cultural experiences, whether sought after or imposed,

> naturally sharpened Somali self-awareness and their sense of the distinctiveness of their culture, language and religion—perhaps most fully in the period before European colonization in their involvement in the medieval religious wars in Ethiopia between Christian and Muslim. This exposure to other cultures and traditions was intensified by alien colonial rule, which included the opportunity for significant numbers of Somali men to serve as merchant seamen all over the world. They then returned to retire to the traditional nomadic life, often coming home with a fund of exotic knowledge and rich store of memories.[50]

Increasingly, these travelers realized that the integrity of Somali dress and culture was not something they could take for granted, but something requiring thought and action to maintain.

Europeans—both scholars and ordinary travelers—were also fascinated by the cultural and physical differences between themselves and Somalis. In the 1920s, anthropologist Nello Puccioni compiled a set of data on Somali facial and body measurements for a German project called the "Archiv für Rassenbilder" (a photographic archive of racial "types"). Patrons could buy sets of cards on the characteristics of groups such as the Somali, Burmese, Watussi, Bambara, and Latvians for two Deutschmarks each.[51] Western concerns with race and "racial purity" shaped the policies of fascist Italian Somaliland as well as the British colonies. In British East Africa, a person's access to public education and facilities was determined according to his or her categorization as "European," "Asian," or "African," with the best resources being reserved for Europeans and the worst for Africans.[52] In the 1920s and '30s,

> Somalis began to agitate for non-Native classification [claiming to be of "Arab" rather than "African" heritage]....One colonial administrator who was quite familiar with the Somalis thought their campaign was motivated by the belief "that Asiatic status would confer, amongst other things, immunity from arrest by African police constables, special accommodation in hospitals and prisons, [and] more favorable treatment in the law courts."[53]

In British East Africa, where Somalis represented a small minority confined to the northeast region of the colony, this campaign was successful. In British Somaliland, however, Somalis were an obvious native-born majority. In view of their long-standing history of intermarriage with Arabs and Persians, however, many Somalis became "resistant to any attempts at their reclassification as native Africans."[54] This battle over race, which continued for the rest of the colonial period, has implications for how Somalis view themselves as well as other Africans and African Americans in the twenty-first century.

The dramatic changes that accompanied colonization also led to a revival of interest in Islam within Somali culture—particularly Sufism (mysticism) and those practices that combined Islamic and pre-Islamic elements, such as ritual dancing, spirit possession, and the veneration of local saints. One Sufi order, the Qadiriyya *tariqa* or school, had already been established in Somali territory for hundreds of years.[55] Yet during the nineteenth and early twentieth centuries, several new orders and branches gained more dedicated followings. Charismatic leaders, such as Sheikh Uways Muhammad Muhyidin al-Qadiri al-Barawi (a famous leader of the Qadiriyya) and Sheikh Abdurahman ibn Abdalla al-Shashi (popularly called "Sheikh Sufi"[56]) spread the message of Sufism and Islam, but they also helped to build new farming settlements, schools, and mosques. These institutions offered educational and religious services and provided a gathering place for all members of the community, including people who were not directly affiliated with the Sufi brotherhoods.[57] Harald Swayne observed that sheikhs were

> enabled to settle down and form permanent villages, and cultivate, on account of the respect in which they are held by all tribes. A looting party must be driven to the last extremity of hunger before it will attack them, and generally in such a case only as many animals would be looted as are needed to provide food. The mullahs are drawn from various tribes, and, being cosmopolitan, have very extended influence. They are a quiet, respectable class, generally on the side of order, and civil to travelers.[58]

The Sufi-led communities offered peace and stability that was an attractive alternative to the disruptive and demeaning nature of colonization. Cassanelli has noted that "by providing within their settlements a degree of economic security and a sense of community, the shaykhs were able to attract many of the marginal elements of southern Somali society to the brotherhoods."[59] These members included many ex-slaves as well as Somalis from the less-powerful minority clans, but also Somalis from the higher classes who were drawn to the spiritual and communal atmosphere of the new settlements. Administrators in British and Italian Somaliland did not see the sheikhs as a major threat to their authority and gave them a certain amount of freedom to carry out their activities. In Italian Somaliland, the government allowed members of the Sufi orders to be judged by Islamic law instead of the colonial courts.[60]

For Somalis, religion offered an alternative to the clan system, which placed a high premium on ancestry, nomadism, and territorial control (which had been severely limited by colonization).[61] Sheikhs were seen as neutral authorities, unaffiliated with the clans. For former slaves, conversion to Islam strengthened their status as free persons, since the Qur'an forbids Muslims to be held as slaves. Even if it didn't improve their real social status, in spiritual terms it made them equal to Somalis. Many slaves who had been captured as children were simply socialized into Islam since it was the dominant religion along the east coast of Africa.[62] Social class became a critical matter during fascist rule in Italian Somaliland, since "people of lower status, especially if they had slaves among their ancestors, were the first to be conscripted into forced labor."[63] Luigi Bricchetti claimed that as many as one-third of the inhabitants of Mogadishu were either slaves or recently freed from bondage.[64]

On a broader level, Islam was also viewed as a basis for unification against Europeans as well as encroachment by Orthodox Christian Ethiopia. Although the Sufi orders were generally advocates of nonviolence, some nomads who had been forced to migrate between the *Haud* grasslands (also known as the Ogaden region) and British Somaliland were provoked by the Ethiopian army into a series of armed conflicts.[65] In other regions of the British Empire—Sudan, Egypt, parts of the Middle East and South Asia—Muslims were engaged in similar struggles. As Muslims gathered in Mecca for the pilgrimage or to further their religious education, news of these resistance movements spread and were carried back to all parts of the Islamic world.

Resistance in the North

It was in this context that a charismatic new sheikh, Sayyid Mohammed Abdulle Hassan, was able to introduce a new Sufi order, Salihiyya, into Somali territory and become the leader of an armed resistance movement against the British. Sayyid—later known to Europeans as the "Mad Mullah"—made the pilgrimage to Mecca when he was in his early thirties and stayed there as a student for three years.[66] In Mecca, he spent much of his time with a Sudanese scholar who advocated for armed struggle against the British and the establishment of a government based on Islamic law—a movement called *Mahdism*.[67] Because of this influence, Sayyid developed a strong attitude that was markedly more conservative and confrontational than was typical among members of the other Sufi brotherhoods in Somali territory.

Upon his return to British Somaliland, Sayyid's objectives were "to inveigh strongly against the prevailing laxity in religious practice," revive "the religious spirit in his people," and fight against "excessive materialism and consumerism." He advised Somalis not to be seen "wearing infidel clothing, sporting foreign hair styles, walking like an unbeliever, or exhibiting outlandish manners of any sort." This included "studying the books of unbelievers or participating in their gatherings or festivals."[68] He also tried to halt practices that he saw as generally harmful, such as the chewing of *qaat* (leaves containing a stimulant) and the use of tobacco. Salihiyya opposition to practices that other Sufi orders accepted, such as visiting the gravesites of local saints to pray for their intercession and guidance, created resentment and a number of enemies for Sayyid, even among other Somalis.[69] These tensions sometimes led to violent encounters. In 1907, some members of the Salihiyya *tariqa* assassinated Sheikh Uways and some of his followers after Uways created a popular poem that was critical of Sayyid and his practices.[70] Others opposed Sayyid on the grounds that his blunt opposition to the British posed a threat to their opportunities for trade. Although the Salihiyya order was not very successful as a spiritual movement, it did serve as a catalyst for another kind of struggle.

Nomads in the northern region were frustrated with Ethiopian army raids and control over their grazing lands and were looking for a strong leader to give them guidance. Sayyid took advantage of these circumstances and framed his movement as a fight against all colonial powers in Somali territory, including the British. By the year 1900 he was able to persuade six thousand men to join his army.[71] They were called "dervishes," a term that has been used in numerous cultures for members of Sufi brotherhoods. As word of the resistance spread, the number of Sayyid's dervishes grew. To symbolize the religious principles underlying their struggle (as envisioned by Sayyid), the soldiers were given turbans along with uniforms that closely resembled the clothing known as *ihram* worn by male pilgrims at Mecca.

> The Dervishes were issued at the outset with a simple uniform consisting of three measures of white American or Indian cloth . . . two to be wrapped or worn around the body while one served as a head-dress. As a result of this, [they] were known as *Duub-'Ad,* men of the white turbans. A black or brown rosary went with the plain, loosely fitting white robes.[72]

The same uniform was worn by some soldiers in Sudan (see figure 7).[73] It is important to note that the turban cloth (called *imamad* in Somali) was sometimes draped over a shoulder and not always wrapped around the head. The turban was not a typical item of dress for Somali nomads; however, clothing made of plain white wrappers was very familiar since it was exactly what most of them (both men and women) were wearing on a daily basis. The turban was really the only thing that distinguished Sayyid's soldiers from ordinary Somalis and called attention to their political and religious principles. And it was this same outfit, minus the prayer beads, that Somali elders in Kenya gave to Senator Barack Obama in 2006.

Interestingly, Sayyid—who was evidently very aware of the political power of dress—seems to have maintained some practices that were not exactly orthodox Muslim, but part of traditional Somali culture. Drake-Brockman recorded a rumor that Hassan was protected from bodily harm by a magical amulet given to him by a lizard.

> Among the many curious stories connected with Mahommed Abdullah is one concerning the small amulet in which is said to be a complete copy of the Koran, and which he carries on his person day and night; he is said to wear it suspended and hidden from view in his left armpit. . . . [He was warned by the lizard] that he must wear it day and night, and never let anyone lay a hand on it, and that if he did this, not one of his enemies could injure him. The Mullah has firmly convinced his followers of the secret powers of this amulet, and the futility of anyone attempting to take his life. There is a story that an Ogaden once wished to kill him when they were alone together. . . . The Ogaden raised his rifle, pressed the trigger, but no report followed; whereupon he reloaded and again attempted to fire, but a misfire was the result for the second time, whereupon the Mullah exposed his amulet and pointed out its secret powers.[74]

Amulets were still a common part of nomadic dress, as were a range of traditional items: wrapped clothing, the use of frankincense and henna, elaborate hairstyles, leather sandals and shields, the *audulli,* and prayer beads. It is worth noting that while Arab dress did have an influence on Somalis in the north during the colonial period—because of the proximity and political relationship to the Middle East—European dress made hardly any impact. Widespread adherence to Islam and resistance to European colonization (whether violent or nonviolent) gave even ordinary Somalis reasons to avoid European-style dress. Nomads did not wear wrapped clothing because they had no other choice; this was a collective and often conscious decision. After five years of fighting Sayyid's forces, the British gave up and retreated to the coast. The colony of British Somaliland still existed, but British expansion into the interior of Somali territory was halted until the 1920s, when advances in military technology made Somali defenses obsolete.

Dramatic Changes in the South Breed New Choices and Tensions

Although the economy in northern Somali territory was somewhat disrupted by the armed conflict with the British and the new border with Ethiopia (which made seasonal migration between the grasslands and the coastline more difficult for nomads), the British did not have a very strong cultural presence. Until 1935, the number of foreign administrators in the colony was never higher than fifty people.[75] Their main interest was in fostering trade with Somalis for livestock and other products, which were needed to support the British colony at Aden (Yemen). The situation in Italian Somaliland, however, was very different. Italians—who had no other major colonies in Africa when they entered Somali territory—considered Somaliland to be "undeveloped," confiscating large sections of agricultural land between the Juba and Shabelle rivers in order to establish European-owned plantations for bananas, coffee, peanuts, sesame, rice, and cotton. This displaced both nomads and farmers and made life even more difficult for former slaves, a problem that would plague the government of Somalia after independence.

> This then is the broad background under which the Somalis lived during the colonial era ... there was no formal or even de facto British *colony* in the north, but there was an ambitious and even aggressive Italian colonization plan for the south, a plan which had no room for egalitarian values, human rights, or the development of the indigenous people.[76]

In 1940 the Italian Chamber of Commerce estimated that in Somaliland "approximately 73,000 hectares of arable irrigated land was owned by Italians, 15,000 by Arabs and Indians, and none at all owned by Somalis, a result of legislation which prohibited native proprietorship of land."[77] This land was tended by slaves and later anyone (including Somalis) who could be captured and forced to work on the plantations. Somalis were also prohibited from exporting livestock or any other commodity without permission from Italian administrators, which severely limited their economic options. These land-use and labor policies were a huge blow to nomadic culture, a blow that the southern region has never fully recovered from.

During the economic depression of the 1930s, Italian Somaliland was stripped of immense quantities of food and other products, which were sent to Italy, the rest of Europe, Arabia, Japan, and the United States. A report from the 1930s recorded export values (in Italian lire) for a range of dress- and fashion-related materials, including leather and fur, cotton, ivory, and incense.[78] The sheer quantity and variety of goods that were drained away from the local economy is striking. Even with severely depressed prices (in the United States cotton was selling for less than ten cents a pound) goods like cotton and leather were exchanged for millions of lire.

EXPORTED PRODUCTS	1932	1933
Cow hides	1,301,390 (lire)	2,170,500 (lire)
Sheep and goat hides	1,395,830	1,878,270
Dig-dig (deer) skins	390,110	202,090
Leopard skins	2,784,100	1,431,230
Sandals	28,350	42,430
Raw cotton	4,350,400	2,522,060
Raw ivory	159,390	103,680
Incense	909,740	630,270

While a good portion of this money undoubtedly went to line the pockets of the colonists and to the government of Italian Somaliland, there was still demand in the local market for imported textiles and thread to make wrapped clothing. There was also a small but growing market for imported soap and perfume, indicating a notable departure from the traditional use of incense and other natural products to clean and scent the body.[79] These changes in dress were probably not obvious to the colonists, but they do offer a glimpse at changing attitudes toward European dress and social customs in southern Somali territory.

While some imported goods were undoubtedly consumed by the colonists, Somalis in the south were also becoming increasingly enmeshed in the global economy, using dress to display wealth, social class, and political power during a time when these resources were in short supply. This was very different from the traditional uses of dress: to signify age and gender, to serve as an outlet for creative expression, and to be worn as part of magical and religious practices. Somalis had a long history of trade with the outside world, but conspicuous consumption and outright capitalism were new developments.

By the 1920s things had also changed in the north, though for different reasons. Increasing trade had driven up expectations for bride-wealth, but at the same time the natural environment was strained by the increasing numbers of livestock, particularly during times of drought. Increasingly unable to rely on their extended families for sufficient wealth to get married, more and more young men were migrating to the coastal towns to look for paying jobs. Women and children also sought refuge in urban areas in situations of extreme poverty or when kinship structures had broken down.[80] A song written and performed a few decades later blamed the decline of traditional, nomadic life on the inflated expectations of young women.

> The girls say:
> We want gold and silver
> Which we would put around our arms
> And wear around our necks
> A *guntiino* of silk
> A scarf which no money can buy
> And linens that have never been seen
> When women set their minds on this
> That is how marriage was destroyed[81]

In spite of the wealth that flowed through the area, the colonial government did not reinvest much in local development. By encoding "tribal customs" into colonial law and interpreting them in ways best suited to the purposes of the Empire, the British also pitted Somalis against one another: those who settled in urban areas and tried to work within the law (or at least manipulate it to their advantage) versus those who stayed in rural areas and refused to engage with the British on their terms. In this way, "Somaliland reached independence with a legacy of deep underdevelopment...the seeds of tribalism, distrustful and opportunistic attitudes toward the state, and an almost complete lack of modern institutions and infrastructure."[82]

Because the experience of colonization was so different depending on the region, Somali dress—even the exact same items of dress—came to have different meanings in different areas. Symbols like amulets, wrapped clothing, and traditional hairstyles that conveyed "pride" in some areas demonstrated "backwardness" in others. For a small (but politically powerful) minority, European-style dress was the new "modern" thing to wear; for others, it was a sign of giving in to the brutality and disruptions of colonial rule. These regional and class differences continued to grow as colonization ended and the nation of Somalia gained its independence in 1960.

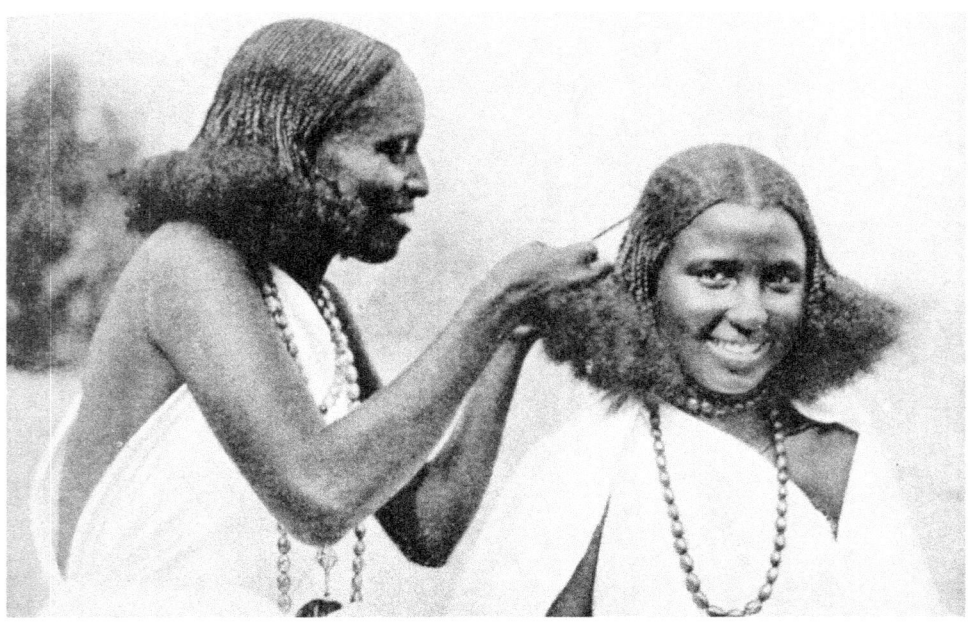

FIGURE 1. Photograph of two young nomadic women braiding their hair into a style that signifies availability for marriage. Published by Harald Swayne (1903) in *Seventeen Trips through Somaliland and a Visit to Abyssinia*.

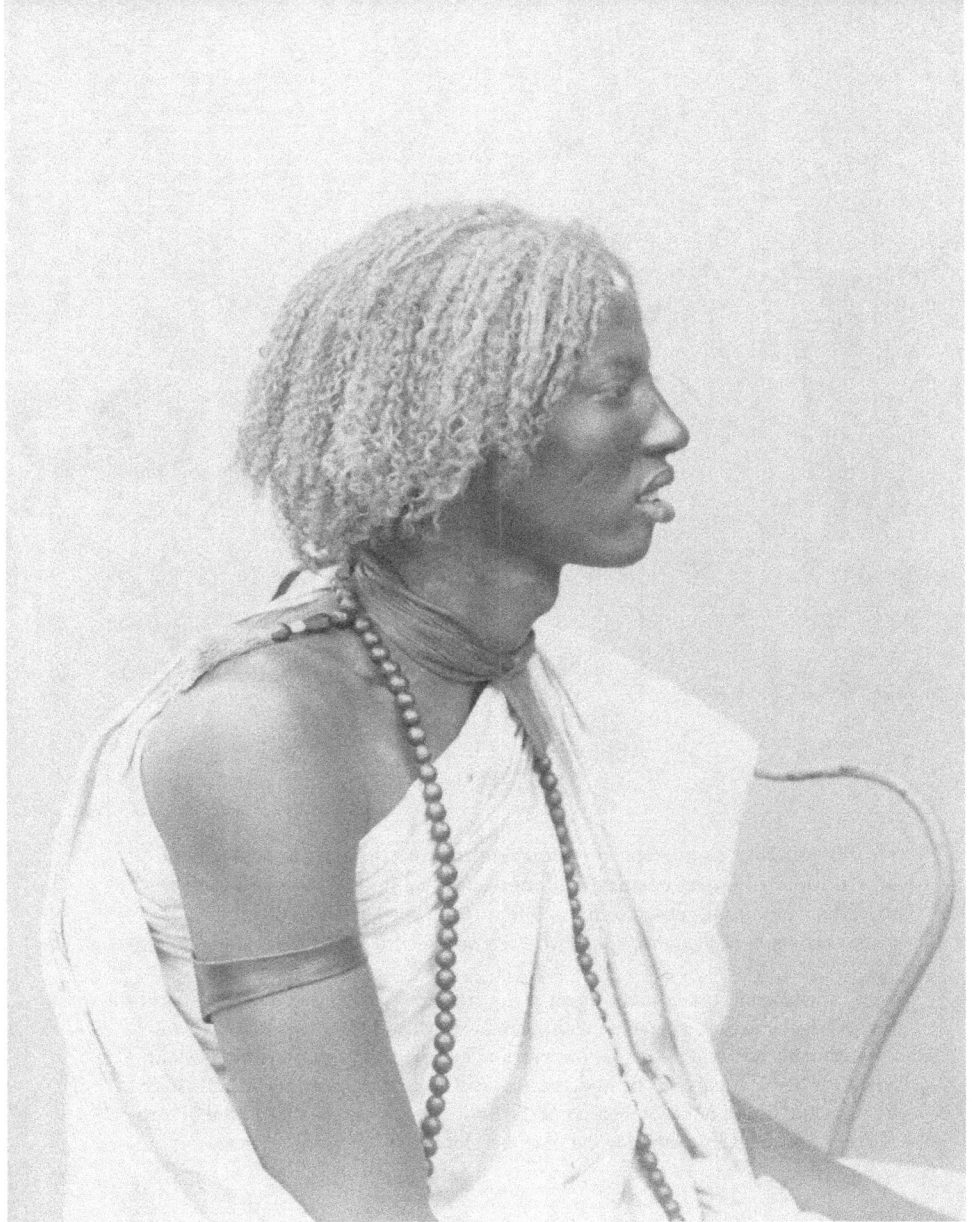

FIGURE 2. Photograph of a young nomadic man from the late 1800s. Notice
his bleached hair, the amulet (*hardas*) strung on a band of leather around his
neck, the band of leather around his bicep, and the strand of prayer beads worn
as a necklace. Collection of the Smithsonian National Museum of Natural
History, National Anthropological Archives, lot 80–52, image #02539100.

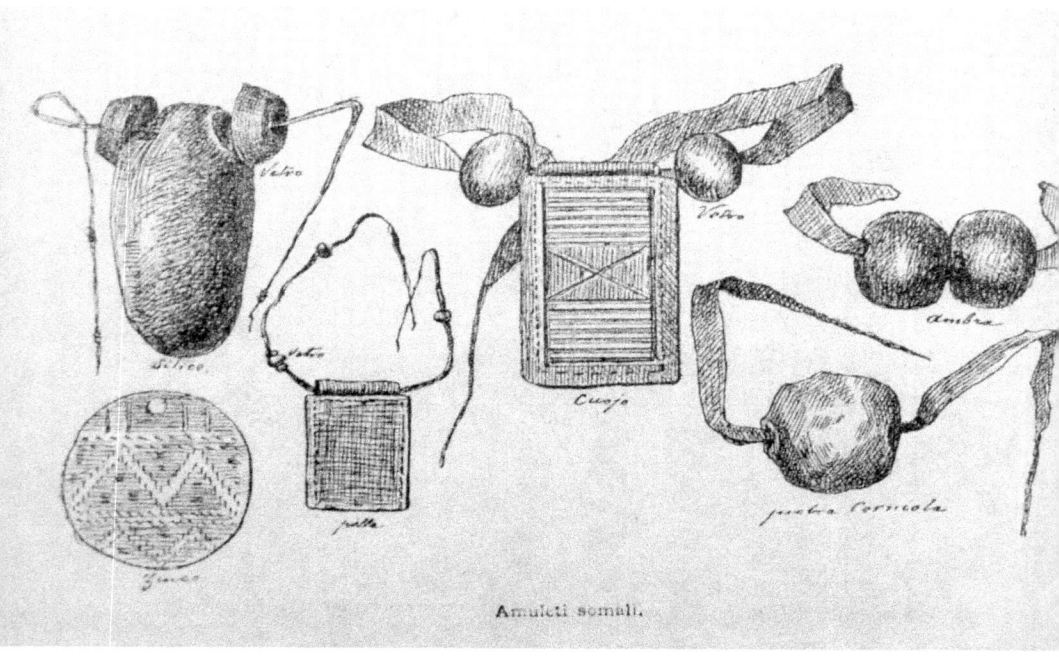

Amuleti somali.

FIGURE 3. *Above,* Lithograph of typical amulets worn by nomadic Somali men until the mid-twentieth century, made of stones, chunks of amber, and packets of leather containing verses from the Qur'an. Published by Luigi Bricchetti (1902) in *Somalia e Benadir: Viaggio di Esplorazione nell'Africa Orientale.*

FIGURE 4. *Facing,* A married woman in the late 1800s wearing an *audulli,* a necklace with a large, crescent-shaped pendant, numerous silver bells, and a chain strung with valuable beads made of glass, silver, and amber. This represented her wealth as well as her participation in an extensive trading network with the Middle East, Europe, and South Asia. Collection of the Smithsonian National Museum of Natural History, National Anthropological Archives, lot 80–52, image #02537300.

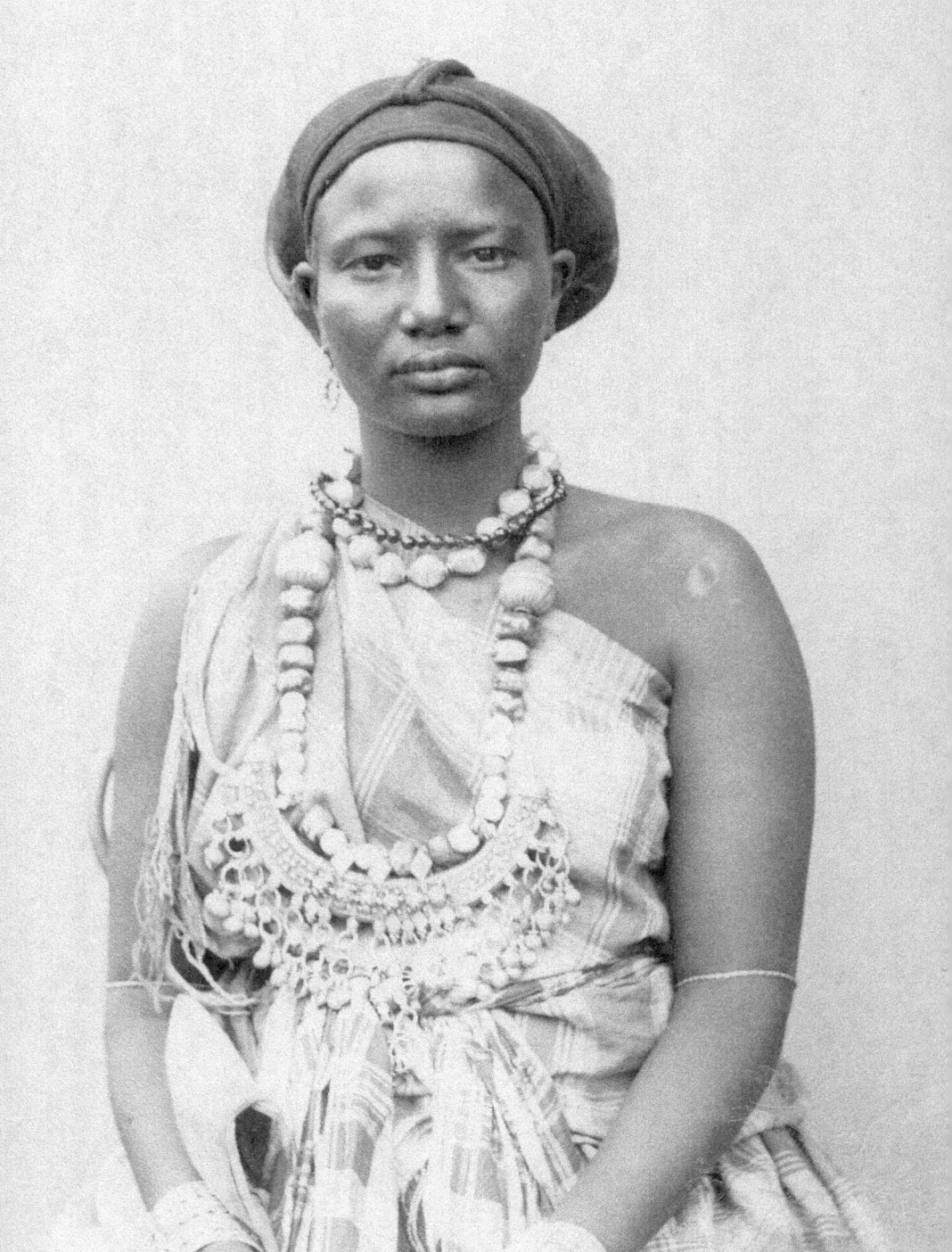

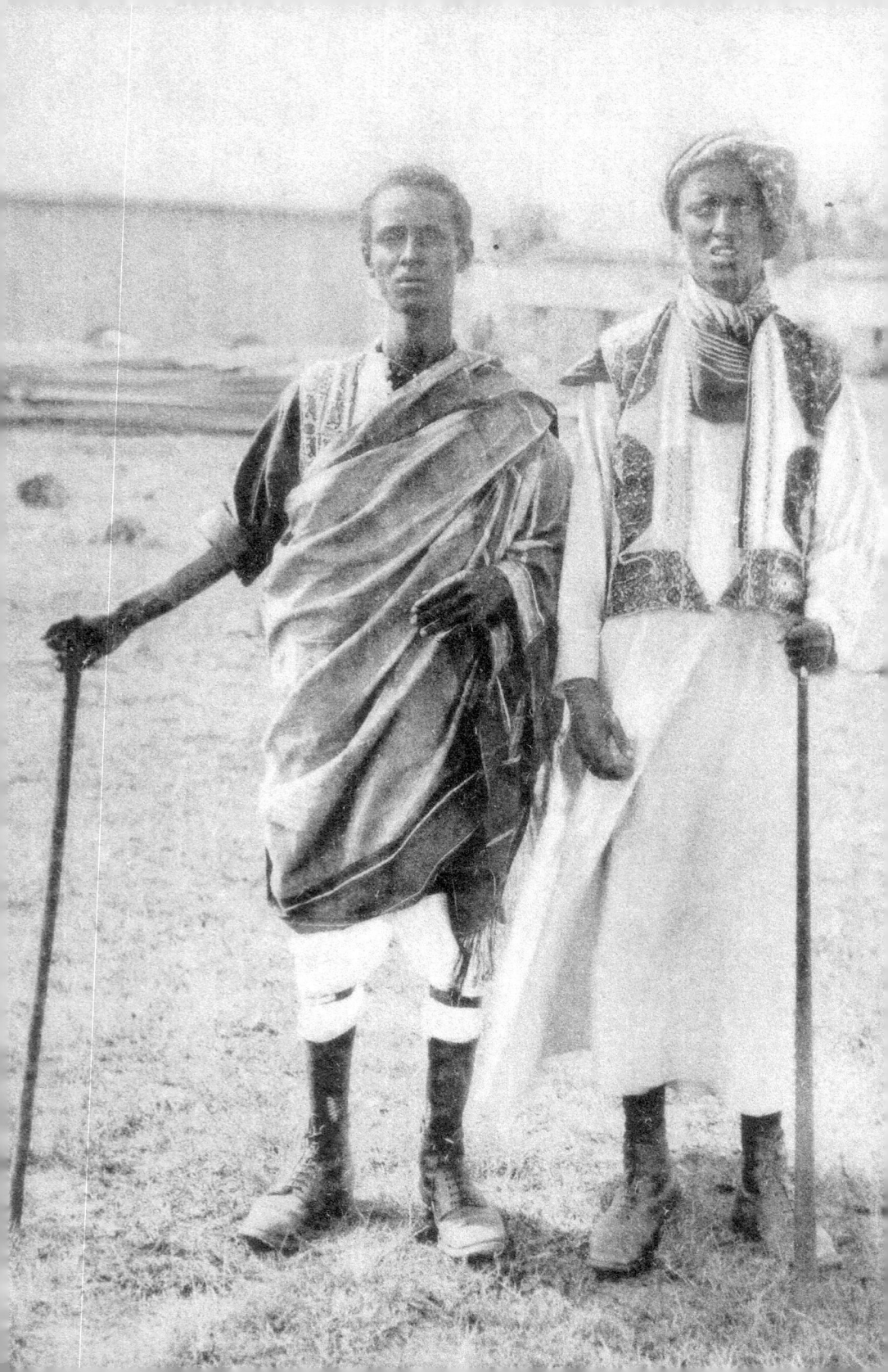

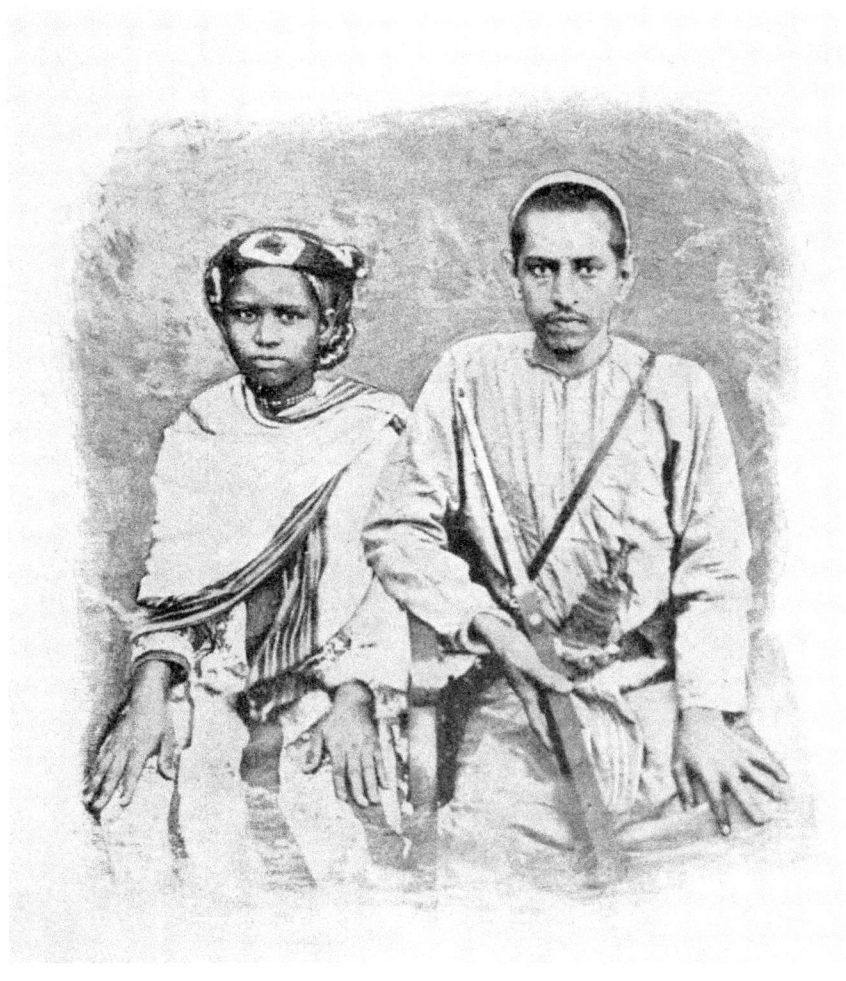

FIGURE 5. *Facing,* Postcard of "Somali traders" from the early 1900s; notice the mixture of Arab, nomadic, and Western-style dress, including lace-up boots and walking sticks. Collection of the author.

FIGURE 6. *Above,* Lithograph of an urban Somali-Arab couple in the late 1800s; notice the man's tunic (*kamiz*) and skullcap (*kufi*) as well as the woman's shawl (*garbasaar*), which probably doubled as a garment to cover her head. At the time, these garments were markedly different from nomadic dress. Published by Luigi Bricchetti (1902) in *Somalia e Benadir: Viaggio di Esplorazione nell'Africa Orientale.*

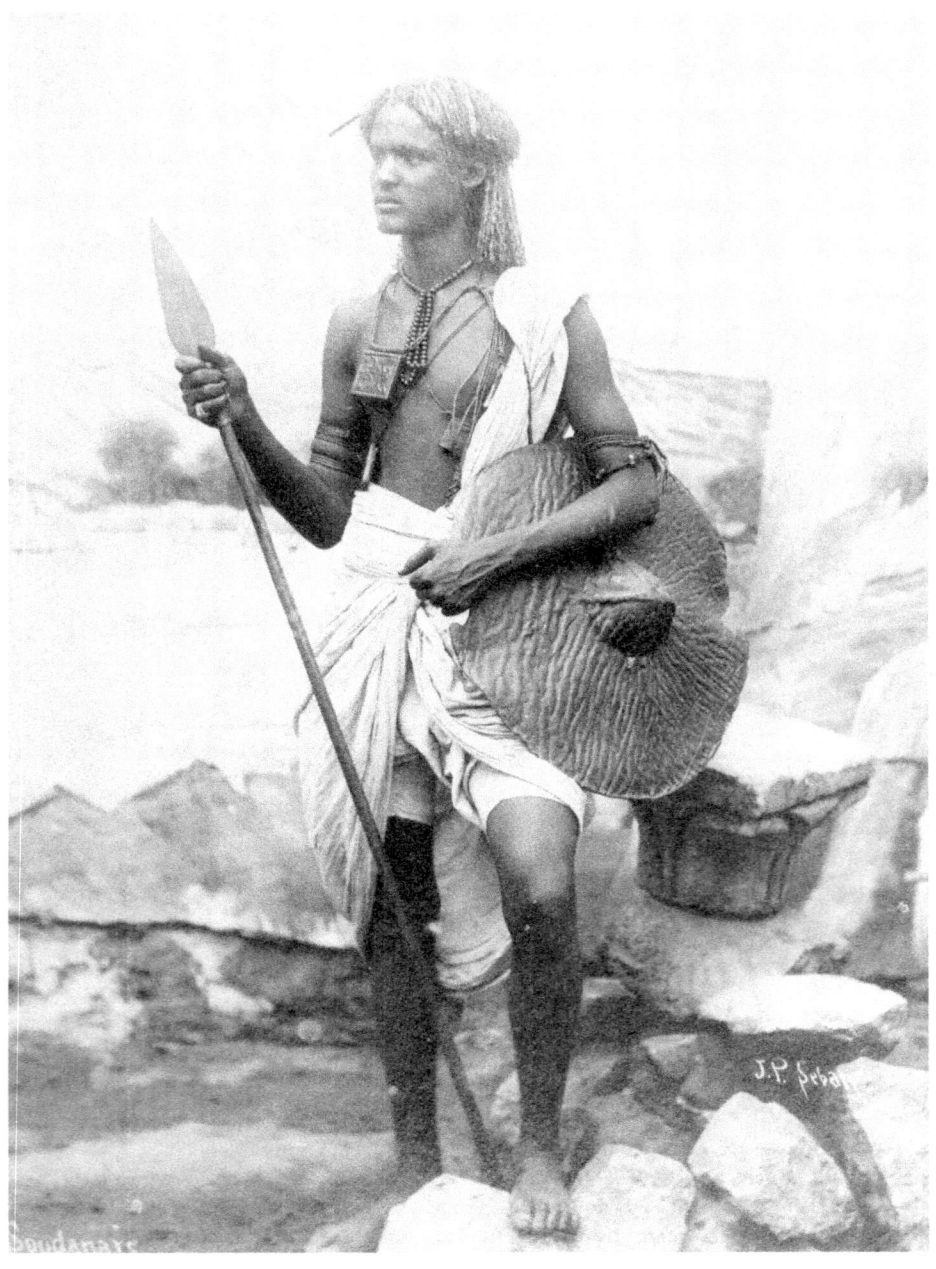

FIGURE 7. Photograph of a "Sudanese warrior" involved in the resistance against British colonization; the same style of dress—based on garments worn by pilgrims at Mecca—was worn by Somalis under the leadership of Sayyid Mohammed Abdulle Hassan. Collection of the Library of Congress (Washington, D.C.), Prints and Photographs Division.

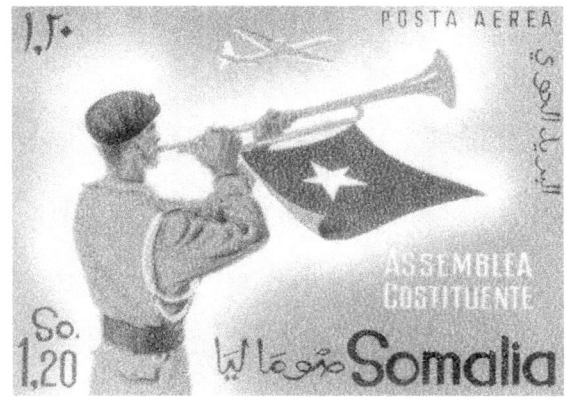

FIGURE 8. *Left,* Postage stamp from the early 1960s depicting a male soldier in the national army blowing a trumpet with the national flag of Somalia; notice the Western-style uniform, which included a long-sleeve shirt, pants, and a beret. Collection of the author.

FIGURE 9. *Below,* Male soldiers in the national army wearing button-down shirts, pants, belts, socks, shoes, and helmets; this kind of Western-style dress was not common until after World War II. Photograph in *Beautiful Somalia,* published by the government of Somalia (in 1971), p. 24.

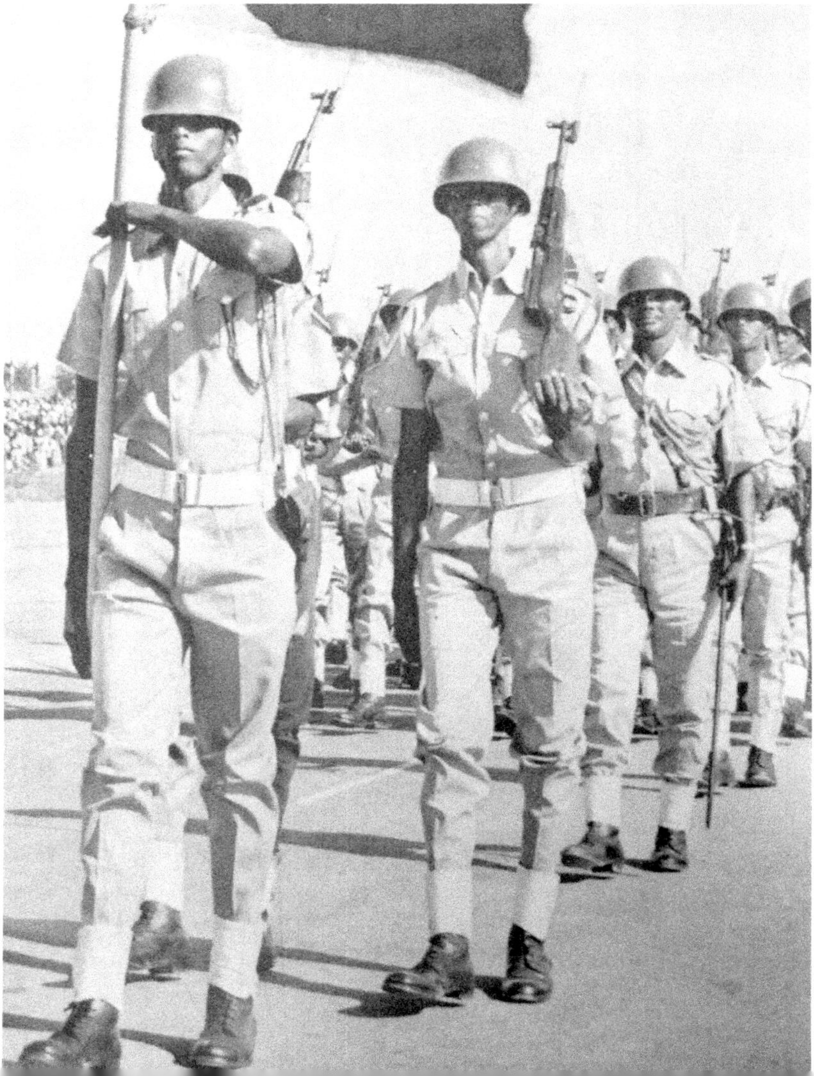

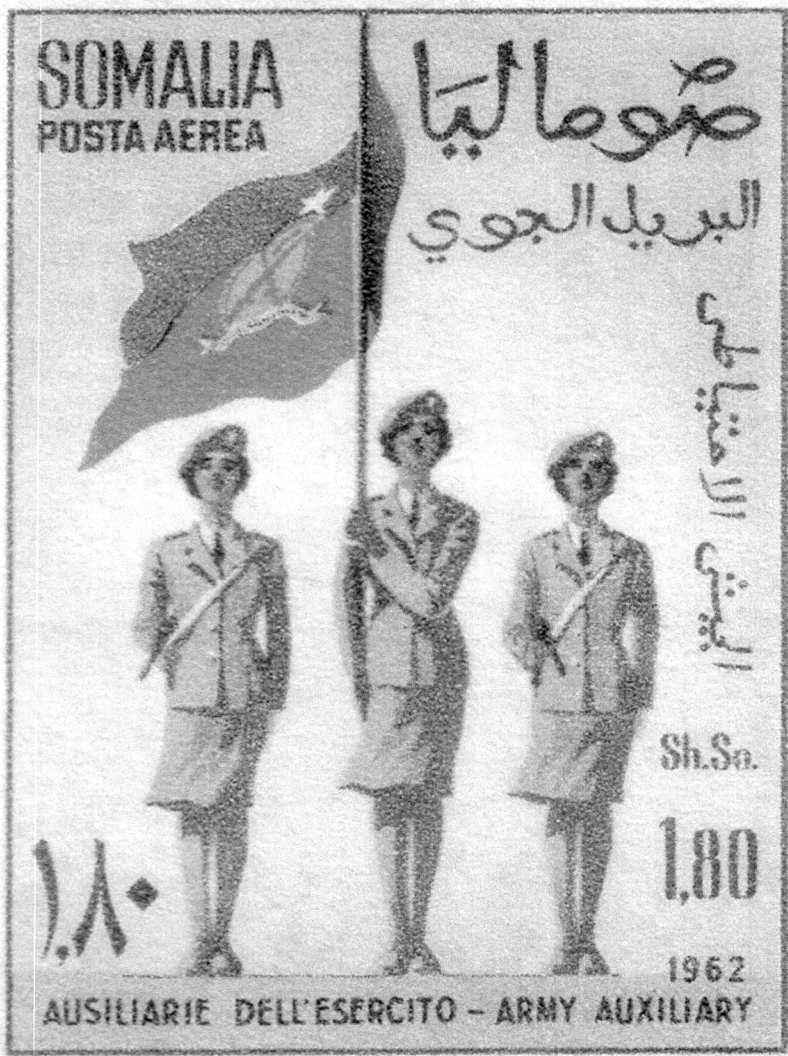

SOMALIA
POSTA AEREA

صوماليا
البريد الجوي

Sh.So.
1.80

1962

AUSILIARIE DELL'ESERCITO – ARMY AUXILIARY

I.P.S.–OFF.CART.VAL.–ROMA   C.MANCIOLI

٥ SHILIN SOOMAALI

5 SHILIN SOOMAALI

5

5 SHILIN SOOMAALI

CENTRAL BANK OF SOMALIA

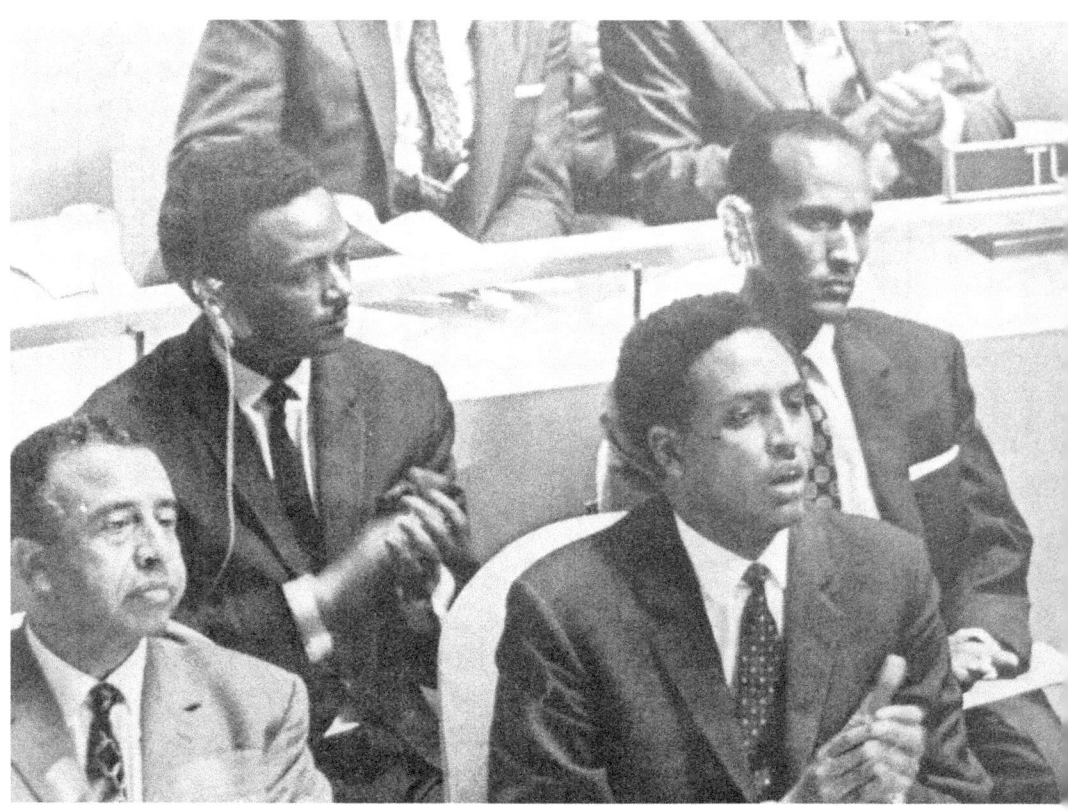

FIGURE 10. *Facing top,* Postage stamp printed in 1962 depicting female soldiers in the army auxiliary forces wearing jackets, knee-length skirts, neckties, and berets; this kind of clothing (particularly the short skirt) was never widely accepted outside of the military since it was associated with prostitutes. Collection of the author.

FIGURE 11. *Facing bottom,* Five shilin banknote from the Central Bank of Somalia; the back side depicts three men picking bananas dressed only in shorts and sleeveless shirts. Collection of the author.

FIGURE 12. *Above,* Male delegates from Somalia to the United Nations wearing three-piece suits. Photograph in *Beautiful Somalia* (1971), p. 17.

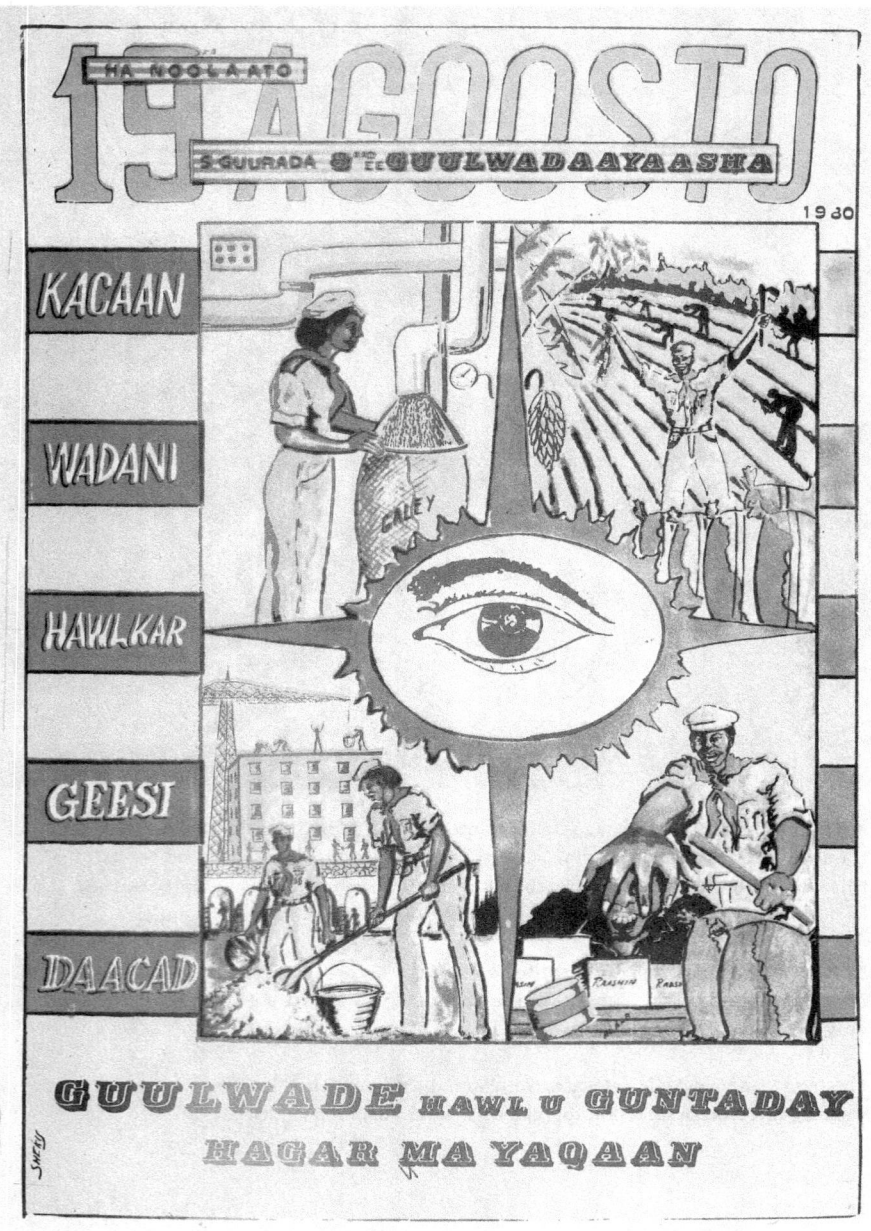

FIGURE 13. Poster showing the *Guulwadayaal* (Barre-era militia) harvesting grain, working in a factory, and threatening miscreants. In the aesthetic of Socialism they were depicted wearing green fatigues, berets, and red kerchiefs, a style that gave rise to the derogatory nickname "Green Dogs." Collection of the Herman B Wells Library at Indiana University, Bloomington.

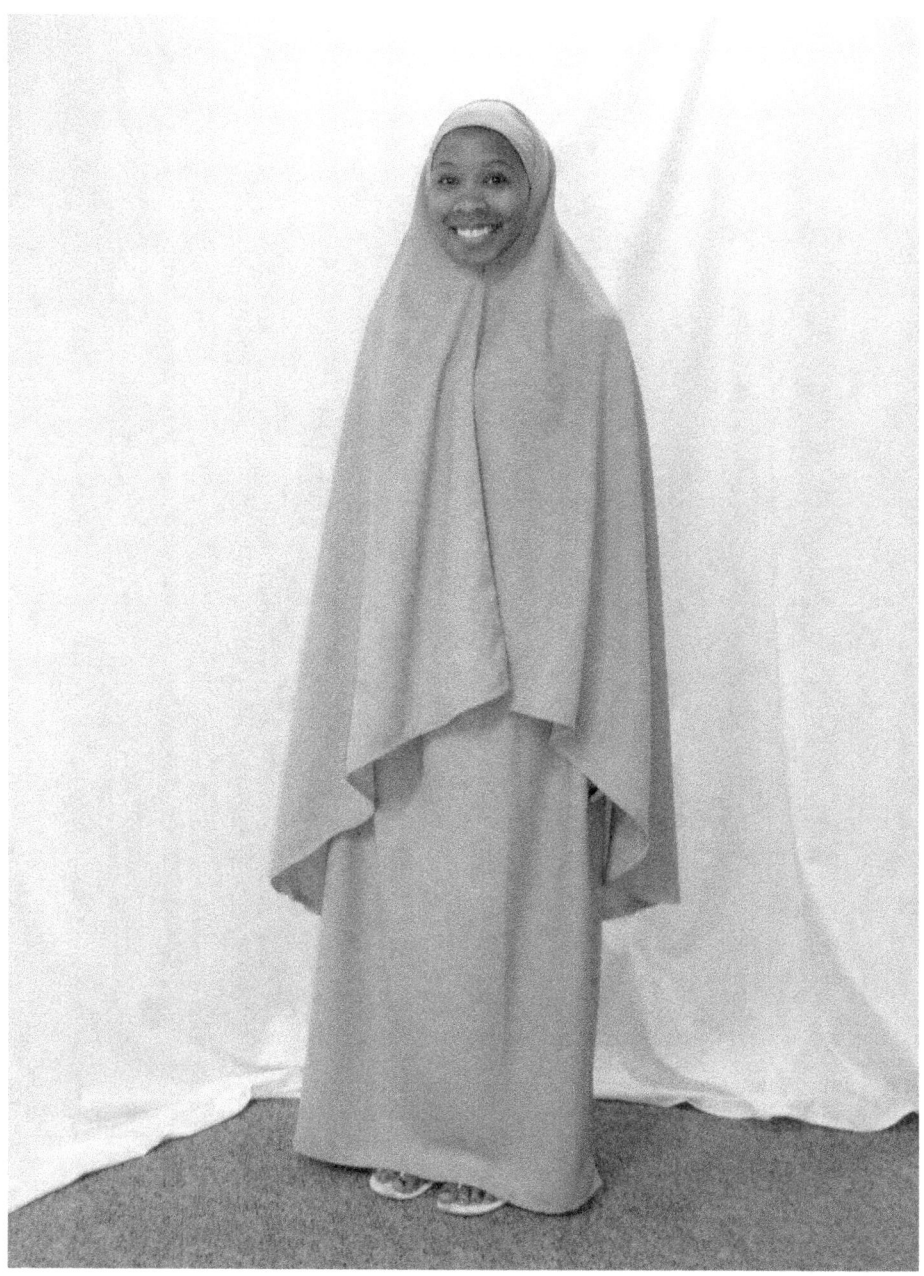

FIGURE 14. *Jilbab* ensemble consisting of a small head wrap (*masaar*), a larger head covering that fits tightly around the face, and a matching skirt; although this style of Islamic dress did not appear in Somalia until the 1980s, it has become very common in the 21st century among refugees and Somalis in the diaspora. Garments in collection of the author.

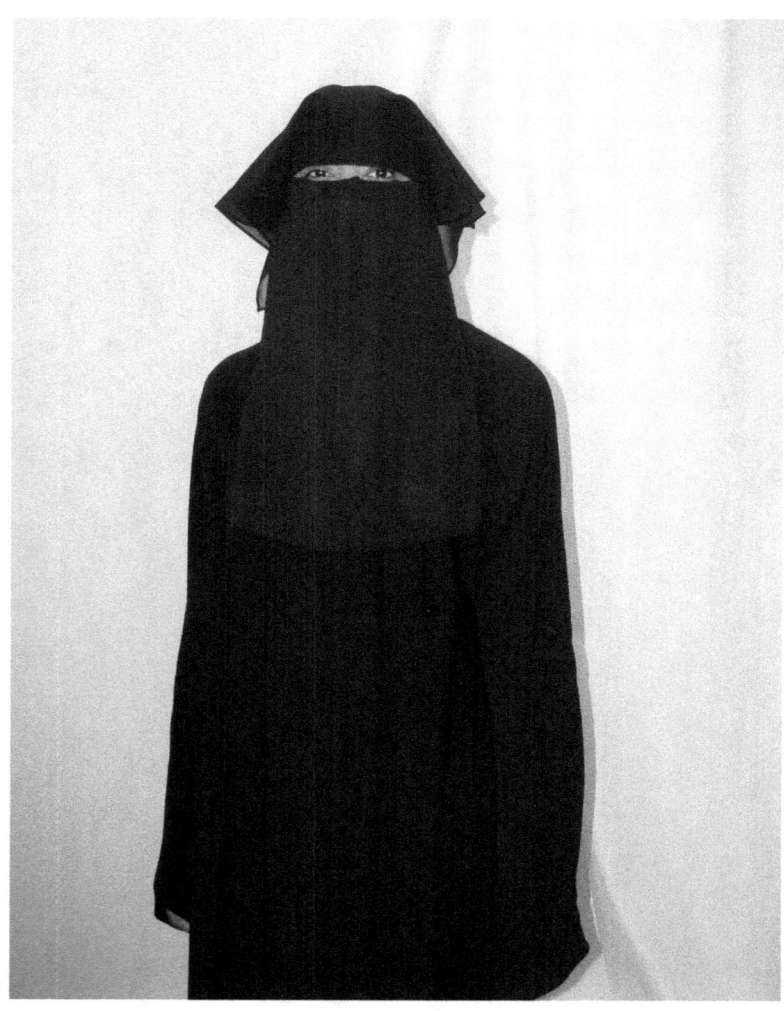

FIGURE 15. *Niqab,* a very conservative and controversial head covering that diffused from the Middle East to Somalia in the 1980s; prior to that time, only the descendants of Arab and Persian settlers would have worn this kind of garment that covers the face. Collection of the author.

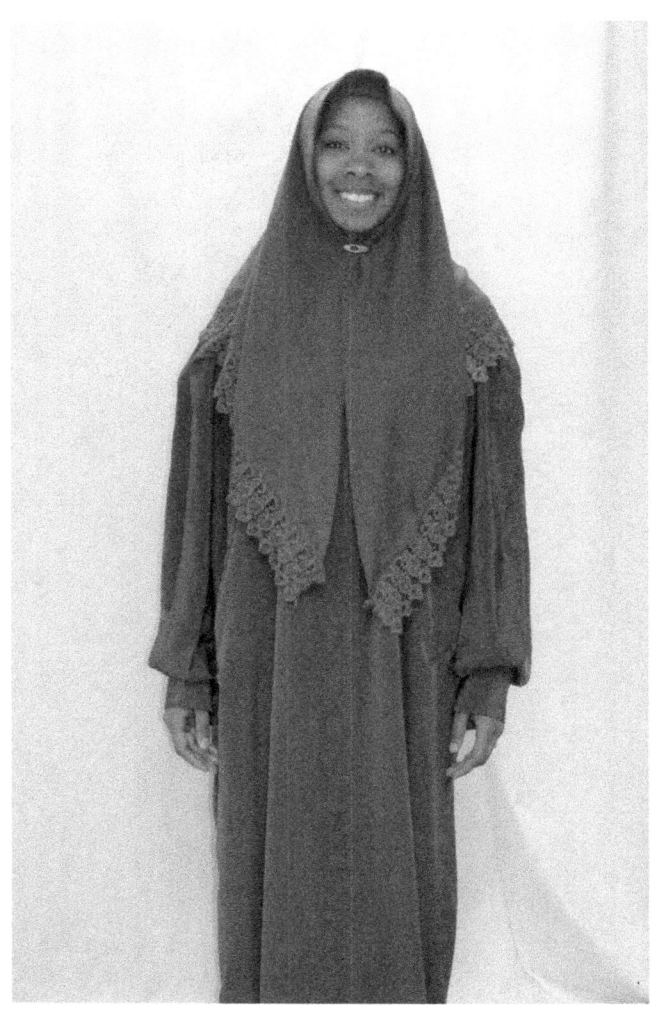

FIGURE 16. *Shuka* (cloak) and *khimar* (head covering), an Islamic style of dress from the Middle East that first appeared in Somalia in the 1970s; *shuka* is a word used in other parts of East Africa as a generic term for a garment (covering). Collection of the author.

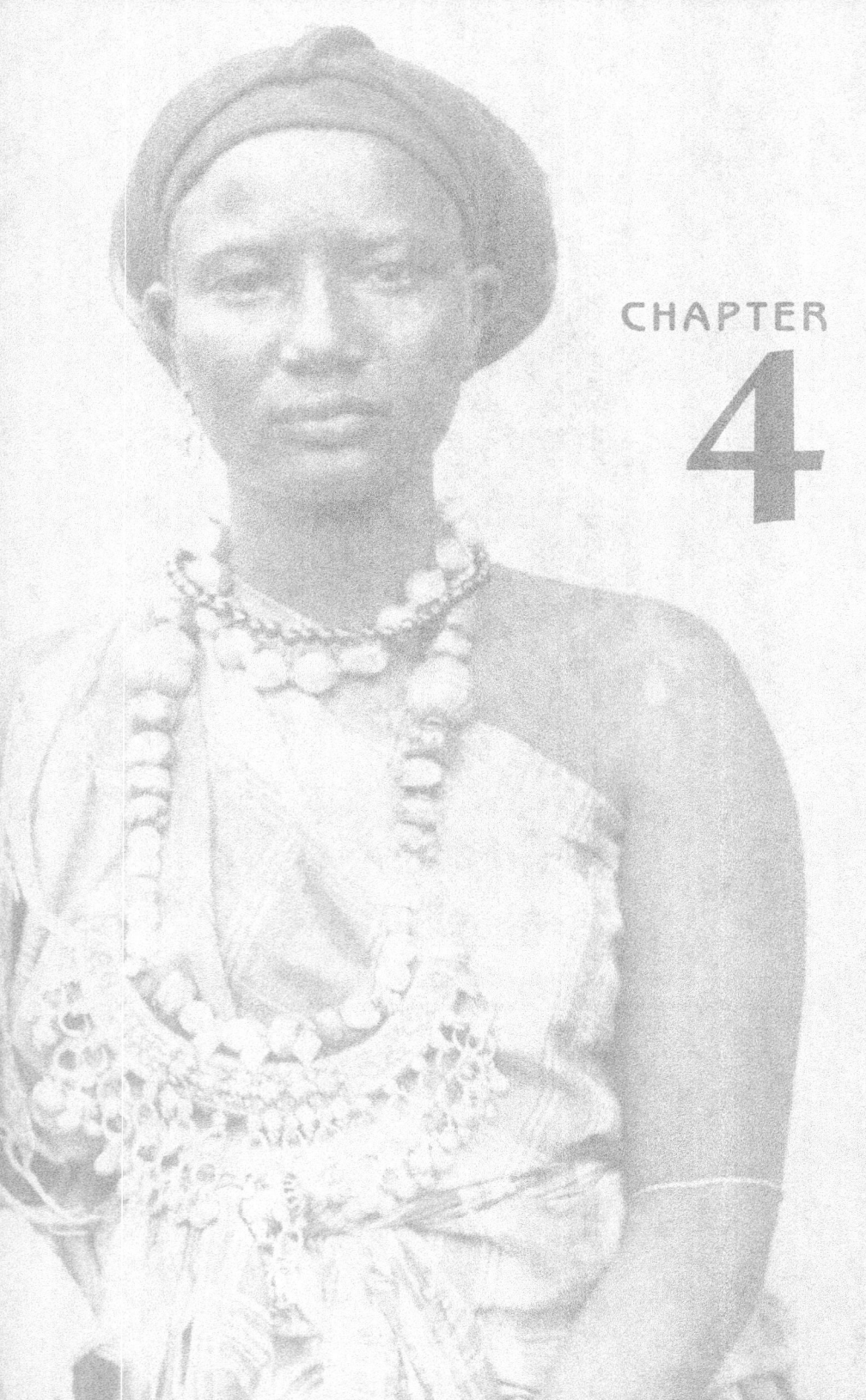

CHAPTER

4

Dressing the Nation—1945 to 1991

The world is a journey
Which leads to a beautiful dream
And modernity is its nose-rope
Don't shortchange yourself
It is a curse to stay behind one's age group
People have emancipated themselves
From these rags and heavy clothes you wear . . .

—Maxammed Jaamac Jaaf and Mariam Mursal, 1960s

From the end of World War II to independence to the total collapse of the government in Somalia—a span of just forty-six years—Somali dress changed radically. Although there had always been some differences in dress between men and women, the gap widened significantly. Among men, European-style dress gained widespread acceptance. Among women, new types of fabric and some garments became fashionable, but European-style dress was not widely accepted and in some cases considered a mark of prostitution. Islamic "veiling" practices also took hold, even among Somalis who were not the descendants of Arab and Persian settlers. As older garments like the *guntiino* and *maro* were replaced by other forms of dress, they became valorized as symbols of traditional Somali nomadic culture. The government used images of men and women wearing these garments on all kinds of official documents and artifacts including postage stamps and currency.

Not surprisingly—since the government of Somalia came to a dramatic and violent end after just thirty-one years of independence—the academic literature about this time period tends to focus on politics. Issues of particular concern include the rise and fall of dictator Siad Barre, Somalia's involvement in the Cold War, neocolonialism, and changes in clan politics. A closer look at dress, however, reveals other tensions: between men and women, between those who were educated under the colonial system and grew to accept it and those who did not, between "noble" Somalis and members of the underclass (including the descendants of former slaves), between those who wanted to romanticize traditional culture and those who were still living it, between long-standing religious practices and radical new ideas about Islam coming from the Middle East. Although Somalia has often been discussed as a "homogeneous" nation—at least in comparison to multiethnic, multi-religious countries like Nigeria and Kenya—there were still vast differences in dress that depended on age, gender, social class, ancestry, region of the country, level of education, etc. Styles ranging from three-piece suits to conservative Islamic dress to updated "traditional" garments like the *dirac* and *gorgorad* reflected and shaped growing currents of misunderstanding and mistrust in civil society. Clothing didn't cause the government to collapse, but as an arena for the expression of political values—one open to all members of society on a daily basis—it was certainly involved in its demise. Anyone who thinks dress could not possibly have that much political significance should consider the ban on Islamic dress in Turkey; until recently women who wore "headscarves" were not allowed to serve in Parliament or attend public universities. While these circumstances are starting to change (in 2003 a former Islamist[1] became the prime minister), the goal of the Turkish government since the 1920s has been to establish and preserve secularism. Although that country, like Somalia, is ninety-nine percent Muslim, clothing reflects and inspires a great deal of tension between different segments of society.[2]

In the 1930s, Petr Bogatyrev observed that politics were a double-edged sword in the realm of dress. Nationalism, for example, could instill great passion and pride for certain styles, but only as long as there was no significant change in power.[3] Once valorized as a symbol of the nation, dress became "subject to the ebb and flow of contested political ideologies."[4] During World War II, the Nazi government promoted the *dirndl* skirt as a "symbol of the feminine ideal—Aryan, healthy, 'natural' and preferably blonde."[5] Although many elite women rejected this image and preferred to wear French couture,[6] Bavarian-style folk dress became a popular national symbol. After Germany was defeated, it rapidly fell out of use.

As in the case of the *dirndl*, the political symbolism of dress is frequently linked to gender. In *Re-Orienting Fashion*, Carla Jones and Ann Marie Leshkowich observed that women tend to be responsible for negotiating ethnic and national identities through dress because they "can simultaneously be

imagined as essentially maternal and iconic of a national body, yet also different, citizens who must prove their worth through high-stakes performances
of identity."[7] In colonial Algeria, the French recognized the symbolic power
of women's dress and attempted to change it as a means of changing the entire local culture[8] (making it more compatible with colonization and French
cultural norms). Conversely, in France during the Revolution, national dress
was primarily a male domain, since it was based on the concept of the citizen-
soldier and "women were never seen as full citizens like men who could perform military service for the nation."[9] In the early 1900s, the dress of Somali
men was more politicized than the dress of Somali women, but that rapidly
changed as colonization came to an end. Resistance to "foreign influences"
shifted from armed conflict to more subtle visual and cultural cues.

Unfortunately, photographs from this time period in Somali history,
particularly images from urban areas, have become difficult to obtain. Many
of the books written by outsiders do not include images of people, which
would be needed to study trends in dress.[10] Photographs taken by Somalis
and archived in Somalia are inaccessible because of the civil war and have
probably been destroyed. Some Somalis in the diaspora have collections of
family photographs; however, many refugees were forced to leave with only
the clothing on their backs. In the Somali community in Minnesota, which
is where I conducted my field research, most people are refugees and do
not have family photographs taken in Somalia before the 1990s. Because of
these extreme conditions this chapter is based on an unusual assemblage of
sources: popular songs, currency, postage stamps, a propaganda poster, and
a book titled *Beautiful Somalia* that was published by Somalia's Ministry of
Information and National Guidance in 1971 for distribution to embassies all
over the world. It must be kept in mind that some of these objects were created by the government and do not give a complete picture of dress from this
time period; they focus on romantic images of Somalis wearing "traditional"
dress and "modern" Somalis wearing European-style dress while leaving out
the new forms of Islamic dress. These distortions highlight the discord that
existed in Somali society during the latter half of the twentieth century.

From Colonialism to Neocolonialism

After its defeat in World War II, Italy was forced to give up its colonies in
Africa, which by that time included Libya, Eritrea, and Italian Somaliland.
Libya was officially recognized as an independent nation in 1951, but Eritrea

was annexed by Ethiopia. Italian Somaliland was turned over to the United Nations to be governed as a protectorate. Despite these changes, some colonial administrators decided to remain in Somali territory with their families, living in urban areas such as Mogadishu and Kismayo. Compared to British colonial officers, the Italians may have had little optimism about what they would find back home. As the twentieth century wore on, these expatriates were increasingly joined in the cities by young Somalis seeking jobs and schooling.

Thousands of Somalis were employed in homes and businesses owned by expatriates. There were also jobs to be found in the colonial government and eventually the new national government as soldiers, police officers, drivers, and office workers. Educated young people (almost all men) returning from universities in Europe and the Middle East served as lawyers, engineers, journalists, doctors, and teachers. In a report by the British government on conditions in Somali territory shortly after World War II, one official noted, "There has been a marked drift to the towns during the recent war, and too many young people have left their stock and gardens to live in townships."[11] Between 1969 and 1990, the population of Mogadishu went from less than half a million to more than two million people.[12]

Although the British emerged from World War II as victors, it left them with little ability to maintain such a large empire. In 1949, the British gave up control over Somaliland, and the two halves of Somalia were joined together as a protectorate of the United Nations (although the British did retain the right to serve as administrators for the U.N.). Under this arrangement, corporations from Europe as well as the United States and the Middle East were allowed to exploit Somalia's natural resources including oil and uranium;[13] however, Somalis fought for and slowly gained more and more control over their own governance. In 1954, the first municipal elections were held and the new council adopted a national flag: a blue field with a five-pointed white star representing the five colonial divisions of Somali territory. It remains the national flag today (see figure 8). In 1960, Somalia was formally recognized as an independent nation, but there were still Somalis living in present-day Kenya, Ethiopia, and Djibouti. In the 1960s and '70s, Somalis on both sides of these borders agitated (and in some cases went to war) to be reunited as a single nation, but were not ultimately successful.

Even though Somalis had previously resisted European-style dress, as they moved into urban areas and came into closer contact with Europeans their clothing, hairstyles, and other aspects of body adornment started to change. One reason for this was employment. Soldiers in the new national army and police force were expected to wear European-style uniforms, which included pants, button-down shirts, combat boots, and helmets (see figure 9). Even women who served in auxiliary divisions as nurses and secretaries were issued knee-length skirts and neckties along with jackets, berets, gloves, and long socks (figure 10). These uniforms, which fit much closer to the body than the *guntiino,* were undoubtedly uncomfortable in a climate where temperatures often climb above forty degrees Celsius. The garments were also very different from styles of dress worn by most contemporary Somali women; since these uniforms did not cover the entire lower body they were considered quite scandalous. Flight attendants for Somali Airlines (which partnered with the Italian national airline Alitalia in 1963) also wore Westernized uniforms.[14] A photograph in *Beautiful Somalia* shows one flight attendant wearing a jacket, a pillbox hat, and a slim watch on her left wrist. Another photograph shows a female DJ for Radio Mogadishu wearing a short-sleeve dress with a scarf wrapped around her neck, simple earrings (unlike the heavier silver jewelry favored in the 1800s), a bangle bracelet, and a wristwatch. Her head is uncovered and she has a short, pixie-style haircut.

In urban areas, young people were also experimenting with European-style dress. Fashionable clothing and jewelry was sold in boutiques owned by British and Italian expatriates. In a life history published under the pseudonym "Aman," one Somali woman described her experiences in Mogadishu after migrating from the countryside to the city with her mother and sisters. As she encountered other young people, she quickly began to feel out of place.

> One night one of my friends took me to a party. There were a lot of handsome men there. There were a couple of whites there too, even though the party was mainly for Somalis—all of them were well educated, and the majority worked in banks or in big offices for the government. . . . I was embarrassed at the way I looked—my clothes, my hair—my dress and the way I acted weren't like the other girls. . . . The girls here didn't wear sarongs like we did in [the village]. Their dresses were sewn together, shorter, prettier. They even had better shoes—European shoes I had never seen before.[15]

Within a generation, a considerable number of men were wearing Westernized dress on a daily basis, and there are hints that this change was not only about appearing fashionable. There is a picture of three men wearing shorts and sleeveless shirts while harvesting bananas on the five shilin banknote (though obviously named after the British "shilling," "shilin" is the official spelling on Somali currency) (see figure 11). This image suggests that European clothes could be standard work wear for laborers.

Starting in the late 1950s, as many countries in Africa regained their independence from Europe, delegates to the United Nations often changed their dress from European styles to new forms of "national dress."[16] The first president of Ghana, Kwame Nkrumah, wore a wrapper made of *kente* cloth and gave a very large and beautiful piece of *kente* to the United Nations as a symbol of his country's dignity and freedom. The male delegates from Somalia, however, continued to wear three-piece suits (see figure 12), while "Somali" dress was the domain of the only woman in the group.[17] Perhaps the mixture of suits and ethnic dress was an intentional strategy, a means of projecting a blend of tradition and modernity that would be more appealing to Western patrons. It seems to have worked: in the 1960s, Somalia was awarded more foreign aid per capita than any other country in Africa.[18]

Instead of investing in infrastructure or long-term projects to benefit society, such as schools and hospitals, however, much of the aid money was used "to pay for increasing numbers of bureaucrats and parliamentarians, who lived ostentatious and opulent lives in Mogadishu, and for a five-fold increase in the size of the Somali army."[19] I. M. Lewis observed that within a few years, many Somalis were disillusioned with the new government.

> [The National Assembly] was now widely regarded cynically as a sordid market-place where, with little concern for the interests of those who had voted for them, deputies traded their votes for personal gain . . . ferried about in sumptuous limousines. . . . A story popular in Mogadishu epitomizing the gulf between rulers and ruled referred to an incident in which one man riding on another's back and making the motions of driving a vehicle was stopped by a puzzled guard at the entrance to Government Headquarters (*Governo*). "What do you think you are doing?" challenged the guard. "Oh," replied the man riding his human mount, "I noticed that in order to get in here you had to be conducted by a chauffeur."[20]

A gulf between the lower and upper classes widened rapidly as politicians siphoned money to build lavish houses, buy expensive clothing and cars, and send their grown children to universities outside of Somalia. Nepotism was rampant. Although some professionals and government officials were undoubtedly hardworking, honest people, others were extraordinarily corrupt. Because of these conditions, many Somalis began to associate Western fashions with arrogance and corruption instead of progress; a sign of neocolonialist policies that placed the personal greed of Western-influenced politicians ahead of the needs of most ordinary citizens.

For young women, Western fashions could also be associated with a loss of morality and sexual purity, leading to accusations of "selling their beauty" instead of entering into a proper marriage.[21] In the growing middle class many young people—both men and women—were pursuing marriage for personal reasons like love and companionship instead of for traditional reasons of collective interest, but came under fire from other parts of society. A popular song painted these nontraditional choices as a form of gold digging.

> Everyone has his own preferences
> And taste is what sets people apart
> One cannot tell who is wealthiest from the way people present themselves
> What I prefer is
> Rich men who turn over lots of wealth and have capital
> Who, while you live with them, put you in a huge house
> And give you a luxurious life
> What about you?
> Dear sister, Ruun
> Don't get rid of the culture in which you were born
> Or run away from your cultural heritage
> Don't throw away the ways of your ancestors
> What I prefer is a man who establishes a home with you
> Receiving you from your male relatives
> With their blessing
> You will live together honestly
> Blessed by the Lord.[22]

Yet, women making life decisions in this period were caught in a difficult position amid the waves of cultural change. While young men gained more and more opportunities for education and employment, choices for respectable young women were increasingly constrained. The nomadic way of life was dying out, but under the new system women and children were largely an afterthought.

The Regime of Siad Barre

It was in this atmosphere that in 1969 the president of Somalia was assassinated. Siad Barre—who started his career as a police officer in Italian Somaliland and had risen through the ranks to become commander of the national army—was installed as the country's new leader, a position that he would hold as dictator for the next twenty-two years. Immediately he declared that Somalia should be called the Somali Democratic Republic. Basing the government on Socialism—a concept that was translated into the Somali language as "wealth-sharing based on wisdom"—he ordered the seizure of many banks, factories, plantations, and other businesses owned by European expatriates. He also started a national campaign to burn effigies in the streets "representing 'tribalism, corruption, nepotism and misrule'" and insisted that Somalis should call one another "comrade" (*jaalle*) instead of "kinsman."[23] Yet, in many ways he continued to behave like a commander, issuing demands and expecting obedience from both soldiers and ordinary citizens. Strikingly, he also wore his military uniform throughout his time in office, appearing as a commander in all official portraits.

At first, the new government had a great deal of popular support. In 1972, Barre hired scholars to create a written form of the Somali language and started a literacy campaign, sending teachers out into the small towns and rural areas to educate both children and adults. He also established Somalia's first university.[24] In this way, he hoped the country could overcome educational and language barriers that had been introduced during the colonial period.[25] One problem, for example, was that without a written language for Somali, all documents had to be recorded in English, Italian, or Arabic. This naturally favored people who were well educated and had loyalties that extended beyond the borders of Somalia. Other popular programs included funding for health care, rural development, and guaranteed employment for all citizens.[26]

Many other decisions were not so popular, such as a new law banning clan alliances and references to ethnic or clan differences. So, for example, if someone died in a traffic accident, the family would not legally be able to claim *diya* or "blood payments" from the clan of the person who caused the accident. The idea behind this was to end discrimination against groups like former slaves, the *Saab,* orphans (since Barre himself was an orphan), and the less powerful Somali clans. This policy might have been well intended, but it was also a serious departure from traditional ways of ensuring order and justice. Another problem was that a vast difference existed between rhetoric and day-to-day reality. Exploiting clan divisions to his own advantage, Barre built himself a loyal cadre of government officials based on the clan system.

three groups in particular exercised special power, a trinity known *sotto voce* as MOD after the initial letters of the corresponding clan names. M (Marehan) represented the president's own clan, O (Ogaadeen) that of his mother, and D (Dulbhante) that of his most prominent son-in-law, head of the sinister National Security Service (NSS) established, with East European advisers, shortly after Siyaad's coup. Although officially dedicated to "Scientific Socialism," it is more accurate to regard this phase of Somalia's existence as "Scientific Siyadism."[27]

Another decision that turned the tide against Siad Barre was the establishment of a militia called the *Guulwadayaal* or "Pioneers of the Revolution." This group was supposed to provide employment for orphans and other marginalized youths, but ultimately served the purpose of spying on households and reporting subversive activity.[28] Reflecting on her family's experiences during Barre's regime, scholar Amina Adan observed that members of the militia were "set loose on the public to ascertain that everyone went to their neighborhood Orientation Center and participated in community service programs (such as cleaning streets) so as to humble everyone docilely to obey state authority."[29] A poster printed in 1980 (figure 13) depicts members of the *Guulwadayaal* harvesting grain, working in a factory, and threatening miscreants with violence. Eerily, the poster also has a giant eye in the center, symbolizing the group's unofficial role as spy agency for the government. Both male and female militia members wore green fatigues, which included pants, a short-sleeve shirt and a beret, along with a contrasting red kerchief— a popular Socialist symbol in many countries including China and the Soviet Union. These uniforms and the unpopular activities of the *Guulwadayaal* earned them the nickname "Green Dogs," an epithet that could bring severe punishment if overheard by a member of the militia.[30]

As the years went by, the government became less responsive to the needs of ordinary citizens and more reliant on tactics of fear and violence. Barre—always dressed in his military uniform—required his portrait to appear "in all public and private establishments; every public institution had an illuminated concrete and glass structure in its front yard where an immense portrait of the *macallinka* (the teacher) was displayed."[31] This was more than just narcissism; Barre wanted all citizens to view him as an omnipotent, omnipresent force. Although officially designated as a Socialist Republic, Somalia was increasingly being run as a military dictatorship. Barre's names for himself, which included "Father of Knowledge," "Father of the Nation," and "Victory Pioneer Siad," multiplied and became increasingly bold.[32] I. M. Lewis described Barre as working "bat-like" throughout the night, "sustained by endless cups of black coffee." He personally supervised all leaves, promotions, and passport applications sought by government employees, making it virtually impossible for any kind of organized resistance to develop within the government and threaten his authority.[33]

The New Islamism Takes Root

Even through these dramatic political changes, Somalia's historic ties to the Islamic world remained strong. In 1974 Somalia joined the League of Arab Nations—the only member state where Arabic was not the primary spoken language. (Siad Barre supported this move because he identified with Arab nationalism and anti-colonialism, not because of Somalia's Islamic heritage.[34]) Relationships with Arab League countries gave more university students opportunities to attend institutions in the Middle East instead of going to Europe. Saudi Arabia offered scholarships, but these were primarily in religious studies and offered only to men.[35] The goal was to offer charity to other Muslims and spread the Saudi version of Islam (Wahabbism), not raise the educational level of all Somalis.

As worldwide oil prices soared in the 1970s and the OPEC countries became fabulously wealthy, employers in countries such as Iraq, Saudi Arabia, Kuwait, Qatar, and the United Arab Emirates also began to hire enormous numbers of teachers, construction workers, and domestic servants. Tens of thousands of Somalis (especially men) were able to migrate to the area for short-term and long-term employment. In the process, they encountered new styles of dress and new ideas about the practice of Islam, mixing with migrant laborers from other parts of the Middle East, Pakistan, India, and Southeast Asia. The wages they sent home through an informal transferring system called *hawaalad* became an important source of income for their families as well as the nation as a whole.[36] In the 1970s it was estimated that workers in the Middle East were putting the equivalent of at least 300 million U.S. dollars into the economy of Somalia annually, accounting for roughly forty percent of the country's GNP. By the late 1980s it had climbed to as much as 540 million U.S. dollars annually.[37]

Another influence during this time was the Iranian Revolution, which fostered a new way of thinking about politics and religion throughout the

Islamic world. Although Iran is not an Arab country, enthusiasm for Islamism and the achievements of the Revolution—which had replaced a highly Westernized president with a government theoretically based on Islamic law—spread quickly. Frustrated with Scientific Socialism and the attitude of secularization that went with it, some Somalis formed an Islamist organization of their own called al-Itaxaad al-Islamiya. Its overarching goal was to depose the existing regime and form a new Islamic government in Somalia, but members also had a cultural agenda, insisting that women should wear more modest clothing modeled after the Iranian *chador* or the *jilbab* worn in Jordan and Turkey, and pushing for men and women to be seated separately, regardless of whether the gathering was religious or secular. Al-Itaxaad and another Islamist group, al-Islah al-Islamiya, were

> allied with other Muslim fundamentalist associations in the wider Islamic world and were supported by endowments, *zakat* [donations to charity], and special funds . . . from philanthropic Islamic associations. Petrodollars also came from Saudi Arabia, Kuwait, and Iran to fund *da'wa* (proselytization). [Leaders] were trained at the Saudi sponsored . . . International Islamic Universities in Pakistan and Malaysia. . . . Both groups established Qur'anic schools and orphanages and provided basic Islamic education.[38]

In addition to these groups, some young Somalis were attracted to the Muslim Brotherhood (al-Ikhwan al-Muslimun), a movement with similar goals that had originated in Egypt.

Due to these influences, during the 1970s and '80s several new types of clothing from other parts of the Islamic world began to appear in Somalia. One garment for men was called the *macawis,* a sarong-like wrapper that Somalis adopted from Indonesian and Malaysian migrant workers. This style did not have much political significance, but was comfortable to wear and resembled the wrappers (*maro*) that Somali men had been wearing before so many of them adopted Westernized clothing. A small number of women descended from Arab and Persian settlers had been wearing Middle Eastern dress for generations, but in the 1970s these styles became more widespread and took on new meanings. In fact, several of the new garments for women—particularly the *jilbab* (figure 14) and *niqab* (figure 15)—made strong political statements and were not at all related to pre-existing forms of dress in Somalia.[39] Many Somalis I spoke with in Minnesota emphasized how shocking it was to see this kind of clothing and how alien it was to Somali culture. In an article on the rise of Islamism in Somalia, Cawo Abdi similarly argued that "This was a new phenomenon . . . signifying an internationalization of more conservative interpretations of Islam."[40] By the late 1980s, there was increasing pressure in Somali society for women to veil, regardless of their social position or religious beliefs.

One of the first garments to appear in the 1970s was the *shuka* (figure 16, a general term used in other parts of East Africa for something that covers the body[41]) also known as a *buibui;* an ankle-length, button-down cloak made from an opaque solid-colored material. Regardless of the season, this garment is worn over other clothing and is usually paired with a head covering called a *khimar.* The *khimar* is typically a solid color (either white or a color that matches the *shuka*) and is sometimes decorated with a lace or crocheted edge. Usually, it covers the hair and ears and is pinned or tucked under the chin, but the wearer can also leave it a bit looser to expose her earrings or a bit of hair. In her autobiography, Aman noted that her sister wore this kind of clothing because she was considered very beautiful and was being secluded in preparation for a good marriage, a very old practice called *purdah* practiced in many parts of the Middle East and South Asia. In this era, a good marriage might have been to someone who had earned a lot of money by working as a migrant laborer in the Middle East.

> [Hawa] was light-skinned, and not only that, she was pretty, pretty, with so much beauty in her. Big lips, her teeth were super white, and her gums were black. Very beautiful eyes and nose, soft hair—everything about her was beautiful. Lighter-skinned girls like that—they keep them in the house because they are afraid that someone will put the evil eye on them. People are jealous of girls like that, so they have to be kept inside. They have to wear a *shuko*, a big long-sleeved black dress to cover themselves.[42]

In countries like Jordan, Syria, and Turkey (which is where these garments originated and are commonly manufactured), the *shuka* is called *jilbab* or *jelaabib* and is a popular style of dress for married women. In Iran, the cloak is called a *manteau* (coat) and the combination of cloak and head scarf is called *rupush-rusari*.[43]

Although the Qur'an does not specify the colors or shapes of garments that Muslims should wear, the words *jilbab* and *khimar* have a special significance because they appear directly in the scripture. Verse 33:59, for example, describes how women following the path of the prophet Mohammed should be dressed: "O Prophet! Tell thy wives and thy daughters and the women of the believers to draw their cloaks [*jilbab*] round them (when they go abroad). That will be better, so that they may be recognized and not annoyed."[44] Interpretations of exactly what this means and what the *jilbab* and *khimar* consist of vary between cultures.

Unlike Syrians or Turks, Somalis use the words *jilbab* and *jelaabib* to describe a style of dress that appeared in Somalia in the 1980s (after the Iranian Revolution) and closely resembles the Iranian *chador*. The *jilbab* is an outfit consisting of three pieces made from opaque fabrics (which can be a solid color or a mixture of prints and solids) that are tailored to fit the individual wearer: a triangular-shaped head wrap (*masaar*), a matching skirt or dress (*guuno*), and a much larger cone-shaped head covering that fits tightly around the face and drapes down over the shoulders and chest. The last piece is frequently referred to as *hijab,* a general term in Arabic for "covering." The only parts of the body left uncovered are the hands, feet, and the face below the forehead (excluding the neck and ears) (see figure 14). Longer head coverings project a more devout appearance and can extend all the way to mid-calf. Unlike traditional wrapped dress, the *jilbab* does not need to be wrapped or readjusted throughout the day. A very conservative head covering called *niqab*—designed as a covering for the face with a small opening for the eyes—was once popular among Arab and Swahili women from wealthy families (who called it *burqa* or *barakoa*[45]) but was never very common among Somali women.

When all three pieces of the *jilbab* are made of the same fabric it gives the wearer a uniform appearance from head to toe, although Somalis tend to wear a range of colors (tan, blue, green, maroon, yellow) and do not restrict themselves to black. In the 1980s, activists from Iran began traveling to other parts of the Muslim world to promote Islamism and the idea of wearing Islamic dress as a symbol of political and social transformation.[46] They may have traveled to Somalia, but Somalis probably also encountered these ideas and styles of dress when they traveled to the Middle East for employment and/or education. Some refugees I spoke with in Minnesota and other parts of the United States insisted that the *jilbab* was *never* worn in Somalia; however, photographs taken in the early 1990s show many refugees wearing these garments.[47] It seems highly unlikely that this was a new fashion trend that developed while the country was collapsing; it had to be something the refugees were already wearing.

As these new conservative forms of dress became more common in Somalia, a woman who left too much of her body uncovered was in danger of shaming her family by being labeled a prostitute. A division of the police called the *buona costuma* (Italian for "good costume") was created to track prostitution by monitoring dress.[48] Although expatriate women were not bothered, many Somali women were arrested outside of nightclubs and bars for the crime of wearing Western fashions. At a public seminar in Minnesota, one woman told me how she had been arrested as a teenager for wearing a miniskirt. When her father (who had a job within the government and was mortified at having to post bail for his daughter) arrived at the station, he ordered her never to wear a miniskirt again.[49] Aman was arrested for the same reason.

> [The police officer] said . . . he had to arrest me because I was a *sharmuuto* [prostitute], I was wearing a short skirt. I was bad for the city, I was a shame to the city, so he had to clean me out. I *was* wearing a short dress with a shawl, but even if I had been a prostitute, he didn't have the right to slap me and kick me.[50]

A Somali woman living in the Washington, D.C. area told me how she left Mogadishu in the early 1980s to attend college. When she returned home after finishing her degree, she found that many people had become more conservative about religion. She explained this by noting that at least in the mosques, Somalis could openly discuss politics—even the government had to respect these places of worship. More and more women were wearing new styles of dress from the Middle East. Although she had never worn a head covering when living in Somalia (and still does not), one day a man threw stones at her, saying that she was "ruining the country" by not dressing more modestly.[51] Cawo Abdi observes that although

> an increasing number of men and women joined this nascent movement, it did not succeed in changing most Somali women's self-representation and way of life until the late 1980s. Most women, and Somali society in general, perceived the new conservatism as a challenge to their freedom of movement, association, and dress, a challenge to the autonomy that women inherited from their nomadic culture and transplanted to urban centers.[52]

A popular song from the 1980s commented on the "heavy clothing" (new forms of Islamic dress) worn by increasing numbers of women in Somalia, arguing that "One covers things only if there is something bad."[53]

Rethinking Traditional Culture

Concerns about personal autonomy and foreign influences (both from the West and the Islamic world) led a significant number of Somalis to reconsider their own history and dress as a source of inspiration. After arguing against "heavy clothing," the same song from the 1980s made a case for wearing traditional dress.

> They call me beautiful like the male ostrich
> I still wear all the finery
> I am the leader of the tradition everyone knows is mine
> Of the ways in which my mother reared me, of [our] cultural heritage
> I love to support this way of life
> Contempt and dishonesty cannot undermine me
> For I know these always cause problems and destruction
> You, lost soul, I tell you
> Of your dress and mine
> Which of the two is more respectful?
> Which one covers the body best?[54]

This reimagining of traditional culture was always supported by the government, but in the 1970s it really took hold. A new public high school was named after one of Somalia's "heroes," Sheikh Hassan Barsane, who led a resistance movement against the Italian colonial government.[55] Siad Barre imagined himself as a modern-day Sayyid Mohammed Abdulle Hassan (the "dervish" resistance leader), and spent a great deal to commission "a towering equestrian statue set on a marble pedestal as a tribute to him."[56] Women were a vital part of this cultural revival. The Somali Revolutionary Socialist Party (SRSP), the only political party allowed after the coup in 1969, had a membership of 20,000 people, sixty percent of whom were women.[57] A subgroup of the SRSP, the Somali Women's Democratic Organization (SWDO), was dedicated to improving "equality and the participation of women in all sectors of Somali life." Although the SWDO's primary focus was on programs for health care and family planning (particularly reducing rates of circumcision, considered by many, including the U.S. government, to be a hazard to women's health),[58] members also promoted traditional cultural activities such as handcrafts, poetry, and folk dancing.[59]

Through banknotes and coins the national mint circulated images of men and women engaged in handcrafts that were rapidly disappearing from everyday life but had come to be recognized as part of traditional Somali culture. The front of the one thousand shilin banknote, for example, shows two women making woven baskets. This was a common household activity (considered a vital skill for young women) before many families switched to using aluminum vessels. Each woman was pictured wearing a *shash* (head wrap) and *garbasaar* draped loosely over her head and shoulders. The front of the fifty shilin banknote shows a man weaving cloth by hand on a wooden loom. Although a few weavers were still using this kind of equipment in the 1970s (*Somalia in Word and Image* shows men making Benadir cloth the traditional way),[60] Mogadishu also had a modern textile factory producing cloth on industrial looms.[61] The man was depicted wearing what appears to be an Arab-style *kamiz* (tunic) with an embroidered collar—a style of dress that was traditional only in urban areas.

This was hardly a trend confined to Somalia. Throughout Africa and the Middle East in the 1960s and '70s, many educated people were rethinking traditional culture and how it might apply to modern life. Anthropologists Robert and Elizabeth Fernea noted that

> In Morocco, in Egypt, in Saudi Arabia, in Jordan and Lebanon, people spoke to us about the need to return to roots, to reaffirm the basics: family ties, parent–child relationships, religious beliefs . . . they wanted the convenience of modern technology, but not the values of the West at the expense of their own ways of life.[62]

For many, this included backing away from Western dress in favor of garments such as the *kamiz, bisht* (cloak), and the *kaffiyeh* (which turned into a popular symbol of Arab and Palestinian nationalism). To a certain degree, this movement extended to the Horn of Africa, where garments like the *kufi* and *salwaar kamiz* regained some of their popularity among Somali men living in urban areas.[63] Instead of wearing a turban or *kaffiyeh* as a head covering, however, Somalis wore this kind of cloth draped over one shoulder, making a visual reference to the uniforms of Sayyid Mohammed Abdulle Hassan's dervish army. Often, elements of dress from the Middle East were mixed with garments from other areas of the world; for example, a *macawis* might be paired with a Western-style button-down shirt.

For women, "traditional" dress became more colorful.[64] In addition to solid colors and the occasional plaid, it expanded to include stripes and prints. One new style of fabric was called *kanga*—a lightweight cotton cloth printed with designs and text. This fashion came from the Swahili-speaking parts of Kenya and Tanzania (where *kanga* prints remain popular), although some versions were printed with text in the Somali language. I purchased a *kanga* print at one of the Somali malls in Minnesota that has a bright red center and a navy blue border decorated with small diamonds that were grouped together to form paisley and flower motifs (see figure 17).[65] The blue border resembles the *pullau* of an Indian sari, a decorative border designed to be displayed at the hemline and chest, while the white diamond motifs look like a type of cloth made in India called *bandani*, where designs are made by tying off tiny sections of the cloth, dyeing it, and then cutting off the ties to reveal light-colored patterns.

This is no coincidence. In line with its history of importing vast amounts of textiles, Somalia in the early 1980s was one of the top three African importers of silk fabrics from India (only Kenya and Mauritius—both of which have large populations of Indian/Pakistani expatriates and their descendants—imported more). Somalia was also one of the top importers of manufactured and synthetic textiles from India, including rayon velvet, chiffon, and filament polyester.[66] The latter two types of material are lightweight and easy to care for, making them well suited to the climate in Somalia. Indian manufacturers even went so far as to produce knockoffs of traditional Benadir cloth.[67] New fabrics also arrived from Japan, South Korea, and the Middle East. These new imported fabrics tended to be very colorful, certainly more colorful than the imported fabrics such as *merikani* that Somali nomads wore in the nineteenth century, which were either white or dyed with earth pigments.

In some cases, Somalis took these newer fabrics to tailors and had them made into garments that resembled either Western or "African" styles of dress but were more suited to local aesthetics and were given Somali names. One woman I spoke with noted that her sister liked to wear a short jacket called *garbagale,* which translates as "the shoulders go through it" (in contrast to the *garbasaar* or shoulder cloth, which is suspended from the body and can be used in multiple ways, the *garbagale* is a pre-shaped garment that fits the body in just one way).[68] Another garment worn by girls and young women was the *ambur,* a short-sleeved blouse made from printed fabrics. A photograph in *The Prophet's Camel Bell* shows a girl (perhaps between twelve and fourteen years old) weaving a basket while wearing an *ambur,* a skirt made of Indian madras or Benadir cloth, and simple bracelets on her upper arms.[69] *Beautiful Somalia* shows another woman wearing an ankle-length, off-the-shoulder dress made using a peach, brown, and white paisley fabric (figure 18). The dress looks like it was wrapped, but it was not a *guntiino,* which is always knotted over one shoulder. Unusually, this woman was also wearing a large head wrap; a style much more common in West Africa (especially Nigeria) than in East Africa.

During the 1970s and '80s the *guntiino* was also quickly being replaced by a new form of dress called *dirac* and *gorgorad.* This style might have come from the French colony of Djibouti, since it was more popular in northern Somali territory and resembles the *boubou* worn in French-speaking West Africa.[70] The *dirac* (figure 19) is a long, loose-fitting dress made by taking three to four yards of cloth, folding the piece in half length-wise, creating an opening for the neck at the top, and then sewing up the sides, leaving room for the arms. The *boubou* is made in the same way but with some minor differences. Unlike the *boubou,* for example, where the armholes are usually left very wide (allowing air to circulate around the body), the *dirac* has armholes that are sewn very close to the top, leaving a space of only four or five inches. The *boubou* is worn with a skirt and head wrap and the entire ensemble is made from opaque cotton fabric with a print, jacquard, or tie-dye design. The *dirac,* on the other hand, is made out of printed cotton voile (a semi-transparent fabric) and is worn with a fancy slip called a *gorgorad* which hangs down several inches below the *dirac.* These two garments generally match in terms of color but are not made from the same material. In fact, the *gorgorad* is a pre-shaped garment with an elastic waistband made from a solid-color fabric with just a band of fancy lace or sequined cloth at the bottom (see figure 20).[71] In West Africa, men also wear a *boubou* with pants instead of a skirt; in East Africa, the *dirac* is exclusively for women.

Although these new styles of ethnic dress were widely accepted, women were also ambivalent about "tradition." Which practices should be kept and which should be discarded? Just as importantly, who should decide? In a popular song on this topic, a male and female singer expressed conflicting points of view.

> *Male (Maxammed Jaamac Jaaf):*
> In the old days it was custom
> That a girl perfumed her hair
> And braided it

She wrapped around her waist
A wide cloth belt with fringes and an ornamental cord
And wore a white dress
But something has changed . . .
You, women, have destroyed our culture
You have overstepped the religious law
And destroyed our religion
Girls, won't you behave?
Female (Mariam Mursal):
What was custom in the old days
And a hundred years ago
And what has been left behind
Don't make us go back on that well-worn road
For we have turned away from it with effort . . .
First get some education and learn how to read and write
Don't try to turn back, you country hick, people who have woken up.[72]

Although women were blamed for all kinds of social problems and treated like second-class citizens, they were also idealized as precious symbols of traditional life. This contradiction was carried into the arena of postage stamps issued by the national government.

The Effort to Define a Nation, Captured on Stamps

As an item of material culture, stamps are remarkable for being "intensively used," widely circulated, and developed through a formal design process. Because of this, "these apparently trivial and ephemeral artifacts can touch the everyday lives (and reflect the attitudes) of both governments and ordinary citizens more readily than grand political rhetoric or state ceremonial."[73] Like dress, stamps encode "the nation" making it available for enactment and critique in daily life. Phil Deans and Hugo Dobson have argued that "stamps can and should be read as texts, often with expressly political purposes or agendas which are conveyed through the images they depict."[74] When Nazi Germany issued a set of folk costume stamps in the 1930s (figure 21), for example, it was intended not just as a celebration of German nationalism, but as a claim to cultural superiority over minority groups and neighboring countries as expressed through dress.[75] Carlos Stoetzer has observed that as "ideal propaganda," a stamp goes from hand to hand and town to town; it reaches the farthest corners and provinces of a country and even the farthest countries of the world. It is a symbol of the nation from which the stamp is mailed, a vivid expression of that country's culture and civilization and its ideas and ideals. By the use of symbols, slogans, pictures, or even loaded words, it conveys its message far and wide.[76]

Currency, billboards, and posters can also serve to foster national identity,[77] but these are generally limited to a domestic audience; few material artifacts undergo such widespread use and circulation as postage stamps. As such, they offer fertile ground for the display and political positioning of a nation and its dress in a global context.

When it came to designing stamps, Somalis had an opportunity to think about how they compared to other nations. Which aspects of their heritage were worth celebrating? Which aspects of the modern world should be pursued? Between 1960 and 1980 the government issued seventy-nine sets of stamps, each set including anywhere from two to eight stamps based around a single theme. Almost half of these sets were commemoratives for external events or other broad international topics: the Olympics, UNESCO, the Boy Scouts, Gandhi, the African Postal Union, "freedom from hunger," telecommunications, the anniversary of Lenin's birth, or the "Year of the Child" (a full list is available in Appendix A). The rest of the sets were about internal events and topics. Sixteen depicted the indigenous birds, animals, trees, and/or flowers of Somalia (some of which, like frankincense, were used in traditional dress practices). Another eleven sets were created to commemorate specific events: national independence, the founding of Somali Airlines, the establishment of a written language for Somali, and the founding of the Somali Democratic Republic under Siad Barre. Nine sets of stamps were about traditional industries (trade, agriculture, animal husbandry, fishing), and five were about handcrafts and folk dancing.

One set of stamps issued shortly after Somalia's independence in 1960 (see figure 22) is both patriotic and romantic, combining images of women wearing traditional dress with an agricultural theme. Although nomadic life had previously been more highly valued than farming, independence meant that Somalis were able to reclaim a great deal of land; images of women picking papayas, corn, cotton, and peanuts, standing in a field of sesame plants, and carrying loads of ripe grapefruit, sugar cane, and bananas thus celebrated both agriculture and women as the "fruits of the nation." Most women pictured on the stamps were wearing a head wrap and *guntiino* without a shawl, but the fabric was contemporary: colorful stripes and even a zebra print (surely too fashionable to actually be worn for such work). Two sets of stamps with children's themes (figures 23 and 24) also gave messages about gender roles. In the first set, one stamp shows a young boy in a classroom wearing white shorts and a striped t-shirt, drawing an image of a giraffe on a chalk board (the other stamps show animal drawings: a zebra, a rhinoceros, and a jaguar). The other set features one stamp with a young girl wearing a *guntiino,* a beaded necklace, and a ribbon in her hair while embroidering pictures of fish on a piece of cloth (the rest have images of fish); the girl's location is not clear, but she is certainly not in school like her male counterpart. The message was obvious: that boys (and men) should get an education, but girls (and women) should focus on crafts and beauty. In contrast, a set of stamps issued in 1962 shows women in the auxiliary divisions of the police force and military wearing uniforms with jackets, caps, and knee-length skirts. Although this was a "modern" image instead of a more traditional one, it pointed to the same kinds of gender divisions. The women were not depicted wearing the same uniforms as the men (who were issued pants) and in real life they were restricted to playing supportive roles as nurses and secretaries.

Sixteen sets of stamps have images of men and women wearing traditional Somali dress, including the *guntiino* and *maro*. One set from 1966–67 (figure 25), for instance, depicts scenes of rural life. In one of the images a woman is wearing a striped *guntiino* and matching head wrap while carrying a load on her back in a handmade basket. Passing by is a man with a nomadic hairstyle, a green wrapper around his lower body, a white wrapper around his upper body, and two spears (which makes it clear that he is a nomad). After Siad Barre came to power there were more and more stamps like this. A set issued in 1975 depicts nomadic men and women wearing very traditional dress—no zebra prints or flashy colors, just plain white cloth. The one exception is a woman wearing a *guntiino* with red, black, and ochre stripes (see figure 26), traditional colors for a wedding. Another set from the same year depicts soldiers in Sayyid Mohammed Abdulle Hassan's army wearing their uniforms, brandishing spears, and riding horses into battle. The release of these stamps coincided with the unveiling of the statue to honor Sayyid outside of the Parliament building in Mogadishu; the images were not meant to depict men in contemporary life.[78]

An interesting set of stamps issued in 1972 (figure 27) brings up questions about what kinds of clothing Somalis considered "traditional." The four stamps depict four different folk dances. Three of them show women wearing the *guntiino* with a head wrap or *garbasaar* (very traditional), but a fourth one shows a woman wearing a blue floral dress and some kind of cap that exposes part of her hair. The men are all wearing white t-shirts with either pants or a *macawis;* some have amulets (*hardas*) or a turban cloth (*imamad*) wrapped in an X over the chest like the soldiers in Sayyid's army. Had t-shirts really become so widely accepted that they could be worn as part of "traditional" dress for a folk dance? A photograph in *Culture and Customs of Somalia* shows female dancers wearing the same kinds of outfits depicted on the stamps,[79] so it is possible that male folk dancers really dressed like this too. If these stamps are accurate, it says a lot about how pervasive Western styles of dress had become.

Considering that Somalia was initiated into the Arab League in 1974, images that reflect connections to the Islamic world are surprisingly few: one set of stamps issued in 1972 to honor the visit of King Faisal from Saudi Arabia, one set issued in 1974 when Somalia joined the Arab League (consisting of a map of the member states and images of their flags), and then a single stamp (out of an eight-part series issued for the ten-year anniversary of Somalia's independence) that shows a hand hovering over the Qur'an. In twenty years, these were the only images on stamps inspired by Somalia's Islamic heritage. Far more show men and women wearing Western-style uniforms, even though increasingly conservative forms of Islamic dress were showing up in Somalia during the 1970s and '80s. Another form of dress omitted from stamps was the *dirac* and *gorgorad*. Perhaps this was not considered "traditional" enough (compared to the *guntiino*) to be portrayed as part of the national heritage. Or perhaps it was omitted because the *dirac* came from the north and the national mint was located in the south. Tensions between the north and south—stemming from cultural and economic differences as well as different experiences under colonial rule—were exacerbated during Siad Barre's regime.

Somalia Breaks Down

By the late 1970s, Somali society was falling apart. Corruption, fear of being arrested for opposing the government, and the suspension of free elections made it nearly impossible for Somalis to hold any kind of open dialogue about social problems. The politics of the Cold War added even more tension. Since the United States was behind Haile Selassie in Ethiopia, the Soviet Union was eager to find a partner in the Horn of Africa; in 1974, Siad Barre signed a treaty in exchange for money, weapons, and advanced training for Somalia's soldiers. In an effort to rally popular support and carry out some of his personal goals (since his family had come from the border region) he used this aid from the Soviet Union to attack Ethiopia, the goal being to conquer the Ogaden and reunite Somalis on both sides of the border.

Just a few months earlier, however, Haile Selassie had been overthrown. When the war between Somalia and Ethiopia started, the Soviet Union broke off its relations with Somalia and shifted support to Ethiopia. Without Soviet financial backing, Somalia's military action quickly collapsed and hundreds of thousands of nomads (Somalis as well as Oromo) became refugees when they fled from the border region. This put an enormous strain on areas where refugees were resettled in towns and semi-permanent camps, especially in the north where the climate is harsh and the population was already underserved by the government.[80] A severe drought in the Horn of Africa in the late 1970s and early '80s made the situation even more desperate. Some of the Oromo refugees were also enticed to join the much-hated National Security Service, causing greater fear and militarization in northern Somalia.

Somalia's brief occupation of the Ogaden alienated some nations in the Organization of African Unity (OAU), which has always tried to maintain national borders by discouraging wars and secessionist movements. Although he dismissed Ethiopian criticism that he wanted to annex Djibouti and reunite all Somalis under one nation, Siad Barre also compared the war between Somalia and Ethiopia to anti-colonial struggles in Angola, Mozambique, Eritrea, Zimbabwe, and South Africa. Provocatively calling the Ogaden region "Western Somalia," Barre stated that the Somali Democratic Republic "appreciates all oppressed nationalities to resort to warring if their legitimate rights to independence are discarded."[81]

After Somalia was defeated in the war with Ethiopia, Barre's critics became even more vocal. In response, Barre turned the national army on his own people, executing commanders that he blamed for the loss in Ethiopia and ordering the military to bomb entire villages.[82] In northern Somalia, Barre resorted to a wide range of abuses, including

> imprisonment and detention without charge, extra-judicial executions, confiscations of businesses and properties, expulsion from schools, rape, demolition of water wells, public humiliation of clan chiefs and elders, exile

to Mogadishu, denial of financial services and import-export licenses, and confiscation of livestock.

Continuing opposition centered in the northern city of Hargeisa resulted in an 8:00 PM curfew, "indiscriminate killings," and denial of permission to bury the dead without a permit.[83]

In response to the bombings and oppression, in the 1980s dissenters formed two major opposition groups, the Somali Salvation Democratic Front (SSDF) and the Somali National Movement (SNM). Both were based outside of the country (the SSDF in Ethiopia, the SNM in London) and relied on guerilla warfare to attack the national army in hopes of undermining the government.[84] In light of these threats, Barre abandoned Socialism and began to personally appoint all military officers and government officials, favoring close relatives and members of his paternal and maternal clans (who ironically, were also from the north). Only those who demonstrated complete loyalty were allowed to stay in office; they, however, were rewarded with food, homes, and other luxuries. Consequently,

> His circle of family members and hangers-on had one aim in mind—to stay in power and endure. Nothing was too sacred too profane, no massacre too heinous to ponder to ensure the interests of the "family." The circle that ran the country had become a mafia. . . . One by one, Barre and his inner circle cut all the bonds that held Somalis together as a nation: solidarity, compassion, decency, humanity, and the sacredness of life and property. In short, the values of Somali society were turned upside down.[85]

Somalia had never really recovered from the split between British and Italian Somaliland. Under Barre's regime, economic and social differences between the north and south became even more magnified and could easily turn into matters of life or death.

In 1986, Barre was involved in a severe car accident. He was airlifted to a hospital in Saudi Arabia and forced to stay there for several weeks. This unexpected absence created a window of opportunity for leaders of the opposition. In *The Road to Hell,* Michael Maren noted that shortly after Barre's accident, Somali banknotes began to appear with "an extra symbol hand-stamped on them. It stood for the Somali National Movement, a northern rebel group that had begun fighting to overthrow the regime. [Some] didn't want to touch the money. It was as if each exchange of the currency slowly eroded the foundations of the regime."[86] As the SSDF and SNM advanced into southern Somalia, circumstances deteriorated in that part of the country too.

Cawo Abdi has argued that there was a direct connection between this violence and the spread of Islamic dress among Somali women regardless of their ancestry or personal beliefs.

> By the very late 1980s, the Somali government turned even more repressive, and rebels against the regime became more active in regions close to the capital, increasing the physical and material insecurity of the whole population. For the first time, most women in Mogadishu began covering their hair with conservative headdress that covered the neck and the shoulders. Those who resisted this new trend received verbal and physical harassment. Whether to veil or not to veil was no longer women's prerogative. The Somali civil war, brewing from the mid-1980s, finally erupted in January 1991, catalyzing a dramatic alteration of Somali women's self-representation and Islamic identity.[87]

In the face of so many disruptions and tragedies leading up to the civil war, religion was also re-emerging as an important way for individuals to cope; religious dress offered both physical and metaphorical protection. It would be a mistake to think that there were not some women who accepted or even welcomed these changes in dress. In addition to those who were looking for relief from vulnerability, some women may have been inspired by the Iranian Revolution or the voluntary readoption of *hijab* in Egypt, a statement not only of faith but of Egyptian-style feminism and hope for improved social conditions for women.[88]

In 1988, Somalia signed a peace treaty with Ethiopia, depriving the opposition of its base of support. When the militias were thus forced to re-enter the country, they took control of the city of Hargeisa, and Siad Barre responded by ordering the national army to bomb it, killing tens of thousands of Somalis. In 1989, an opposition group called the United Somali Congress (USC) formed in Rome. Originally, the USC's intention was to unite all opposition groups and restore democratic institutions by taking over the government. Forces gathered outside of Mogadishu, but they could not agree on who should lead the group. As a result, the movement split into several factions. These forces began shelling each other along with the city, destroying many buildings in Mogadishu and killing many more tens of thousands of citizens. Mohamed Haji Mukhtar dedicated his revised edition of the *Historical Dictionary of Somalia* to his son, "Suleyman Mukhtar, who died at age eleven from the indiscriminate shelling in Mogadishu in 1990, and to all the innocent young people who suffered the same fate."[89]

In January 1991, Siad Barre was forced to flee Mogadishu for a safe position in the countryside. Hundreds of thousands of Somalis were killed in the civil war that ensued between Barre's forces and the opposition, but many also died of starvation after soldiers destroyed crops and caches of grain.[90] Lying just north of Mogadishu, the agricultural region between the Juba and Shebelle rivers became known as the "triangle of death." After a year and a half of fighting, Barre was forced to flee the country; he went into exile in Nigeria and died in 1995. Since then, Somalia has not had a functioning central government. There is no police force, no border patrol, no functionaries to issue official documents such as passports and birth certificates, and there are no foreign embassies. A region in the north known as "Somaliland" has formed its own government and established a certain level of calm, but has not been formally recognized by any other sovereign nation. Attempts to restore order in the south have been defeated by widespread access to automatic weapons, continuing internal chaos, and external interference (particularly from Ethiopia and its allies in the "War on Terrorism").

From Somalia to the Diaspora

This history of competing ideologies and suppressed social dialogue—going as far back as the end of the colonial era—has profoundly affected how Somalis interact with one another as well as with outsiders. Racial tensions stemming from slavery and colonization were hardly resolved during Somalia's brief existence; this has affected how many Somali refugees in the United States interact with African Americans (a topic explored further in the next chapter). Although the official position of Barre's government was that clans did not exist and all Somalis were equal, groups such the *Saab* (the artisan caste) and the "Somali Bantus" (the descendants of slaves from Central Africa) were never fully integrated into Somali society. I have observed that many Somalis even in academic contexts have a difficult time discussing issues such as race or what role the Somali Bantus should play in the new national government. Another lingering effect of Barre's regime and the ensuing civil war has been widespread fear of the police and government, making it difficult for many Somalis to cope with certain aspects of their new lives such as passports, paperwork, and even answering questions for a census.[91]

In the face of such difficulties, dress might seem unimportant. However, in many ways this era made Somalis more sensitive than ever to the symbolism of dress and the embodiment of ideology through clothing. Consider a stamp from the 1970s which shows two young men—the "future of Somalia"—standing together in front of the flag, wearing the uniforms of the *Guulwadayaal* (figure 28). As socialists and citizens of the Somali Democratic Republic these boys embodied Somali identity, but not in the traditional sense; they were living a life very different from what the generations before colonization had experienced. Whether Somalis adopted Western fashions, Islamic dress, military uniforms, or some of the new "ethnic" garments like the *dirac* and *macawis,* their clothing said a great deal about their economic and social position in Somalia. Traditional dress—for both men and women—was no longer just something to wear; it had become idealized and charged with allusions to a way of life that was disappearing for good. The symbolism attached to dress did not simply evaporate when the government of Somalia collapsed; in many ways, dress took on an even more important role as it became one of the few tangible reminders of home. And yet, like memories that grow and change as the years pass, Somali dress has also continued to change and accumulate new layers of meaning.

Dress in a Time of Extreme Change—1991 to 2010

> In Somalia, a society at war with itself, and where sexual violation has also become a tool of war, the tendency towards more extreme religious practice has been reinforced by the perceived need for protection and protective clothing. . . . As a Somali woman, I have seen that the recent increase in veiling has been accompanied, for the first time in Somali history, with extreme forms of censorship of women's behavior, as extreme versions of Islamic interpretation have found fertile ground. Women who refuse to conform are harassed by both sexes, and peer pressure is exerted on them to veil.
>
> —*Sadia Ahmed, 1999*

In 1991, the conflicts that had been brewing in Somalia for more than a decade erupted into a full-blown civil war, causing the total collapse of the central government. At least 50,000 people were killed in the initial violence, but ten times as many died from starvation due to the "scorched-earth" style of fighting and the disruption of supply chains. In a survey conducted in 1999 by the International Red Cross, more than half of Somali refugees said they had lost contact with a family member, fifty-eight percent said their home had been looted or seriously damaged, and sixty-five percent said that a close family member had died because of the chaos (the only country with a higher percentage was Cambodia). In 2007, the U.N. High Commission for Refugees estimated that there were still 400,000 internally displaced Somalis plus an additional 464,000 Somali refugees living in other countries, with the highest concentrations being in Kenya, Yemen, the U.K., the United States, and Ethiopia. Somalis have also continued to apply for asylum in record numbers all over the world.[1] In some cases, Somalis have integrated well into their new circumstances. Ayaan Hirsi Ali, for example, left Somalia with her family when she was eight years old, living in Saudi Arabia, Ethiopia, and Kenya. In 1992 she was granted political asylum in the Netherlands and in 2003 was elected to the Lower House of Dutch Parliament. Many young Somalis in the United States are finding it possible to learn English, get an education, and integrate very quickly into American society. Others have found it difficult to cope with new languages, radical changes in social life (both inside and outside of the Somali community), post-traumatic stress from the civil war, and living in difficult economic circumstances while trying to support family members back home.

Refugees have a lot of practical challenges to deal with, but they must also consider the fate of what it means to be "Somali." As long they are unable to return home, the preservation and reproduction of Somali culture—through language, food, religion, poetry, oral history, and even dress—is very important to many people. This is literally all that Somali refugees have left of their country. Whether young people choose to wear Islamic dress, Western fashions, elements of traditional dress, or a combination of these styles, their clothing and other aspects of body adornment say volumes about their priorities and cultural loyalties. Their dress also represents their efforts to negotiate very complicated social circumstances. Little things like a hairstyle or the pattern of a headscarf can mean the difference between assimilation and the preservation of Somali culture. As hard as outside forces like the media and local culture can pull young people to change their styles of dress, pressures from inside the Somali community also push them to resist changing. Somali dress has not disappeared, but—much like Somalis themselves—it has been forced through some radical changes in both form and meaning.

In this chapter I take stock of what has happened to Somalis and their dress since the start of the civil war in 1991, particularly outside of Somalia. Although the highest concentrations of Somali refugees are still found in East Africa (especially in Kenya), differences between the countries of resettlement are introducing new layers of complexity and fragmentation to Somali culture. Even if peace is achieved and expatriate Somalis eventually return to Somalia, what will those who grew up in Canada think of their counterparts who grew up in Saudi Arabia or South Africa? Vast differences in local language, culture, and climate are bound to influence how different groups of Somalis conceptualize themselves. As noted by the editors of the anthology *From Mogadishu to Dixon,* the Somali community in Egypt, for example, consists of persons who migrated from Somalia to Egypt before the civil war of 1991, émigrés who moved from Somali diaspora communities in the West for cultural and religious reasons, and individuals from the Somali diaspora in Kenya, Yemen, or Ethiopia. Moreover, Somalis in Egypt may join the Somali diaspora in Finland as a result of family reunification policies. Yet, after they establish themselves in Finland, they may decide to settle and raise their family in Egypt—and again the process continues.[2]

Two decades of exile have profoundly affected both voluntary migrants and refugees, especially young people born in the diaspora who have no living memory of Somalia.

Between a Rock and a Hard Place

Somalis started leaving the Horn of Africa in significant numbers as early as the 1980s. In some cases, they were able to join other Somalis in cities such as Cairo, London, and Florence where expatriate communities had been established for decades.[3] As the situation in Somalia grew worse, some individuals went on the pilgrimage to Mecca and simply never returned home. Others relied on their personal and business connections to get them out of the country. One woman I spoke with in Minnesota explained how her mother had been importing textiles from India. In 1990, she took her two daughters to India on the pretext of a business trip, which is where they happened to be when the government in Somalia finally collapsed.[4]

As opposition forces gathered outside Mogadishu and began shelling the city, order quickly broke down. Residents would leave their homes in the morning and find bodies lying in the streets. Many were hopeful that they could outlast the fighting and stay in Somalia with their friends, family members, homes, and businesses—everything they had worked so hard for over the years. In his book *Yesterday, Tomorrow: Voices from the Somali Diaspora*, Nuruddin Farah noted that he was teaching in Uganda when Siad Barre was forced out of Mogadishu in 1991. His family fled to Kenya, but he assumed they would quickly be able to return home.

> I remember flying into Nairobi [the capital city] when I received an urgent phone call from my immediate family and thinking that I would sort out what I took to be a pushover problem, in a matter of weeks. I was then of the optimistic belief that reason would reign, and that full-scale strife would be averted.[5]

Unfortunately, like many Somalis (especially in southern Somalia), Farah's family found that the only safe solution was to continue living in exile.

Between 1990 and 1991, Kenya took in approximately 400,000 Somali refugees, but there were hundreds of thousands more who starved or were killed along the way. In a series of fifteen interviews with Somali women refugees who had resettled in Minnesota, Dr. Catherine Daly found that more than half had witnessed an act of violence or been victimized themselves as they tried to make their way out of the country. One woman noted, "We were going to stay in Somalia, but they were searching for boys. We left so they wouldn't be killed . . . we just ran for our life!" Another woman left Somalia after finding her sister's dead body and lost her daughter along the way. Not all of the women were able to talk about their experiences; among those who did was one woman who watched as her husband, brother, and father were killed and was then shot in the face and left for dead.[6]

In some cases, even once Somalia was behind them Somalis turned on one another. In the refugee camps in Kenya, one young woman observed that

> There were some people who pinpointed those who used to work for the government, even the women. A neighbor of ours used to work for the government; she was a policewoman. They came to our hall and raped her; they tortured her and beat her badly. They asked her where the property of the government was, even though she was just a policewoman! In Somalia, the policewomen used to wear the same clothes as the men. They took her clothes, the trousers, from her. Her husband was also a policeman and they took his clothes also. Then, they raped her in front of him and just left her on the ground. She was seriously injured.[7]

After walking for days to cross the border with no food or water, or escaping from one of the coastal cities in a rowboat, some refugees arrived in other countries only to be attacked by the police or the local population. In a book documenting the lives of refugees, one woman noted that when her family crossed the southern border they were stopped by the Kenyan police, who took all the women into the bush and raped them.[8] Being refugees without any money, resources, or immediate connections had left them in a very vulnerable position.

When the war broke out, the government of Kenya established several refugee camps along the northeastern border with Somalia.[9] This area has a harsh climate as well as a native population of Somali nomads that has long been at odds with the Kenyan government; locals referred to these native Somalis as *shifta* (bandits). (The meaning of this term has expanded to include all Somali men who commit criminal acts such as rape, theft, and murder against women in the camps, even when the men themselves are refugees.)[10] In many cases, the refugees discovered that the camps were nearly as dangerous as the conditions they had left behind in Somalia.[11] One woman who spent more than nine years living in the camps recalled

> When we fled Somalia and settled in Dagahaley, I became the women's leader. . . . I have seen many things and I have listened to many problems. . . . Hundreds of women [have been] attacked in the surrounding bush when they ventured away from the camp to fetch firewood. Sometimes we walk for many hours to gather enough fuel for the family. It is there, in the bush, that we are at our greatest risk of rape. When such things happen to girls, they will no longer be marriageable. But still, with the inter-clan feuds, women don't want the men to go into the bush because the women will only be raped but the men will be killed.[12]

In her dissertation about the Dadaab refugee camp, Cindy Horst found that victims of rape were often reluctant to report the attacks due to shame, fear of revenge, and lack of protection for witnesses; the police could not be counted on to arrest their attackers.

Refugees with more financial resources sought housing outside of the refugee camps in Mombasa or Nairobi. Citing concerns about how this might affect the tourist industry in Kenya, the government tried to discourage self-resettlement by forcing Somalis to stay inside the camps unless they had "explicit permission to be elsewhere, such as for medical reasons or educational purposes."[13] However, since many of the refugees were lacking basic documents (passports, birth certificates) and there was already a long history of cross-border migration by nomads, this policy turned out to be difficult to enforce for refugees who had never been in the camps.

In 1992, photographer Fazal Sheikh went to Kenya to interview Somali women, take photographs, and try to understand what the refugees were going through (his goal being to bring human rights abuses to international attention). The resulting images and text—including materials from a return visit in 2000—were published in two volumes, *A Camel for the Son* and *Ramadan Moon*.[14] Some of the children he photographed—both boys and girls—were shown wearing Western clothing, mostly t-shirts and dresses. Most of the women, however, were shown wearing a shawl (*garbasaar*) wrapped around their head and upper body, making it difficult to tell what kind of clothing they were wearing underneath. With one exception—a woman wearing a cardigan over a *guntiino*—none of the adults was obviously wearing Western-style dress. Some were wearing the head wrap for married women known as *shash*, either alone or in combination with another head covering. Others were wearing the Islamic style of dress called *jilbab* (often crudely sewn) or a piece of dark, opaque, solid-colored cloth (the kind that might be used for *jilbab*) wrapped around their head and upper body as a *garbasaar* instead of the more traditional lightweight fabrics with stripes or printed patterns. A few of the women were shown breastfeeding or with exposed shoulders, but the majority left only their hands and faces uncovered.

How can we account for this? Western clothing was not very widespread among women in Somalia, but it did exist. Yet, photographs of the refugees show very little evidence of it. With regards to the images taken by Fazal Sheikh, this could be explained by his personal bias; perhaps he thought that a Western audience would not be as sympathetic to Somalis in Western-style dress, even though some of the children were dressed this way. Another possibility is that this is how the women chose to be depicted for a Western audience (assuming they had a choice; this might have been their only clothing) or chose to dress for their personal safety in the camps. It also seems possible that women who wore Western-style dress on a daily basis in Somalia— women who had received an advanced education or served in the military auxiliary forces—did not end up in the refugee camps in large numbers.

As the civil war has dragged on for almost two decades, the refugee camps have become a dead end for many Somalis. Unless they can get the funds and permission to join friends and family members in the city or migrate to another country, there is little hope for a better future. Factors that prevent refugees from migrating include a lack of official authorization (identity cards and visas), lack of money to pay for transportation, and problems with mental or physical health. One older woman in Minnesota explained to me that her husband could not join her because he had two other wives; being aware that the United States does not recognize polygamous marriages, he decided to remain behind in East Africa. Without a central government, returning to southern Somalia is not much of an option. Although there is some economic activity going on, the situation can deteriorate at any moment.[15]

In desperation, some refugees have turned to criminal activity or religious extremism. As Sadia Ahmed observed, this includes a

> large number of young [men and women] who have grown up with little experience of life beyond conflict, with high unemployment rates and a lack of alternatives due to the destruction of schools. It is a well-known

fact among Somalis that some extremist religious groups create business and employment opportunities for loyal followers.[16]

Before the civil war these kinds of groups were generally shunned as a threat to traditional Somali culture and religious practices, but the breakdown in civil society has created a situation where extremism can easily take hold and spread. Without a central government, Somalia itself has become fertile ground for fundamentalist groups such as Al-Shabab.[17]

Sheikh's photographs, as well as the photographs of other journalists working in Somalia (which are not plentiful since the southern region is still an active war zone) almost always show women wearing the *jilbab* or a *garbasaar* with only their hands and faces showing; no exposed arms, legs, or even ankles. Certainly, not everyone who wears this kind of clothing has extreme political views. There is pressure for all women in the refugee camps and Somalia to dress this way, regardless of their beliefs. Also, for many women Islam has become a coping mechanism and a source of guidance in difficult times. During her research from July 1999 to August 2001, Cindy Horst observed that a majority of women were wearing the *jilbab*. Cawo Abdi made the same observation, arguing that

> The Somali political crisis and the permanent insecurity experienced by Somali women resulted in women drastically changing their attire. . . . Whether this change was directly imposed on women or indirectly enforced through the violence ensuing from the civil war—rapes, harassment, and so on—is hard to assess. What is unambiguous is that the civil war brought about conditions that heightened women's vulnerability. I was struck by the uniformity of women's dress while doing my first fieldwork in Dadaab [refugee camp]. Almost all women are now wearing long, thick, flowing dresses, accompanied by a veil covering the head and shoulders and descending all the way to the knees, covering the dress and leaving only the face showing. Somali women call these *jalaabiib* or *jilbaab*. These are very colorful, in contrast to black chadors with gloves and face coverings worn by a minority of refugee women. One cannot help but be amazed by the dramatic transformations in Somali women's public self-representation in Dadaab compared with the dress habits in prewar times.[18]

Although conservative versions of the *dirac* and *guntiino* have returned to northern Somalia and the diaspora communities (the most physically safe places to live), in the refugee camps the *guntiino* has practically disappeared. Somalis who were alive just fifty years ago would hardly recognize contemporary dress. This says a great deal about the incredibly dramatic changes that have occurred and the vulnerable position many Somali women have found themselves in since the start of the civil war. The lack of a central government has meant that all Somalis—whether living in Somalia, the refugee camps, or the diaspora—are essentially on their own.[19] Whatever crime or difficulty might occur, there is rarely anyone to protect or advocate for them; small wonder then that so many are desperate for any source of support. For many refugees, Islamic dress is more than just clothing or a "choice": it represents a stabilizing force in their lives.

Why Minnesota?

Some of the first countries outside of East Africa to accept refugees for resettlement were Italy, Great Britain, and other members of the British Commonwealth such as Canada, Australia, and New Zealand—not surprising since northern Somalia had been a British colony. Although the number of Somalis in East Africa is still much larger than on any other continent, some of the largest diaspora communities outside of Africa are in London and Toronto.[20] The United States began accepting Somali refugees in the mid-1990s after the failure of Operation Restore Hope.[21] Immigration policy reforms in the early 1990s, which were intended to keep certain states such as New York and California from being overwhelmed by large numbers of refugees (who often need intensive social services to adjust), meant that most Somalis did not get to choose where they would initially be placed. All they knew was that they were being allowed to leave the refugee camps and settle somewhere in the United States.

Today, the largest Somali community in the United States is located in Minnesota, concentrated in the "Twin Cities" of Saint Paul and Minneapolis. The second- and third-largest are located in Ohio (Columbus) and Washington (Seattle). Smaller communities are scattered throughout the country in cities both large and small: Phoenix, Atlanta, and Washington, D.C., as well as Lewiston, Maine; Pelican Rapids, Minnesota; and Barron, Wisconsin. The city of Barron had fewer than 3,000 residents before Somalis started moving there, mostly to work in the Jennie'O turkey processing plant. By 2003, they constituted more than twelve percent of the town's population.[22]

For more than a century, the state of Minnesota was known for its large number of Scandinavian immigrants, who probably had the easiest time adjusting to the extremely long and cold winters.[23] That began to change in the 1970s after immigration reforms allowed families, church groups, and nonprofit organizations like Catholic Charities and Lutheran Social Services to sponsor tens of thousands of Hmong, Vietnamese, Liberian, and Oromo (Ethiopian) refugees for resettlement in the United States. Social workers and volunteers helped them find necessities such as housing, jobs, and clothing. They also offered advice about laws and standards of living in the local community. With good intentions, new immigrants were often invited to church services in order to bring them into the fold both culturally and spiritually.

With its history of resettlement success, Minnesota seemed like an appropriate place to send Somali refugees. Unfortunately, misunderstandings often erupted over things that non-Muslims did not recognize as religious issues, such as food preparation (*halal* food), rules for giving and receiving charity, and the cleanliness of donated items (particularly clothing and mattresses).[24] Relations with African Americans were often awkward. In my experience, most Somalis do not see themselves as "Africans" or as part of an underclass, which makes it difficult for them to identify with the racism African Americans have experienced, much to the dismay and confusion of African Americans. Distrust among both volunteers and Somalis grew after the events of September 11, 2001. Despite these failures, the initial placement of Somali refugees in Minnesota did establish a core population that was able to sponsor friends and family members coming from other parts of the United States or from other countries. In the booming economy of the late 1990s, many were able to find jobs working as parking lot attendants, taxi drivers, hotel housekeepers, assembly-line workers, and janitors cleaning floors at the airport and the Mall of America. Although affordable housing was not always easy to find (a situation made worse by welfare reforms and intense demand), families also found reasonably good public schools where students could catch up on years of patchy or missed education. As the number of Somalis grew, so did the number of mosques, *halal* grocery stores, and restaurants selling specialties like camel meat and *injera* bread. Such a high concentration of Somalis made it possible for those with limited skills in English to shop, work, and spend their entire days speaking only Somali. Within a few years Minnesota became known throughout the Somali diaspora as "the de facto 'capital' of the Somali community" in the United States.[25] When I meet Somalis living in other parts of the United States or even other countries, they inevitably have at least one relative living in Minnesota.

Important landmarks in the Minneapolis–Saint Paul community include the Somali malls (entire shopping centers where all of the merchants are Somalis), the Brian Coyle Community Center (staffed by Minneapolis Parks and Recreation), and a neighboring cluster of high-rise towers known as Riverside Plaza (which are highly visible on the edge of downtown Minneapolis and house many low-income immigrants and native-born tenants in addition to Somalis). Smaller groups of Somali immigrants have found housing in South Minneapolis along Lake Street, Minnehaha Avenue, the Midway and Frogtown neighborhoods of St. Paul (stretching along I-94), and some of the suburbs north of Minneapolis including Columbia Heights, Fridley, and Brooklyn Park. Fridley is where the Islamic Center of Minnesota is located along with a small Islamic school for kindergarten through twelfth grade called Al-Amal.

Suuqa Karmel, the first "Somali mall" built specifically for Somalis, is located just off of Lake Street, not far from the Uptown neighborhood (although, as is common in many big cities, there are vast socioeconomic differences between these two neighborhoods). Its opening in early 2001 was financed by Basim Sabri, a Palestinian immigrant and real estate developer who also owns Mercado Centrale (a Latino marketplace) and the International Bazaar (a multicultural marketplace) located just a few blocks away. Prior to these ventures, the neighborhood was known as a magnet for prostitutes and drug dealers. In an interview with Sabri, a reporter for the Minneapolis *City Pages* observed,

> It's a sunny spring day and business is bustling at Karmel Square. At the center of the building is Karmel Coffee, where a group of Somali men have gathered around an ornamental fountain to sip coffee and trade the day's news. When Sabri talks about this spot at 2942 Pillsbury Ave. S., just off Lake Street, he beams with pride. It has become a key meeting place for members of the Somali community. Before he arrived, Sabri claims, the spot was "a ghost street."[26]

Suuqa Karmel is the bottom floor of a two-story building and is divided in half. The northern half is the coffee shop mentioned in the *City Pages*. It has a few tables, an area for cooking and serving food, a computer kiosk with Internet access, and a fountain (which, oddly, has a statue of a nude woman). The other half of the floor contains approximately thirty businesses owned and operated mostly by women. Each space is very tiny (most are about six feet wide and four feet deep), so customers stand in the halls while they look at the merchandise and goods are hung from every available surface.

Since there are no doors to the shops (only metal gates), it gives the marketplace an open, bazaar-like quality. Bargaining is expected, and many of the owners do not arrive until the afternoon, when customers are getting done with work. Shops line the outer walls of the room and a row of back-to-back shops fills the middle. There is a small area for prayers (close to the bathrooms, so men and women can easily perform ritual washing before entering) and a window that looks out into the café so people can order drinks and food without going to the other side. The merchants sell mostly textiles, ready-made clothing, and accessories, but some sell books, tapes, and videos (especially discussions of religious issues and Somali-English dictionaries) or household furnishings (tea sets, bedspreads, prayer clocks, curtains, etc.). Other shops offer services such as faxing, haircutting, tailoring, money transferring, and travel arrangements. A newer and much larger market in Minneapolis near the corner of Lake Street and Chicago (an area notorious for violent crime in the 1990s) has many of the same types of businesses (see figure 29).

These marketplaces are a major attraction for Somalis living in other parts of Minnesota and the neighboring state of Wisconsin. In the town of Barron (Wisconsin),

> the stores and public services ... were not prepared to provide for the needs of Somalis. For example, the grocery stores in Barron were not aware of the special food needs of Somali Muslims. They did not stock halal meats, or the seasonings that the Somalis use in their food preparation. Even though there would be a considerable profit to be made from selling these items to the Somali community, the stores still do not supply the items, and the Somalis are forced to drive to the Twin Cities (Minnesota).[27]

An outsider driving through Barron would not have any idea that the town has such a large number of Somali residents, as I can attest from growing up nearby and visiting several times since 2003.

In contrast to life in the Twin Cities, Barron provided a true culture shock to both Somali immigrants and local residents. High school students protested that Somalis were receiving "special treatment" by being allowed to wear head coverings (*hijab*) since the rest of the students were not allowed to wear hats or even hooded sweatshirts to class, an argument couched in fears about Muslims, immigrants, and their own job prospects.[28] Finding Somali food in Barron is a problem, but so is finding appropriate clothing. Many of the refugees wear some elements of typical American dress (jeans, khakis, t-shirts, athletic shoes, etc.), but certain items—especially the *guntiino, garbasaar, shash, dirac, gorgorad,* and the *macawis* for men—are available only in shops owned by Somalis. These garments were common in East Africa, but have become some of the most difficult items to find in the United States. Accordingly, fancy sets of *dirac, gorgorad,* and *garbasaar*—which are sought after for weddings—are also some of the most expensive items of clothing in women's wardrobes.

Women also go to the Somali malls to buy Islamic dress. (A man might wear a *kufi* or a *kamiz* for Friday prayers, but these garments are not typically worn on a daily basis.) Head coverings (*hijab*) and garments like the *jilbab* are not exactly sold at Wal-Mart. Long skirts and loose-fitting tunics might turn up in mainstream shops, but it depends on the season and the current style.[29] This is an issue not only of modesty or fashion, but of being viewed as a "respectable" woman in the Somali community. Although Islam places a strong emphasis on marriage and the family, many women in the diaspora have found themselves living as single mothers, struggling to work and raise children on their own without the help of extended family members.[30] Data from the 2000 U.S. census showed that among adult Somali refugees, nearly one-third of the women were serving as "head of household" for various reasons. "11% were widows, 20% were divorced, 22% were never married, and 38%, although married, were not living with their spouses."[31] Many Somali women have no choice but to work long hours at "low-status, low-income jobs shunned by most men."[32] At the same time, the ideal within Islam is that a woman should not have to work outside the home. Wearing modest dress is a way to bridge the gap between these two opposing values. In effect, it communicates the idea that "Yes, I may be working long hours outside the home, but I am doing this for the good of my family." In both visual and practical terms, it also separates a woman from mainstream society, sending a strong message to both sides about her loyalties.

The Attractions and the Dangers of Fitting In

In contrast, some Somalis in Minnesota view acculturation—wearing local styles of dress and speaking English—as the right thing to do. Children spend much of their time in school with American classmates and learn English more quickly than their parents. Although there are Somali-language television and radio programs available in Minnesota as well as several Somali community newspapers, mainstream media is far more accessible and abundant. Many Somalis have been in the United States for a decade or more, making long-term decisions about buying a house, getting an education, or starting a new career. These are not just economic choices; they also move the individual away from being a refugee. Every step in this direction means that it becomes more and more difficult to drop everything and return "home." During Catherine Daly's interviews with Somali women, some said they would not return to Somalia even if they could. "Given a choice, I wouldn't go back but to another country." Others expressed that they missed being in Somali society and would be happy to go home if peace could be restored. One older woman struggling to find employment stated, "If [it is] safe to return I would like to."[33]

For many refugees, safety is one of their greatest concerns. Although the United States is better in many ways than the war zone they left behind, Somalis have found themselves living in a country with racial, ethnic, and religious tensions they do not fully understand, often in neighborhoods with a long history of violence. "Fitting in" by speaking English and wearing local styles of dress might be good if it leads to a job, but not if it leads to violence. Whether it is widely recognized or not, items of dress—tattoos, bandanas, certain brands and colors of clothing—have long been used in the United States to signify membership in violent gangs. After several young Somali men were murdered by other Somalis in 2008, debates erupted over the value of fitting in and how to protect young people from the violence.[34]

Acculturation can occur through many different avenues. Political activism has brought Somalis into closer contact with African Americans, other Muslims, and the larger community of Minneapolis–St. Paul. After a mentally disturbed Somali man was shot to death at a bus stop by the police when he failed to put down his crowbar and machete, community leaders met with police and the mayor of Minneapolis for discussions.[35] While the circumstances were difficult, this event opened lines of communication between Somalis and government officials. In 2000, a Somali woman who was fired from her seasonal job at the main post office in Saint Paul for wearing the *jilbab* (in violation of a new dress code) filed a lawsuit with help from the Council on American Islamic Relations (CAIR) and won an out-of-court settlement.[36]

In 2001, a Somali immigrant who had recently become a U.S. citizen ran for mayor of Minneapolis under the "New Voices Party," focusing on education, affordable housing, and the role of the police in the community.[37] During the 2008 election campaign, the office of Senator Norm Coleman hired a member of the Somali community to serve on his staff and facilitate outreach to other Somalis in Minnesota. Controversy arose during the hotly contested senate race of 2008, when this staffer worked as a translator at one of the polling stations without revealing his connections to the Coleman campaign and was accused of trying to covertly influence the votes of Somali immigrants.[38] Nonetheless, each of these steps brought Somalis closer to understanding the politics and cultural standards of their new home while giving them a chance to add their own voices.

Although no Somalis were involved in the terrorist attacks of September 11, 2001—the hijackers were all Arabs from the Middle East—the aftermath of that event created some additional challenges. Somalia was declared a harbor for terrorists, which meant that all male Somali immigrants were required to be interviewed and to register with the U.S. government.[39] Some were even deported to Somalia, despite the ongoing civil war. Al-Baraakat—a money-transferring business that Somalis had been using for years to support their relatives in East Africa—was shut down by the U.S. government along with some grocery stores that were accused of food stamp fraud and funneling money to terrorist organizations. In the end, none of the owners were formally charged and the businesses were allowed to reopen, but these events created a great deal of mistrust toward the U.S. government. Like many Muslims, Somalis were simply in the wrong place at the wrong time. In daily life, they were also subjected to harassment based on their appearance and other cues such as having an Arab name (Mohammed, Abdullah, etc.) or making regular visits to a mosque.[40]

The *jilbab* ensemble, which also closely resembles the "habit" of Catholic nuns, is easy for both Muslims and non-Muslims to recognize as religious dress. Although women who wear the *jilbab* make easy targets for harassment and discrimination, some employers, for example Target, allow Islamic head coverings to be incorporated into their uniforms. Compared to ethnic dress like the *guntiino*, the *jilbab* is clearly religious and therefore protected by law, which makes it relatively easy to wear (not as easy as Western-style dress, but easier than "traditional" dress like the *dirac*). Due to this ease of recognition, this has become the dominant style of "religious" dress for women in the Somali community, even though all types of Somali dress have been influenced by Islam.

The issue of what constitutes "Islamic dress" is a complicated one, both in theory and in practice as individuals make daily choices about their dress. Subtle distinctions between more and less conservative types of Islamic dress are not always understood by outsiders who get most of their information about Islam from the media. From one perspective, conservative styles like the *shuka* and *jilbab* are not only acceptable for Somali women to wear, but actually preferred. In her book on the Somali communities in London and Toronto, Rima Berns McGown observed that many Somalis view Islam not just as a personal religious practice but as a safeguard against the potential loss of faith and identity that could come from living in a foreign (non-Muslim) country.[41] From this point of view, the more conservative the dress, the better. Even in the refugee camps, Somalis heard about gang violence, discrimination, and other strains on immigrant families living in the West. A popular cassette tape circulating in Kenya warned about the dangers of migration:

> [One] song tells the story of a Somali man living in Canada who . . . feels as if he has lost his wife and children to a different culture. His wife has changed her appearance by using make-up and wearing high heels and tight clothes. She has become "arrogant" and he fears the effect of her changed behaviour on his children, their mother being responsible for their upbringing. His main concern is that his family loses Islam-hood, and he therefore discourages others to go to Western countries.[42]

Many young people are growing up thinking that these garments are simply normal for Somalis. Unless their parents and grandparents choose to educate them differently or they have opportunities to see photographs from before the civil war, there is little reason for them to think otherwise.

From another perspective, some Somalis view this kind of dress as the "Arabization" of their culture, a danger that could be just as great as Westernization (a point of view shared by intellectuals in countries such as Iran, Pakistan, and Indonesia, where enormous numbers of people are Muslims but not Arabs). Why should Somalis wear Arab dress? Islam requires modesty, but not the wholesale adoption of Arab culture. Somalis have been Muslims for centuries and do not need to prove their loyalty to Islam or pretend to be Arabs when they are not. It would be easy to think that Somali immigrants are simply making a choice between Islamic dress and Western dress, but in reality they have a rich history from their own culture to draw from.

Not all types of traditional dress have been maintained—especially not whole ensembles—but there are definitely elements that continue to be part of daily life. Many women use frankincense, for example, to change the scent of their clothing and interior spaces; the only major difference is that incense burners are now powered by electricity instead of charcoal.[43] Older women use henna to dye their hair and fingernails instead of using nail polish; younger women use it to decorate their hands and feet for celebrations such as weddings. The benefit of these body modification practices is that they can easily coexist with both Islamic and Western dress. Henna is used for celebrations throughout North Africa, the Middle East, and South Asia; in the West henna "tattoos" are fashionable among teenagers and young adults.[44] A henna artist in New Jersey, for instance, advertises that henna is "Fashion Fun! Applying pure natural henna is beneficial for skin . . . a safe organic product alternative to harmful hazardous chemical and laser tattoos."[45] Frankincense and henna are also used throughout the Islamic world. In fact, since the *boswellia* tree (the source of frankincense resin) is native to Somali territory, for centuries the Horn of Africa was known as a source of high-quality frankincense for body modification practices and the religious rituals of many non-Somali groups, including the Catholic and Greek Orthodox Churches.

Other subtle ways of incorporating traditional Somali dress into daily attire include substituting a *shash* for part of the *jilbab* head covering—which adds a different color to the typically single-color ensemble—using a perfume favored by Somalis such as "Secret Man" perfume (which has a very strong, musky scent), or wearing a piece of filigree jewelry made of yellow gold or imitation gold (a style and color favored in the Middle East). Unfortunately, when the civil war broke out many Somalis either lost or had to sell their heirloom jewelry from the nineteenth and early twentieth centuries— like the very elaborate, expensive *audulli* necklaces. Even so, owning and wearing expensive jewelry is still something that many women aspire to. As one refugee in Finland expressed, "We like to show, to dress gold and make our body full of gold."[46]

Weddings, folk dances, and other cultural events represent opportunities to wear whole ensembles of traditional dress. The most popular is the *dirac, garbasaar,* and *gorgorad.* In Minnesota, I bought a set for nearly one hundred dollars (see figures 19 and 20): a hot pink *gorgorad* with a large band of silver and hot pink lace at the hemline (imported from India), a light pink *dirac* made of thin cotton voile with a tie-dye pattern (imported from Japan); and a sheer, hot pink polyester *garbasaar* with a pattern of large gold and gray roses. I later found out that my purchase was a bargain because the colors change at least three to four times per year; hot pink was already out of fashion. Skillfully matched sets in the most fashionable colors of the season (with fancy features like sequins, glitter, and lace) can easily sell for two or three hundred dollars. Women who want to create a good image for themselves will not wear the same outfit more than once. Friends and relatives often exchange outfits to get more use out of them, but once an ensemble has been seen at "too many" weddings it will either be passed off to an older relative who doesn't care about the latest fashion or reserved for wearing around the house. Although weddings are a popular form of entertainment on the weekends, buying the proper clothing can be a drain on the household budget. *Kanga* fabrics (which are common along the Swahili coast[47]) can also be purchased at the Somali malls, but outfits made of printed cotton are not nearly as popular as they are among immigrants from West Africa. These ensembles are almost never worn on the street in Minneapolis–St. Paul, partly because they are not well suited to the climate. Until I started going to the Somali malls I was not aware of their existence.

On the Backs of Women

As Somalis in the diaspora have interacted with new people and new cultures, many questions have been raised about appropriate styles of dress. In many cases, these questions revolve around gender and what it means to be a proper man or woman in Somali society. On one end of the spectrum is a country like Saudi Arabia where all women—regardless of citizenship, ethnicity or professed religion—are required to wear *hijab;* only their hands and face can show in public. Some women in these circumstances (including Somalis) have chosen to wear *niqab* along with their head covering, an additional piece of material that covers the face. Saudi Arabia is noted for having a very conservative culture and style of Islam; Wahabbism has sometimes been compared to Puritanism.[48] On the other end of the spectrum is a country like France, which has officially banned all religious symbols (including Christian symbols like the crucifix) from public schools. This has forced many young women to either leave their heads uncovered or enroll in private schools to finish their education. In the United States, Equal Employment laws guarantee that all residents have the right to wear religious dress (beards, head coverings, etc.), but in practice some employers simply avoid hiring workers who might seek accommodation for religious practices. Unless they become citizens of the country they live in—which is not always possible—Somalis have no say in how these laws are written or enforced; they simply have to live with them or try to migrate to another country.[49] While these circumstances may have narrowed the range of Somali dress within particular countries of resettlement, globally the diversity of Somali dress has only increased due to the myriad of new cultural influences.

Elements of "world fashion"[50] such as business suits and blue jeans are very common in the Somali diaspora among boys and men. Despite what outsiders might think, this clothing is not a reliable index of assimilation to life in Western countries, as these styles of dress were widely accepted among Somali men long before the civil war. However, the same is not true for women; a young woman in a miniskirt would in no way be considered as wearing "Somali" dress. Furthermore, not all Western fashions are considered equally acceptable by Somalis. In the 1990s, urban (hip hop) men's fashions like team jerseys and baggy pants were relatively easy to adopt since they were loose-fitting and modest, conforming to the most basic principles of Islamic dress (which requires at a minimum that men should be covered from navel to knees).[51] Fashions for women in the 1990s, which included tight-fitting shirts and low-rise jeans designed to display the midriff, were hardly adopted at all by Somali women, being considered far too revealing. Scholars like Joanne Eicher and Fred Davis have observed that in the West the display of skin is often linked to gender.[52] Business suits for men typically cover the body from neck to ankle while suits for women include features such as skirts and low-cut necklines. For Somali men "appropriate" dress is usually compatible with Western fashion, but the same is not true for Somali women.

When young women do adopt Western fashions they tend to wear garments that conceal the body, such as long skirts and jackets, leading to a preference for conservative versions of fashion trends, such as a long denim skirt instead of blue jeans. Small items of dress like handbags, shoes, nail polish, and cell phones are also used to add touches of Western fashion to non-Western outfits. Although the process of choosing what to wear is often very intimate and personal, the elements of dress that are seen in public make powerful statements about how the wearer fits into society. For young Somalis—walking a tightrope between cultures—every single item of dress must be carefully considered. Since the range of acceptable choices for women is limited, their clothing as a whole is not a very good indicator of how they see themselves fitting into American society.

Garments like the *jilbab* (figure 16) have a very different aesthetic from Western dress since they are designed to obscure the silhouette of the body. A head covering, for example, might also hide the curves of the neck, shoulders, arms, and chest; an extra-long garment could even drape over the waist and hips. Outsiders might view a simple head wrap (*masaar*)—one that covers the hair, but not the neck—as a bandana, "scarf," or a symbol of African heritage, but a head covering that obscures the outline of the neck is automatically recognized as "Islamic" dress. This immediately creates a visual separation from non-Muslims. Underneath these garments, however, it is not uncommon for a woman to wear a cardigan, a winter coat, or even pants. These hidden garments are worn for practical instead of symbolic reasons.

Pants are almost universal among Somali men, but for women they are a controversial garment. Close-fitting pants have become common among women living in the refugee camps as an undergarment (worn under a skirt), but pants by themselves (without a skirt or another outer garment such as a *shuka*) are generally considered unacceptable because they look too much like clothing for men.[53] In Finland, Anu Isotalo recorded conversations about the clothing of a young woman who Somalis thought was becoming too assimilated.

> She is proud and she doesn't listen to what other [Somalis] say. . . . And little by little, things get worse, and every day she hears "they said this and this and this about you." And it gets worse. Now it can be that she is wearing trousers but has done nothing bad. She has only taken off her skirt and wears trousers, nothing else. But they may say that if she is wearing trousers, she has given up on her faith, or that she has changed from a decent girl into a whore. She was not a whore, but if some people say "whore whore whore" and she hears it, it can be that she gets tired of what other people say. And then she may even become a whore.[54]

In cases like this, calling a young woman a "whore" does not mean that she is literally selling herself as a prostitute; instead, the term is meant to shame her into changing her behavior. As many Somalis see it, a young woman who does not resist assimilation is endangering not only herself but her future children, threatening the integrity of the entire culture. She might be able to get away with small touches of the West—nail polish or a fancy cell phone— but daring to wear a t-shirt or a pair of jeans without a skirt calls into question her respectability as a woman and ultimately her long-term commitment to upholding Somali culture.

In Minnesota, the Somali population is large enough to support Somali-owned tailoring shops where a woman can order an extra-long skirt or a custom-made *jilbab*. In places like Finland, however, where Muslims (Somalis, Turks, and even some native converts) make up a small minority, garments like these are more difficult to obtain. This affects a woman's ability to express her sense of individuality and taste, as a study of Muslims in Finland has shown.

> "In Finland it is not possible to dress according to one's personality, because it is difficult to get clothes. If someone comes from Syria, others snatch [clothes] from her hands. If someone sends you clothes, they are not necessarily to your taste," says Maryah, a Finnish woman. These limitations are faced even more by immigrant Muslims, who have developed their own strategies for the acquisition of clothes. One Somali woman has opened a shop that imports long skirts and scarves. Some women have started a more private way of helping themselves and their friends. They travel to the Middle East or Somalia to buy clothes that they then sell to other women of the community. They function not only as sellers but as fashion brokers too, since the Arab countries, and Syria in particular, are centers of Arab-Islamic or Muslim fashion that is followed in Finland right alongside Western fashion. Muslim fashion is also followed through digital television channels and satellites.[55]

In contrast to the typically narrow color palette worn by Middle Eastern Muslims, Somalis tend to sport a much broader range of hues: muted beiges and greens, but also vivid colors such as sky blue, yellow, eggplant, and maroon.[56] In Minnesota, Somali women scour the local fabric stores looking for new materials. This sets them apart from Arabs (such as Palestinian immigrants) who wear the same garments, and it also reflects a more individual, improvisational, recognizably African sensibility about colors.

Until the 1980s, Somalis who wore this kind of dress were a rarity: the descendants of Arab and Persian settlers, young women trying to preserve their beauty for a "good marriage," or extreme religious conservatives. These meanings have changed as Islamic dress has become much more common. In Minnesota I have seen girls as young as three years old wearing *hijab*. While doing fieldwork in Kenya and Somalia, Cawo Abdi noted that even

> textbooks produced by UNESCO depict Somali girls as young as four or five all wearing the *jalaabiib* [*jilbab*], reflecting the current situation. This contrasts with the pre-1990s culture of Somalia, where preteen girls were never expected to cover their hair. One looking at these books would never guess that this is a new tradition dating only to after the civil war. Such reified representations of Somali girls are being reproduced in various images, as well as in patterns of dress, contributing to the reconstruction of gender norms for Somali women and girls. With this new trend we witness a new culture under construction, part of the ongoing project of the re-Islamicization of Somali women and girls.[57]

Since the war began, photographs of Somali girls and women in the Horn of Africa almost always show them wearing the *jilbab*, making this the new (albeit controversial) icon of Somali women's dress in the twenty-first century. Western viewers see garments like the *jilbab* and the Afghan *chaadaree* as evidence of extremism and oppression to women, nudging them in the direction of military intervention (even though the *jilbab* exists in a number of other countries such as Indonesia where the outfit is commonly worn only for prayers).[58] In the twenty-first century large numbers of Somali women are wearing the *jilbab* on a daily basis. Some Somalis view this as a positive development; others see it just as negatively as any non-Somali could.

While Islam has been part of Somali culture for hundreds of years and Somalis have internalized the principles of Islamic dress (modesty, separation of gender, etc.)—incorporating them into everything they wear, not just the new forms of specifically "Islamic" dress—the events of the last two decades have complicated how they view themselves as Muslims. Outwardly they might give the appearance of increasing conservativism and adherence to trends in the Middle East, but there are subtle differences and forces within the Somali community that prevent the wholesale adoption of another culture (even a global Islamic culture). Fashions that are common among Arabs and Arab immigrants are not necessarily popular among Somalis.

For example, some young Somalis wear a head covering called a *shayla,* a rectangular scarf that is wrapped over a close-fitting underscarf and held in place with a fashionable pin. This is a common style of dress in the Middle

East among both young and middle-aged women, especially in urban areas. Among Somalis, this trend is restricted to unmarried girls in their teens or early twenties; older women rarely wear such trendy scarves and pins. Beyond the cultural implications, this is also an issue of social class. Most Somalis did not come to the United States with much money and have not been established long enough to make a good living. Using figures from the 2000 U.S. Census, Franklin Goza estimated that 42 percent of Somali households were living under the poverty line; this is dramatic considering that only 22.1 percent of African Americans and 21.2 percent of Hispanics (two groups that have long been economically disadvantaged) had the same income levels.[59] While working as taxi drivers, cashiers, parking lot attendants, housekeepers, and child care workers, many Somalis have been struggling to support not just themselves but family members who are still living in the refugee camps or in Somalia. Although an exception is made for the expensive *dirac* and *garbasaar* (an outfit worn in the United States only by Somalis), wearing the latest Western or Islamic fashion is not a high priority and could even be viewed by other Somalis as a waste of money.

The *guntiino* is another point of contention. This solid marker of Somali identity is still worn in the diaspora by some brides and for cultural events such as folk dances. (Women in Uganda wear a similar wrapped garment—in fact, my Somali garments and slides have often been mistaken for Ugandan at African Studies conferences—but the Ugandan version is generally more colorful and reveals the lower legs.) However, the original nomadic style—where one shoulder was left bare—now seems far too revealing. To compensate, the fabric is made thicker and the *guntiino* is typically worn with a matching shawl (*garbasaar*) over the shoulders (see figure 30). Islamists object because the head and neck are left uncovered. Is this an appropriate representation of Somali womanhood? Because of these conflicting viewpoints, the *guntiino* has fallen out of fashion in the diaspora; Somali women rarely wear the *guntiino* outside of the house. When it is worn, the colors are always red, black, and gold; they do not change with the seasons like the *dirac* and *gorgorad*.

Men's dress has not been affected by these politicized religious expressions to the same degree as women's dress. Although men struggle over accommodations for beards and prayers (particularly time off from work to attend congregational prayers on Fridays), most Islamic garments—which are almost always imported from the Middle East or South Asia—are worn only for prayers and for holidays such as the end of Ramadan. These include the *kufi* (a close-fitting, brimless cap), *salwaar kamiz*[60] (a long tunic and loose-fitting trousers that taper at the ankles), and *imamad* (known as a *ghutra* or *kaffiyeh* in the Middle East). In contrast to Arabs who wear the *kaffiyeh* as a head covering, most Somalis drape the scarf over one shoulder. This recalls the uniforms worn by Sayyid Mohammed Abdulle Hassan's soldiers during the struggle against the British in the early 1900s. For Somalis, wearing the *kaffiyeh* as a head covering is a departure from tradition. This is what the Arab-influenced extremists in Al-Shabab wear; it is not something expected or even widely accepted among Somalis in the diaspora.

While Somali women in the diaspora are just as likely as Somali men to be employed outside the home (especially in the estimated one-third of households where a woman is the sole breadwinner[61]), women face greater discrimination at the time of hiring based on their dress. In principle, Equal Employment laws require that decisions be made strictly on the basis of merit. For example, a large law firm in the United States includes a statement on its website that

> Brink Hofer Gilson & Lione is committed to the principles of equal employment opportunity. Firm practices and employment decisions regarding employment, hiring, assignment, promotion, compensation, and other terms and conditions of employment shall not be based on an employee's race, color, sex, age, religion, national origin, mental or physical disability, ancestry, military discharge status, sexual orientation, marital status, source of income, parental status, housing status, or other protected status, in accordance with applicable law.[62]

In practice, however, discrimination is still quite common. Somali women face pressure to dress according to the expectations of employers, but they also face tremendous pressure from within their own community to project their loyalty to their culture and faith through dress. Finding an employer who understands the dilemma or is at least willing to compromise on dress codes can take a great deal of additional time and effort.

Looking toward the Future

Never before has Somali dress been so important as a marker of identity. Somalis have a long history of interacting with people from other cultures, but—with the exception of the worst years of colonization—there was always a choice; interact and experiment with new styles of dress, or retreat knowing the risks and benefits. When nearly everyone was Somali, there was no need to display one's ethnic identity through dress; it was taken for granted. Dress was used to make distinctions between men and women, young and old, noble and subservient, urban and rural, but these distinctions were not nearly as politicized. There was no need for "Somali" dress until non-Somalis became part of daily life.

For the hundreds of thousands of Somalis who are now living outside of East Africa, the situation is very different. Anyone who wants to hold a job, go to the grocery store, or even just watch television is forced to adapt in some way to the new, majority culture. For some people, adjusting to the new country in which they have resettled becomes an all-encompassing process (assimilation), although success depends on how much the local culture is willing to let them in. The change in others is not as noticeable unless you compare their dress, behavior, and thoughts to earlier times. Until the last two or three decades, Islam was something many Somalis took for granted; dress was shaped by Islam, but very few people wore "Islamic dress." In the twenty-first century, however, the situation is very different. Islamic dress has been highly politicized, associated with extremism and violence, but also worn as a refuge against violence. When a Somali woman chooses to wear an outfit like the *jilbab,* the reasons for her decision are vastly different from what her grandparents or even parents might have considered. Dress has become much more than just a material possession; it has become an outward manifestation of a battle for the future of Somali culture.

In the right circumstances, Somali dress can be a welcome marker of difference, a sign of ongoing commitment to Somali culture. Through cues like language and dress women can have a critical impact on the next generation, teaching their children love and respect. For Somalis who identify strongly with their country of resettlement, however, Somali dress can be an unwelcome marker of difference, a "backwards" practice that speaks to a country and a history some people would rather forget. The experiences of young people in the diaspora—whether positive and affirming of Somali culture or negative and isolating—will play a tremendous role in whether Somali dress is maintained, celebrated, changed, or cast aside all together.

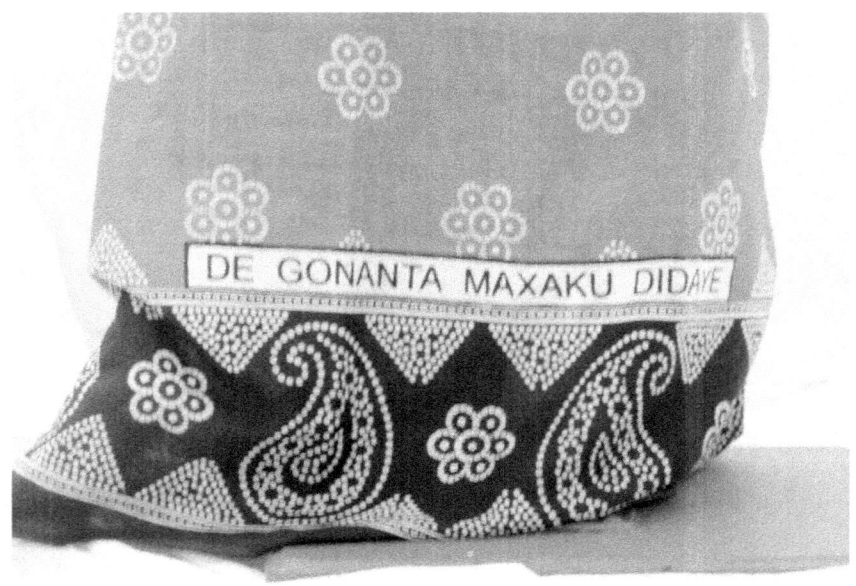

FIGURE 17. *Kanga* print worn as a *guntiino* (wrapped dress); although most fabrics have slogans in Swahili, this one has a Somali text that reads "DE GONANTA MAXAKU DIDAYE" (translated for me as "why don't you settle down"). Collection of the author.

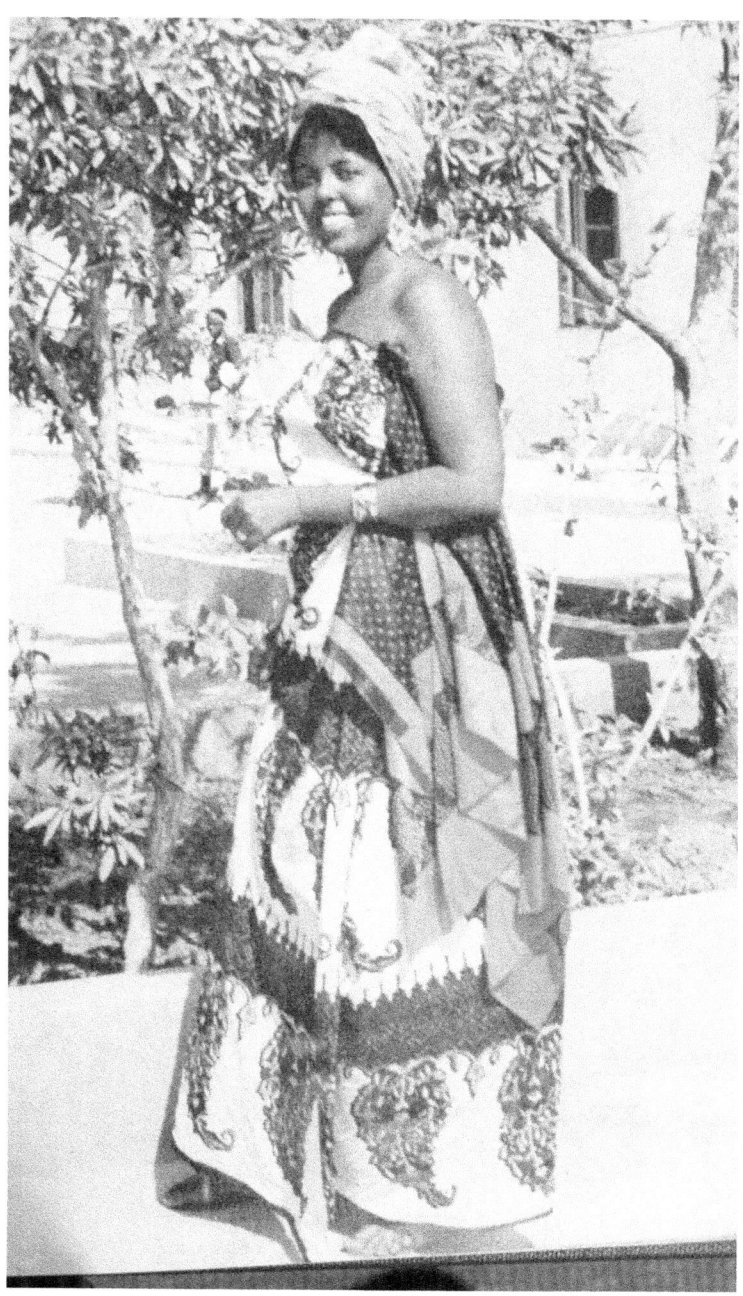

FIGURE 18. A fashionable young Somali woman in the early 1970s
wearing a Nigerian-style head wrap and dress made from a lightweight
paisley fabric. Published in *Beautiful Somalia* (1971), p. 41.

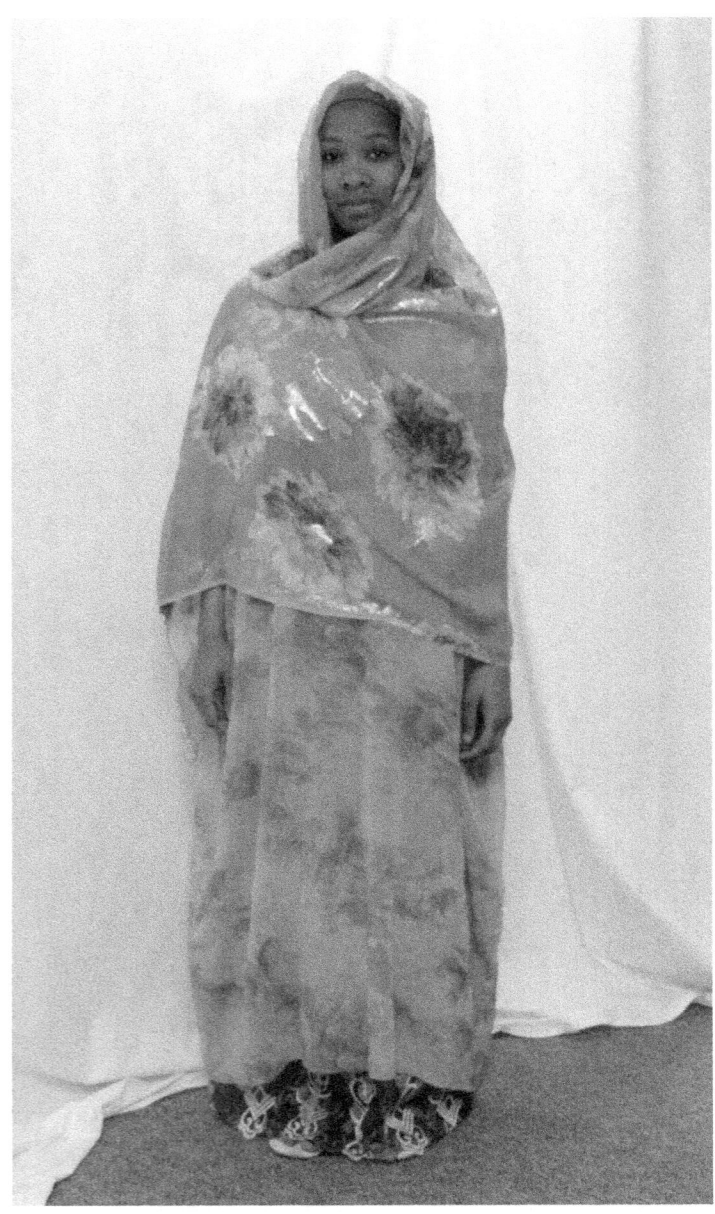

FIGURE 19. *Dirac* (dress), *garbasaar* (shoulder cloth), and *gorgorad* (petticoat); a new style of "traditional" dress made from colorful, imported fabrics that became popular in the 1970s, particularly in northern Somalia; in the diaspora this ensemble is commonly worn for weddings. Collection of the author.

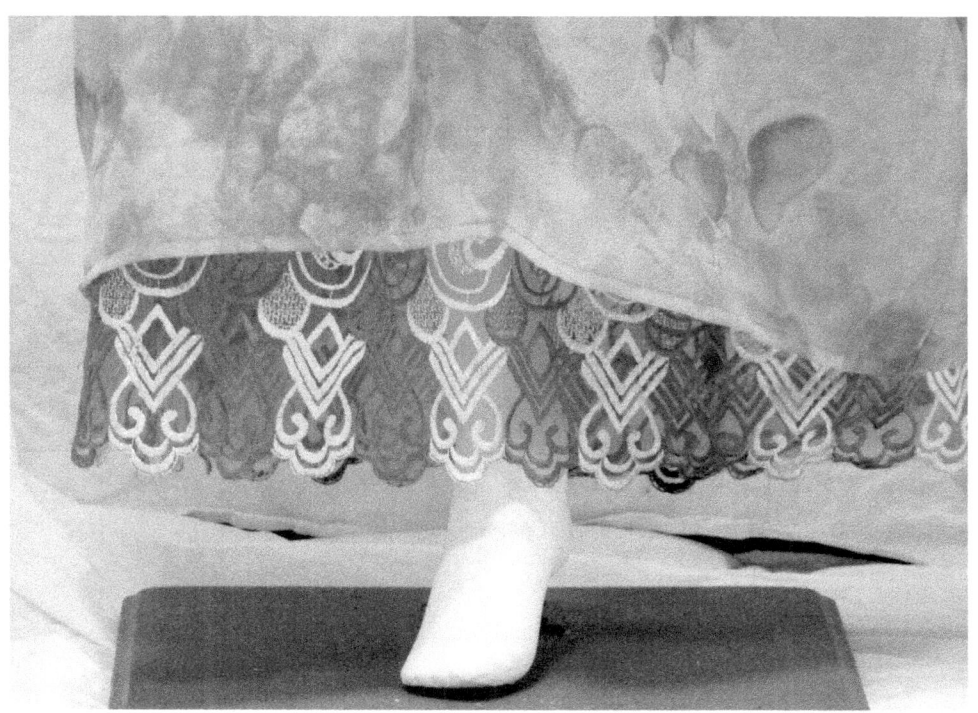

FIGURE 20. Detail of the *gorgorad* (petticoat), which has an elaborate band of machine-made lace designed to be shown at the bottom of the *dirac* (dress); on this particular ensemble (purchased by the author in Minnesota), the *gorgorad* came from India and the *dirac* fabric was made in Japan.

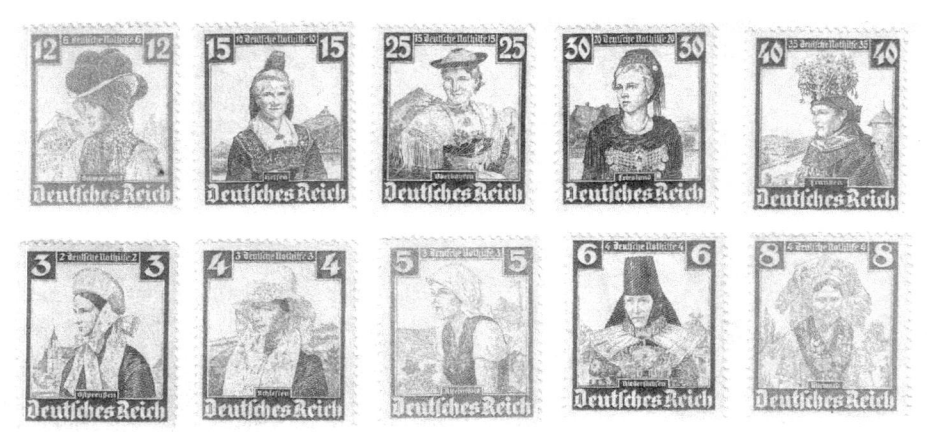

FIGURE 21. Stamps issued by the Nazi government depicting traditional German dress, a symbol of *Volk* (folk) culture. Collection of the author.

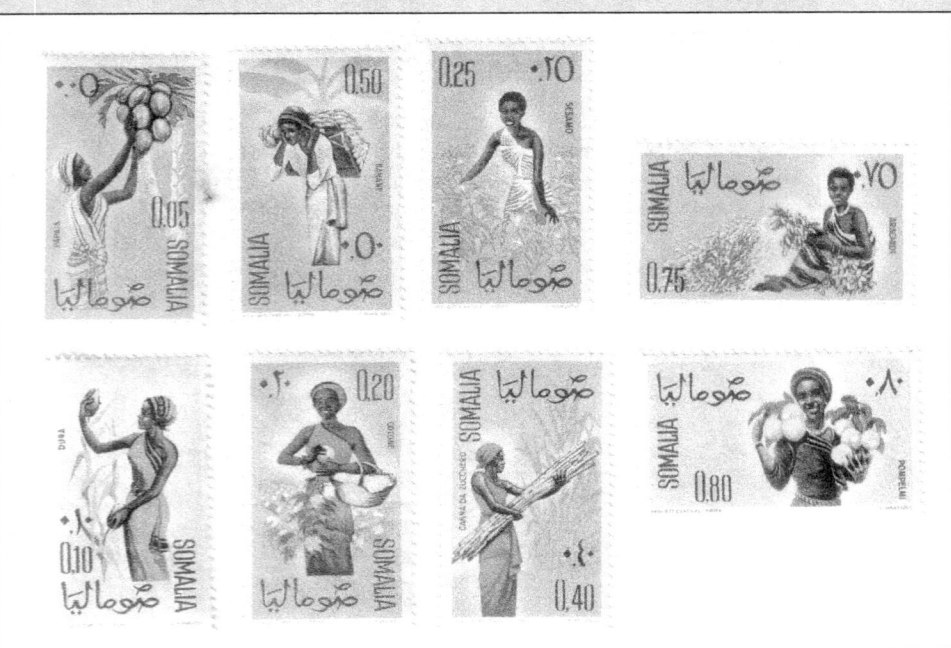

FIGURE 22. Stamps printed shortly after Somalia's independence depicting women in *guntiinaha* performing agricultural work (symbols of fertility and wealth). Collection of the author.

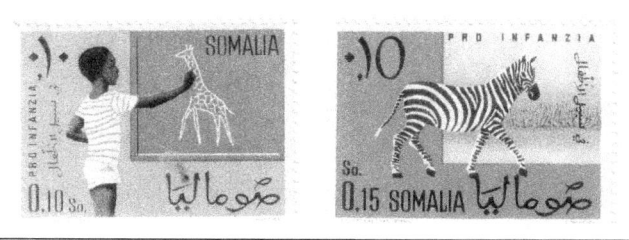

FIGURE 23. *Above,* Two stamps from a block (1960–61)
depicting a schoolboy at a chalkboard drawing African animals
(the other stamps show various animals); his outfit consists
of a striped t-shirt and shorts. Collection of the author.

FIGURE 24. *Below,* Two stamps from a block (1960–61) depicting
a young girl embroidering fish on a piece of cloth (the other
stamps show varieties of fish); in contrast to the boy at school,
the girl is wearing a more traditional outfit consisting of a
guntiino and beaded necklace. Collection of the author.

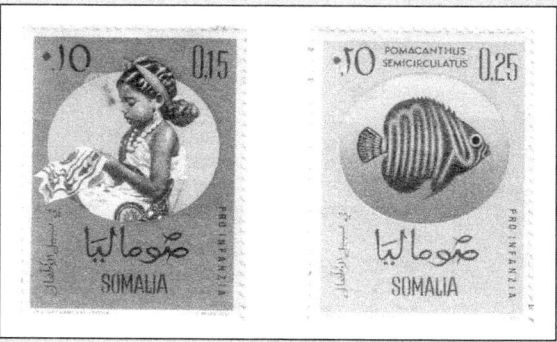

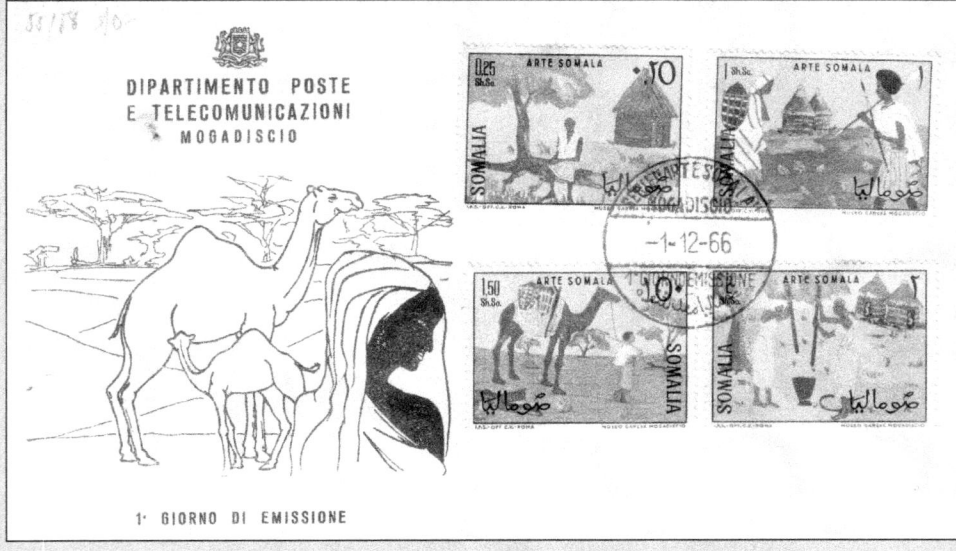

FIGURE 25. First day cover (1966) depicting scenes of rural life. The figures are depicted in historically accurate nomadic garments from the nineteenth and early twentieth centuries, the *guntiino* for women and *maro* for men. Collection of the author.

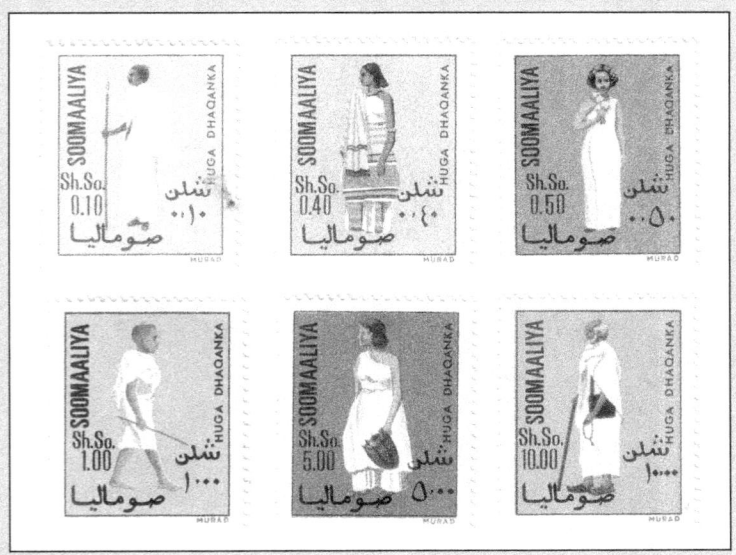

FIGURE 26. Series of stamps (1975) depicting men and women wearing very traditional nomadic dress; with one exception (a red, black, and gold-striped wedding outfit) all of the garments are made of plain white fabric. Collection of the author.

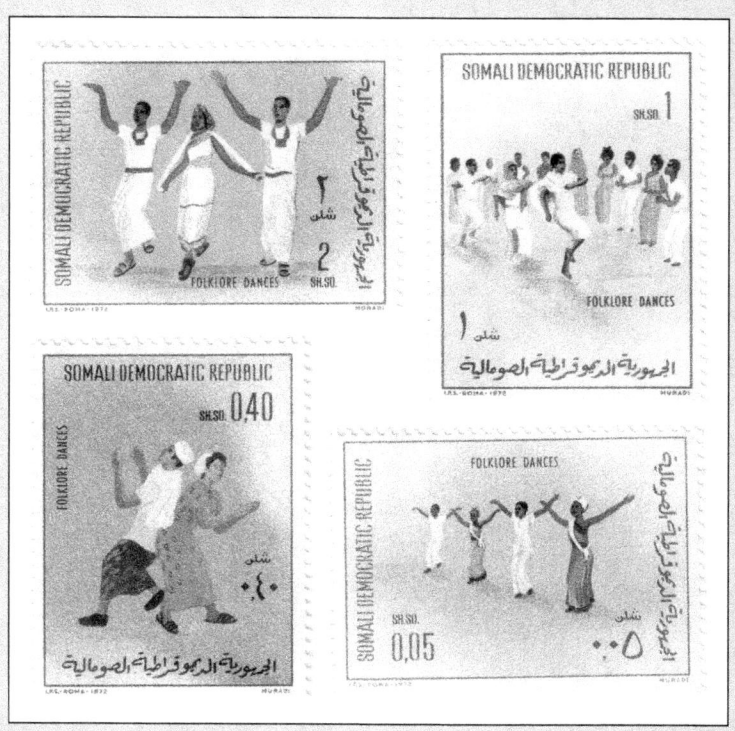

FIGURE 27. Set of stamps about folk dancing (1972–74); interestingly, some of the outfits include t-shirts and the *sarong*-like *macawis,* a "traditional" garment for men that first appeared in the 1970s. Collection of the author.

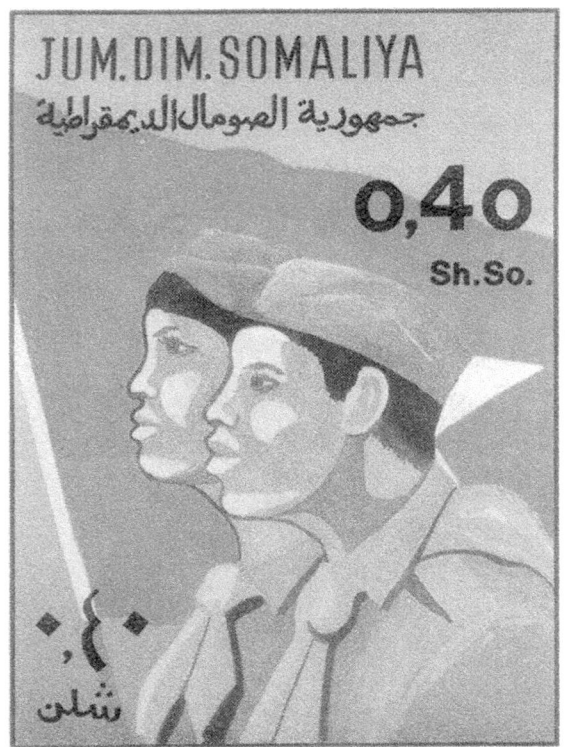

JUM.DIM.SOMALIYA

جمهورية الصومال الديمقراطية

0,40

Sh.So.

٠,٤٠

شلن

FIGURE 28. *Left,*
Postage stamp from the
Siad Barre era showing
two young men in
Socialist uniforms.

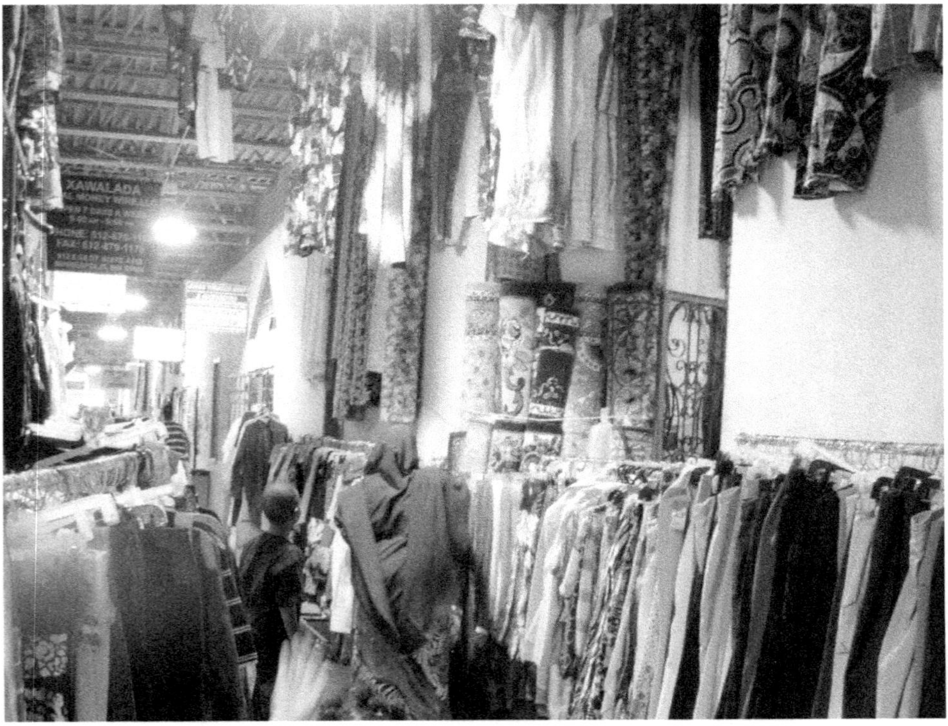

FIGURE 29. *Below,*
Interior of a "Somali
mall" in Minneapolis,
2009. Photograph
by author.

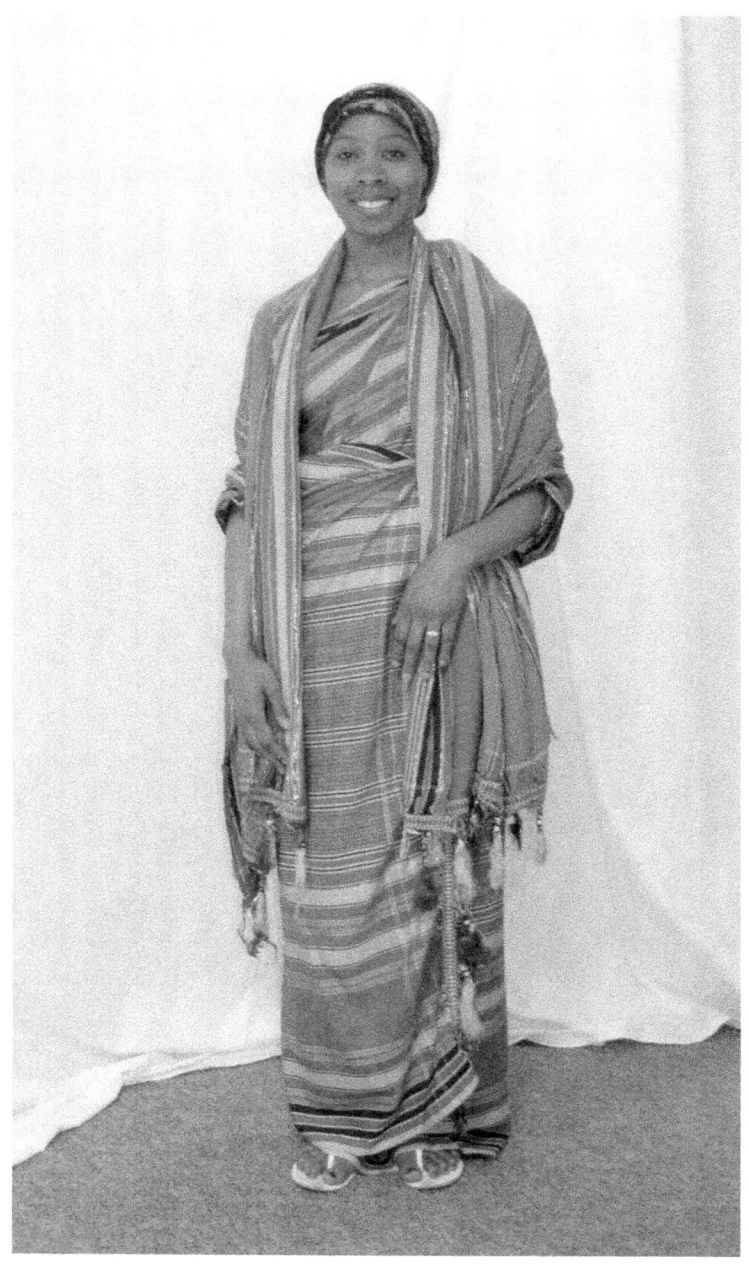

FIGURE 30. Contemporary *guntiino* (wrapped dress) with *garbasaar* (shoulder cloth) and *shash* (head covering for a married woman), all made by Indian manufacturers for the Somali market. Collection of the author.

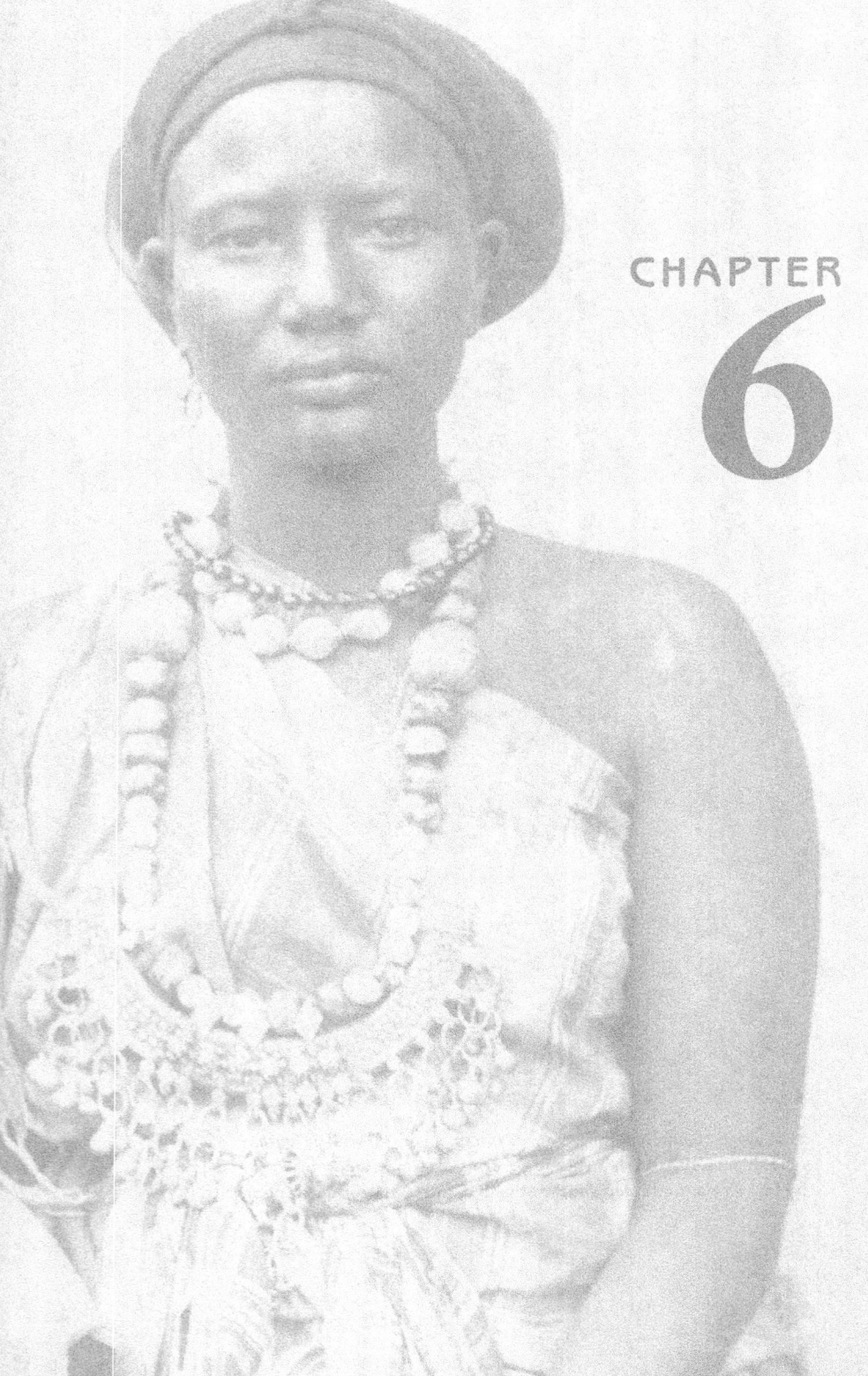

6. The Relevance of History

> The coast off Somalia has become a hotbed of piracy as the Somalian state has collapsed, offering safe haven for pirates targeting the nearby Gulf of Aden, one of the world's busiest shipping lanes. Some 18,000 ships sail through the gulf every year, delivering Saudi oil and China-made iPods to Europe and Porsches to Dubai.
>
> —Wall Street Journal, *January 31, 2009*

In November 2008, Somali "pirates" attracted international media attention by capturing a Saudi supertanker filled with two hundred million barrels of crude oil, a feat accomplished with rocket-propelled grenade launchers from the ongoing war in Somalia. A journalist for the *Times* of London called the supertanker, the *Sirius Star,* "the biggest booty ever taken on the high seas,"[1] a prize that the Somali fishermen-turned-pirates released two months later in exchange for three million U.S. dollars. Although the men who captured the ship were roundly condemned as "pirates" and even "terrorists," there was also an element of romanticism in the media coverage. Many Americans—whose interest in pirates had been aroused by Hollywood's *Pirates of the Caribbean* trilogy—couldn't help but view the media coverage as a fantasy come to life. Missing from the story was an explanation for why Somalis had begun hijacking ships in the first place. An editorial in the *Seattle Times* observed,

> For many Americans, the 21st century resurgence of piracy off the Horn of Africa was a distant, exotic curiosity until an attack on a U.S. cargo ship [The *Maersk Alabama* in April 2009] and the dramatic rescue of the ship's captain by Navy SEALs.... Pirates operate out of Somalia, home to a failed economy, failed government and 1,900 miles of coastline. Piracy passes as a national industry, offering employment and income.... Actual progress [at

stopping the pirates] will be linked to stability and economic opportunity ashore in Somalia, bloodied by 20 years of chaos, with no credible central government or even territory held by a civil authority.[2]

In the absence of any real economic opportunities or government to stop them, hijacking ships for ransom is not necessarily "terrorism," but a mark of desperation. The captain of the *Maersk Alabama* described his hijackers as "very thin" young men wearing t-shirts, sweatpants or shorts, and flip-flops; they were not wearing uniforms and did not seem to be part of any organized group (although the level of organization is now changing as Al-Shabab has taken advantage of piracy as a source of income to fuel the group's violent activities).[3] For the owners of the *Sirius Star,* three million U.S. dollars was a small price to pay for the safe return of more than ten billion dollars in cargo; other ships have paid bribes up front to protect them from being hijacked. What the pirates probably do not realize is that some of their ancestors did this kind of thing before (see chapter 3). In the 1800s there were Somalis making a living by robbing and often killing the survivors of shipwrecks and stealing the ships' cargo, a development made both possible and necessary by the economic disruptions of European colonization in Africa and the Middle East. History is repeating itself in the twenty-first century.

When Senator Obama visited northeastern Kenya in 2006, did the Somali elders who dressed him understand the history behind their actions and the historical moment they were creating? The ceremonial outfit they gave to Obama—which was based on the uniforms worn by Sayyid Mohammed Abdulle Hassan's soldiers in the late 1800s—was originally designed to be read as "Islamic." Sayyid resented the disruptions of British colonialism and wanted to make a strong visual statement of opposition, mixing nomadic garments with an Arab-style turban cloth. Over the years, however, Somalis had come to see this outfit as "traditional." As increasing numbers of young men migrated to urban areas and these garments fell out of use in daily life, they became easier to valorize as proud symbols of Somali history, depicted by the new government on objects such as currency and postage stamps. Also, in comparison to the new forms of Islamic dress coming from the Middle East in the 1970s and '80s, this kind of wrapped clothing looked like ethnic dress and not religious dress, more "Somali" than "Islamic." Americans, on the other hand, immediately recognized the Islamic symbolism of the turban in Obama's outfit. Without any real knowledge of historical trends in Somali dress, they simply read their own interpretations into the outfit based on stereotypes of turban-wearing Muslims. What does this outfit really mean to Somalis in Kenya and elsewhere today? Do they still identify with (or even know about) Sayyid Mohammed Abdulle Hassan? There is still research left to be done to understand current interpretations of this outfit.

Questions Unanswered

Although I have greatly enjoyed assembling the pieces that make up the puzzle of Somali dress, I regret that there are some topics I could not fully explore. Sources like oral history and archives in nearby countries (Yemen, Sudan, Ethiopia, Djibouti, etc.) could be an exciting source of information for a person with the right language skills, preferably a native speaker of Somali.[4] Unfortunately, the literature on dress in these other countries is practically nonexistent, so this would be another exercise in puzzle assembly.[5] Some of the Arab and Persian influences on Somali dress are clear, but what about influences from southern Asia? Women in India wear petticoats like the *gorgorad*. The crescent shape is part of the repertoire for jewelry makers in Afghanistan.

A scholar with skills in Asian languages who was interested in textiles could track down manufacturers in India, Japan, and Korea who produce materials for the Somali market. These textiles (used for garments like the *dirac, gorgorad,* and *garbasaar*) have become an important part of the new "traditional" dress for Somalis, but the origins of these styles and the impact of the Asian manufacturers has not been explored. A colleague of mine, Hazel Lutz—who speaks Hindi and does research on the Indian export market to West Africa—visited one of these manufacturers in Mumbai.[6] Rajsi Brothers produces imitation Benadir cloth and *shash* head coverings (I found packages with the company's address at the Somali malls in Minnesota). What I did not know is that the same factory produces similar textiles with minor variations for consumers in Yemen, Uganda, Nigeria, and Europe. How have these cultures and styles influenced one another? This topic is very complicated and one that I was not able to pursue in my own research.

Another avenue for future research is the Somali diaspora, particularly how young people are using the Internet to rapidly share ideas and images. In an article published in 2009, Lidwien Kapteijns argues that the Internet has become the primary site of public discourse in the twenty-first century (at least for those who are literate). "Hundreds of Somali websites compete to promote and disseminate the interests and interpretations of their (often clan-identified) target groups. . . . It is here that the discursive battles about communal identity, the nature of the state, the role of Islam and Islamism, and (often implicitly) gender norms are waged."[7] Although dress is worn in the physical world, the virtual world is increasingly where people buy and sell garments and share images. Like Kapteijns, I expect this to be a very exciting area for research as Somalis express new visions of what it means to be and dress "Somali."

Navigating a Path

A popular saying along the Swahili coast is that "when elephants fight, the grass suffers." For more than a century, Somalis have been caught up in the powerful forces of colonialism, the Cold War, globalization, and the War on Terrorism. Dress has changed along with these political trends, but dress has also offered Somalis opportunities to "speak" and make their political views known when other avenues have been closed. Dress is not just something to wear; it allows the wearer to embody history and envision a new future through a medium that is intimately personal but also visible to the public. As Hobsbawm and Ranger noted in *The Invention of Tradition*, "traditions" are not static.[8] We blend our thoughts about the past with our experiences in the present and our hopes for the future, investing objects like dress with great meaning. The clothes we wear do much more than serve a functional purpose.

Without a safe home, Somalis must have something to be proud of if Somali culture is going to continue. As crushing as the civil war has been, in the twenty-first century Somalis have an opportunity to take control of their destiny and construct a new image of what it means to be "Somali." But what should it be based on? Who should decide? During Somalia's thirty-one years of national independence, Somalis had many different ideas about how they should think, speak, look, and act. Their dress was a dazzling mixture of styles: nomadic and urban, local and imported, old and new, Islamic and Westernized. This variety of styles only continued to increase as the government of Somalia collapsed and refugees were dispersed throughout the world. Considering this fractured history, how should Somalis represent themselves? Is it even possible to find common ground and a common sense of heritage? What is "Somali" about the clothes Somalis wear? As a young woman asked on a blog, "Are you a guntiino girl or dirac goddess? . . . It's time for all Somali girls to unite and embrace their culture."[9]

Some see Islam and Islamic dress as the banner under which Somalis can unite. One problem, however, is that Islam is not unique to Somalis; some wonder where to draw the line between Somali and Arab culture, particularly in matters such as the rights of women. While Islamic law is progressive in giving women certain rights, such as property ownership and the right to divorce, Arab culture is sometimes very restrictive (in Saudi Arabia, for example, women are not allowed to drive). Another problem is how to reconcile an Islamic identity with the aftermath of September 11, the War on Terrorism, and the rise of religious extremism in Somalia. Somalis living in the West are under enormous pressure to choose sides: assimilate and downplay their identity as Muslims, or stand against the tide and defend their religion—sometimes even at the cost of downplaying their Somali identity. For hundreds of years Somali dress and culture has been infused with the principles of Islam, but this moderate history is not always recognized or acknowledged.

The major alternatives to this vision—Westernization on the one hand and a return to "traditional" culture on the other—are also fraught with difficulties. If Somali refugees in the West fully embrace their new lives, are they giving up hope of returning home and sharing a culture with other Somalis? Even if they do return, what will other Somalis think of them? Some see any influence from the West as corruption, a throwback to colonization. This attitude resonates with the more recent experiences of Arabs in the Middle East, who are deeply affected by the Israeli–Palestinian conflict and the American-led war in Iraq, and who are so close to Somalis both geographically and culturally. Rebuilding "traditional" culture might be even more of a challenge, however. For better or worse, the days of truly nomadic life—when all the important decisions could be made by a group of men sitting under a tree—are long gone, destroyed by European colonization.[10] Although there is still much to be proud of and to celebrate from this history, as a practical way of life it would be nearly impossible to resurrect. Time cannot be turned back. In an era of supertankers and AK-47s, Somalis must interact with the outside world to protect themselves from further harm. Perhaps the best thing to do is embrace the diversity of people who call themselves "Somali" and build a new path into the future. This is something only Somalis can make happen.

Appendix: Stamps Issued in Somalia, 1960–1980

Postage stamps issued by the government of Somalia commemorating external events and other international topics

Year(s) of issue	Theme
1960–61	In support of refugees
1960–61	Olympics*
1960–61	In support of children*
1962	In support of children†
1962	Campaign against malaria
1963–65	Telecommunications
1963–65	Freedom from hunger
1963–65	In support of refugees†
1963–65	Olympics*
1966	United Nations anniversary (20 years)
1966–67	UNESCO anniversary
1966–67	Boy Scouts (international jamboree in Idaho)*
1967–68	Visit from King Faisal of Saudi Arabia
1967–68	World Health Organization anniversary*
1968–69	Olympics*
1968–69	International Labor organizations†
1969–70	Mahatma Gandhi
1969–70	Birth of Lenin (first set produced by Siad Barre's government)*
1971–72	Telecommunications

* = shows Western-style dress (including uniforms)

† = shows historical forms of Somali dress

Year(s) of issue	Theme
1971–72	Congress of Somali Studies
1971–72	African Postal Union
1972–74	Olympics*
1972–74	Arab League (coinciding with Somalia's initiation)
1972–75	UNICEF*†
1972–75	African Postal Union
1975–76	World Women's Day
1977	Scenes of life in Africa†
1977–78	Air transportation (ICAO)
1977–78	Olympics*
1977–78	Palestine (shows the al-Aqsa Mosque)
1979	Year of the Child
1980	Congress of Somali Studies

Postage stamps issued by the government of Somalia commemorating internal events and others aspects of Somalia's national heritage

Year(s) of issue	Theme
1960	Proclamation of independence
1960–61	Ancient trade
1960–61	Women in *guntiinaha* doing agricultural work†
1960–61	Butterflies
1961–61	Handcrafts†
1962	Women in the military auxiliary forces*
1963–65	National independence (5 years)*
1963–65	Urban architecture
1963–65	Somali Credit Bank
1963–65	Somali Airlines (founded in 1963)*
1966	Agricultural and nomadic industries†
1966	Animals and flowers
1966	Birds and vegetation
1966–67	Rural life†
1966–67	Antelope
1966–67	Folk dancing†

* = shows Western-style dress (including uniforms)

† = shows historical forms of Somali dress

Year(s) of issue	Theme
1967–68	Fish
1967–68	Antelope
1967–68	Women in *guntiinaha* displaying agricultural products†
1968–69	Birds and vegetation
1968–69	Women's handcrafts†
1968–69	Flowers
1969–70	Butterflies
1969–70	National independence (10 years)*†
1971–72	Anti-slavery (?)
1971–72	Savannah wildlife
1971–72	Animal husbandry
1971–72	Anniversary of the revolution (2 years)*
1971–72	Livestock
1972–74	Anniversary of the revolution (3 years)*
1972–74	Folk dancing†
1972–74	Establishment of a written language for Somali†
1972–74	Establishment of the *Guulwadayaal**†
1972–75	Anniversary of the revolution (5 years) †
1975–76	Nomads (historical dress and other objects) †
1975–76	Sayyid Mohammed Abdulle Hassan's "dervish" army†
1976	Freedom from hunger*†
1976	Seashells
1977	Anniversary of the revolution (8 years)*
1977	Indigenous animals
1977–78	Trees
1977–78	Spice plants
1979	Ships and fish
1979	Anniversary of the revolution (10 years)*†
1979	Fish
1980	Urban architecture
1980	Birds

* = shows Western-style dress (including uniforms)

† = shows historical forms of Somali dress

Glossary

A word of caution: many of these terms have multiple spellings depending on the native language and culture of the author. There is some confusion of terminology even within the Islamic world. For example, the garment that Somalis refer to as *shuka* is called *jilbab* in Turkey. Somalis use the word *jilbab* for a completely different style of clothing that resembles the ensembles worn by Catholic nuns (similar to the Iranian *chador*).

Ambur. A blouse worn with a *futa* or skirt.

Audulli. A necklace with a large crescent-shaped pendant made of silver, worn by Somalis but made out of elements from the Middle East, South Asia, and Europe.

Barkin. A wooden headrest used by a nomadic man to keep his hair from being flattened or tangled at night and to stay alert to danger.

Bilawi. A nomadic-style dagger, often worn tucked into a scabbard at the waistline; made by *Saab* craftsmen.

Bisht. An Arab-style cloak for men.

Boqor. Hand-made rope used by women as a belt for the saddexqayd.

Buibui. See *shuka* (cloak).

Caftan. A knee- or ankle-length tunic worn primarily by men in Somalia, originally from the Arabian Peninsula (also called *kamiz* or *qamis*).

Dirac. A knee- or ankle-length, thin, loose dress worn in agricultural and nomadic areas; a fashion that came from northern Somali territory in the 1960s.

Futa. An Arab-style short wrapper for women worn around the lower body, often as a layer under other garments.

Gaashaan. Shields made by *Saab* craftsmen out of very tough leather from animals like the hippopotamus and rhinoceros.

Garbasaar. Somali for "shoulder cloth"; a short piece of fabric worn with *dirac* or *guntiino*.

Gorgorad. A petticoat worn with *dirac*.

Guntiino (plural: *guntiinaha*). A nomadic-style dress worn by knotting a long piece of cloth over the left shoulder and wrapping it around the torso.

Hardas. An amulet worn by nomadic men; a leather packet tied around the neck with a thick band of leather.

Hijab. For Somalis, this refers to an Islamic-style head covering (not just a head wrap, but something that covers the neck); in Arabic it simply means "covering."

Imamad. Somali word for turban; typically, Somali men do not wear it as a head covering, but simply drape it over one shoulder.

Jilbab. An Islamic style of dress for women consisting of a head wrap, another head covering that frames the face and drapes down over the chest (sometimes down to the waist or knees), and a matching skirt or dress.

Kabo. Nomadic sandals made by *Saab* craftsmen by sewing layers of leather together to form a platform up to an inch thick.

Kaffiyeh. A checkered scarf (usually black and white, but sometimes red and white) commonly worn as a head covering in the Middle East and sometimes as a shawl by Somali men.

Kamiz. See *caftan.*

Khimar. A triangular head covering designed to cover the hair, neck, and upper chest.

Kufi. A close-fitting head covering without a brim (skull cap).

Macawis. A sarong-like garment adopted by Somali men in the 1970s; an alternative to pants that recalls nomadic-style wrapped garments.

Makkawi. An amulet for men made by stringing two large chunks of amber on a leather choker.

Maro. Somali word for "cloth"; a nomadic garment for men worn by wrapping around the waist and sometimes draping an edge over the shoulders.

Merikani. Undyed cotton cloth of the late 1800s, typically imported from America.

Niqab. A veil that covers the face; until the 1970s in the Horn of Africa, this was only worn by the descendants of Arab and Persian settlers.

Saddexqayd. A wrapped nomadic dress made with up to twenty yards of cloth.

Salwaar. Loose-fitting trousers that taper at the calves; an Arab style of dress worn by men (also called *sirwal*).

Shash. A black or dark blue headwrap; signifies that a woman is married.

Shuka. A button-down, ankle-length overcoat, usually imported from the Middle East; the word *shuka* is also used in other parts of East Africa as a generic word for "covering."

Sunna. A practice advocated by the prophet Mohammed; includes some aspects of dress such as growing a beard and dyeing it with henna.

Tobe. An Arabic word for a wrapped garment; often used interchangeably with maro.

Tusbah. A strand of Islamic prayer beads used to recite the ninety-nine names of Allah.

Waran. A long spear that could also be used as a walking stick.

Xersi. A metal amulet (silver or gold) containing a verse from the Qur'an worn as part of a woman's necklace.

Notes

Note that since there was no written version of the Somali language until 1972, spellings often vary from one publication to another depending on the native language of the author (e.g. "Mogdisho," "Mogadishu").

1. The Political Symbolism of Dress

1. "Ethiopia: U.S. Senator Obama Visits Flood-hit Town in East" (BBC Worldwide Monitoring, 9/1/2006).

2. Ethiopia is a multiethnic country with a large population of Somalis in the southeast region.

3. Issa Hussein, "Why All the Fuss? Asks Elder Who Donned Obama," 3/8/2008, http://allafrica.com/stories/200803071072.html.

4. Ewan MacAskill, "Obama Camp Claims Smear Over Turban Photograph" (*The Guardian* [London]: 1, 2/26/2008).

5. Alec Rawles quoted from "Who Told USA Today that Obama's Muslim Outfit is Not Muslim?" (2/25/2008, http://errortheory.blogspot.com/2008/02/who-told-usa-today-that-obamas-muslim.html). For a more detailed critique of this view, see Heather Marie Akou, "Looking Like a Terrorist," in *September 11 in Popular Culture: A Guide,* ed. Sara E. Quay and Amy M. Damico (Santa Barbara, Calif: ABC–CLIO, 2010).

6. Fred Myers, "Introduction: The Empire of Things," in *The Empire of Things: Regimes of Value and Material Culture,* ed. Fred R. Myers (Santa Fe, N. M.: School of American Research Press, 2001), p. 20.

7. See Wendy Parkins, "Introduction: (Ad)dressing Citizens," in *Fashioning the Body Politic: Dress, Gender, Citizenship,* ed. Wendy Parkins (Oxford: Berg, 2002), p. 10.

8. On hair-straightening, see Shane White and Graham White, *Stylin': African American Expressive Culture, from Its Beginnings to the Zoot Suit* (Ithaca, New York: Cornell University Press, 1999). On dreadlocks, see Petra Slinkard, "Dreadlocks in Babylon: Techniques and Motivations for Wearing Dreadlocked Hair in Southern Indiana" (unpublished M.S. thesis, Indiana University, 2008).

9. The *Black Hawk Down* franchise—inspired by an incident that took place during the U.S.-led occupation of Somalia in 2003 in which eighteen marines were killed in a battle with militias and their bodies dragged through the streets of Mogadishu—includes Mark Bowden, *Black Hawk Down: A Story of Modern War* (New York: Atlan-

tic Monthly Press, 1999); *Black Hawk Down,* directed by Ridley Scott, Sony Pictures, 2001; and *Delta Force: Black Hawk Down,* a video game by Microsoft Windows, 2003. The language "harbor for terrorists" has been used repeatedly by the U.S. government in reference to Somalia since September 11, 2001; see, for example, a 2006 press release from the State Department titled, "Somalia: Expanding Crisis in the Horn of Africa," http://www.state.gov/p/af/rls/rm/2006/68515.htm. For some of the many other negative portrayals of Somalia, see Alexander T. J. Lennon, *The Battle for Hearts and Minds: Using Soft Power to Undermine Terrorist Networks* (Cambridge: MIT Press, 2003); Dan Ephron and Mark Hosenball, "Recruited for Jihad? About 20 Young Somali-American Men in Minneapolis Have Recently Vanished" (*Newsweek,* 1/24/2009, http://www .newsweek.com/id/181408); and Robyn Hunter, "Somali Pirates Living the High Life" (BBC News, 10/28/08, http://news.bbc.co.uk/2/hi/africa/7650415.stm).

10. The first product of this research was my dissertation: Heather Marie Akou, "Macrocultures, Migration, and Somali Malls: A Social History of Somali Dress and Aesthetics," unpublished Ph.D. dissertation, University of Minnesota, 2005.

11. For a good example of these debates, see Ali Jimale Ahmed, ed., *The Invention of Somalia* (Lawrenceville, N.J.: Red Sea Press, 1995).

12. I conducted archival research at the Smithsonian (African Arts and Natural History) and the Library of Congress. Similar (colonial-era) collections exist in the U.K. and Italy, but are not as readily accessible to an American graduate student.

13. Dr. M. Catherine Daly, personal communication.

14. Joanne B. Eicher, "Dress," in *Routledge International Encyclopedia of Women: Global Women's Issues and Knowledge,* ed. Cheris Kramarae and Dale Spender (New York: Routledge, 2000), pp. 422–423.

15. For more on the use of frankincense, see Heather Marie Akou, "More Than Costume History: Dress in Somali Culture," in *Dress Sense: Emotional and Sensory Experience of the Body and Clothes,* ed. Donald Clay Johnson and Helen Bradley Foster (Oxford: Berg, 2007), pp. 16–22. Male circumcision—as commonly practiced by many Muslims, Jews, and Christians—is not particularly controversial (at least in the U.S.). Female circumcision, on the other hand, is much more controversial and is sometimes referred to as FGC ("female genital cutting") or even more negatively as FGM ("female genital mutilation"). Literature on this topic includes: Waris Dirie and Cathleen Miller, *Desert Flower: The Extraordinary Journey of a Desert Nomad* (New York: Quill, 1998); and Leo R. Chavez, Immigration and Medical Anthropology, in *American Arrivals: Anthropology Engages the New Immigration,* ed. Nancy Foner (Santa Fe, N.M.: School of American Research Press, 2003).

16. Wendy Parkins, "Introduction"; Richard Wrigley, *The Politics of Appearances: Representations of Dress in Revolutionary France* (Oxford: Berg, 2002); Judd Stitziel, *Fashioning Socialism: Clothing, Politics, and Consumer Culture in East Germany* (Oxford: Berg, 2005); John R. Bowen, *Why the French Don't Like Headscarves: Islam, the State, and Public Space* (Princeton, Mass.: Princeton University Press, 2007); Joan Wallach Scott, *The Politics of the Veil* (Princeton, Mass.: Princeton University Press, 2007); Emma Tarlo, *Visibly Muslim: Fashion, Politics, Faith* (Oxford: Berg, 2010); Nira Wickramasinghe, *Dressing the Colonised Body: Politics, Clothing, and Identity in Colonial Sri Lanka* (New Delhi: Orient Longman, 2003); Jean Allman, ed., *Fashioning*

Africa: Power and the Politics of Dress (Bloomington: Indiana University Press, 2004); Mina Roces and Louise Edwards, eds., *The Politics of Dress in Asia and the Americas* (Brighton, U.K.: Sussex Academic Press, 2007).

17. Alison L. Goodrum, *The National Fabric: Fashion, Britishness, Globalization* (Oxford: Berg, 2005), p. 62.

18. Allman, *Fashioning Africa*, p. 1.

19. Hildi Hendrickson, "Bodies and Flags: The Representation of Herero Identity in Colonial Namibia," in *Clothing and Difference: Embodied Identities in Colonial and Post-Colonial Africa*, ed. Hildi Hendrickson (Durham, N.C.: Duke University Press, 1996), p. 239.

2. The Origins of Somali Dress—Prehistory to 1800

The epigraph is from C. P. Rigby, "On the Origins of the Somali Race, Which Inhabits the North-eastern Portion of Africa," *Transactions of the Ethnological Society of London* 5 [1867]: 91–95.

1. Pre-shaped clothing includes garments such as jackets and trousers, made from pieces of cloth that have been cut to fit the shape of the body and sewn together. See Eicher, "Dress," pp. 422–423.

2. William H. Schoff, *The Periplus of the Erythraean Sea: Travel and Trade in the Indian Ocean by a Merchant of the First Century* (New York: Longmans, Green, and Co., 1912), p. 26. (Annotated translation from Greek.)

3. Information in this paragraph comes from Schoff, *The Periplus*, pp. 63–64; Ali Abdirahman Hersi, "The Arab Factor in Somali History: The Origins and the Development of Arab Enterprise and Cultural Influences in the Somali Peninsula," (unpublished Ph.D. dissertation, University of California, Los Angeles, 1977), pp. 84, 87, 91–92; Ahmed Hamoud Al-Maamiry, *Oman and East Africa* (New Delhi: Lancers Publishers, 1979), pp. 42–43 (quote); and Hersi, "The Arab Factor," pp. 94, 97.

4. Battuta quoted in Said Hamdun and Noël King, *Ibn Battuta in Black Africa*, rev. ed. (Princeton, N.J.: Marcus Wiener, 1998), pp. 16–17.

5. Hersi, "The Arab Factor," p. 66.

6. Kathryn McMahon, "The Former Museums of Somalia" (unpublished report collected by the Smithsonian National Museum of African Art, 1991), p. 36. The National Museum of Somalia in Mogadishu was completely looted when the government was overthrown in 1991.

7. G. Edward Nicholson, "The Production, History, Uses and Relationships of Cotton (Gossypium spp.) in Ethiopia," *Economic Botany* 14, no. 1 (1960): 9–10.

8. On cotton production in Somalia, see Lee V. Cassanelli, *The Shaping of Somali Society: Reconstructing the History of a Pastoral People, 1600–1900* (Philadelphia: University of Pennsylvania Press, 1982) p. 167; and Catherine Besteman, *Unraveling Somalia: Race, Violence and the Legacy of Slavery* (Philadelphia: University of Pennsylvania Press, 1999), pp. 49–50. The quote about sheep is from Roy Bridges, "The Visit of Frederick Forbes to the Somali Coast in 1833," *The International Journal of African Historical Studies* 19, no. 4 (1986): 691.

9. On evidence of the China trade, see Matthew Gervase (1961), "Chinese Porcelain in East Africa and on the Coast of South Arabia," *Oriental Art* 2 (1961): 52;

and Richard Pankhurst, *An Introduction to the Economic History of Ethiopia from Early Times to 1800* (London: Sidgwick and Jackson, Ltd., 1961), p. 407. The quote from Pankhurst is from *Economic History of Ethiopia* (Addis Ababa, Ethiopia: Haile Selassie I University, 1968), p. 365.

10. Pankhurst, *Economic History of Ethiopia,* p. 285.

11. Ibid., p. 359. See also Richard F. Burton (1987), *First Footsteps in East Africa or, An Exploration of Harar* (Mineola, N.Y.: Dover Publications, 1987), p. 51.

12. Duarte Barbosa, *A Description of the Coasts of East Africa and Malabar in the Beginning of the Sixteenth Century* (London: Hakluyt Society, 1866), p. 15. (Translation from a Spanish version of the original Portuguese.)

13. Hamdun and King, *Ibn Battuta in Black Africa,* pp. 18–19.

14. McMahon, "The Former Museums of Somalia," p. 34.

15. Rigby, "On the Origins of the Somali Race," p. 92.

16. Georges Révoil (1889), *Voyage aux Pays Çomalis: Dix Mois a la Côte Orientale d'Afrique* (Paris: Challamel et Cie, Éditeurs, 1889), p. 356. Translation mine.

17. Burton, *First Footsteps in East Africa,* p. 170.

18. G. D. Carleton, "Notes on a Part of the Somali Country," *The Journal of the Anthropological Institute of Great Britain and Ireland* 21 (1892): 165.

19. Labelle Prussin, *Nomadic Architecture: Space, Place, Gender* (Washington, D.C.: Smithsonian Institution Press, 1995).

20. S.B. Miles, "On the Somali Country," *Proceedings of the Royal Geographical Society of London* 16, no. 3 (1871–1872): 151.

21. The "Handle of Allah" described in Jeanne D'Haem (1997), *The Last Camel: True Stories of Somalia* (Lawrenceville, N.J.: Red Sea Press, 1997), p. 166. Carleton's remark from "Notes on a Part of the Somali Country," p. 165.

22. I. M. Lewis, *Peoples of the Horn of Africa: Somalis, Afar and Saho* (London: International African Institute, 1955).

23. Harald G. C. Swayne, *Seventeen Trips through Somaliland and A Visit to Abyssinia,* 3rd ed. (London: Rowland Ward, 1903), p. 11.

24. Quoted in Bridges, "The Visit of Frederick Forbes," p. 690.

25. Rigby, "On the Origins of the Somali Race," p. 91.

26. By the time of his trip to northern Somali territory in 1854, Burton was famous for writing about his pilgrimage to Mecca (an experience forbidden to non-Muslims). In the 1880s he translated *The Arabian Nights* (also known as the *Tales of 1,001 Nights*), the *Kama Sutra,* and was knighted by Queen Victoria. This quote is from *First Footsteps in East Africa,* p. 75.

27. Ralph E. Drake-Brockman, *British Somaliland* (London: Hurst & Blackett, 1912), pp. 139–140.

28. Deardre Godbeer, *Somalia* (New York: Chelsea House, 1988), p. 44.

29. Révoil, *Voyage aux Pays Çomalis,* p. 330. Translation mine.

30. Rigby, "On the Origins of the Somali Race," p. 92.

31. Phillip Paulitschke (1893), *Ethnographie Nordost-Afrikas: Die Materielle Cultur der Danâkil, Galla und Somâl* (Berlin: Geographische Verlagshandlung Dietrich Reimer, 1893), p. 93. (Copal is essentially a soft, lighter-colored version of amber.)

32. There is a great deal of debate in the academic literature concerning the origins and settlement patterns of the Somali. As a result of Somali territorial expansion, the *Boni* were scattered along the coastlines as well as an agricultural area in the south between the Juba and Shabelle rivers.

33. Drake-Brockman, *British Somaliland*, pp. 214–216. Paulitschke, *Ethnographie Nordost-Afrikas*, pp. 82, 90.

34. Drake-Brockman, *British Somaliland*, p. 214.

35. Nello Puccioni, *Anthropology and Ethnography of the People of Somalia*, trans. Kathryn A. Looney (Human Relations Area Files, 1960; originally published by Reale Società Geografica Italiana, Bologna, 1936). The quote is from p. 80.

36. Carleton, "Notes on a Part of the Somali Country," p. 162.

37. Purissima Benitez-Johannot and Jean Paul Barbier, *Shields: Africa, Southeast Asia and Oceania, from the Collections of the Barbier-Mueller Museum* (Munich: Prestel, 2000), p. 106.

38. For examples, see illustrations in Paulitschke, *Ethnographie Nordost-Afrikas*, as well as Révoil, *Voyage aux Pays Çomalis;* both books catalogue various forms of bracelets, armlets, and earrings made by the *Tomal.*

39. Vinigi L. Grottanelli, "Asiatic Influences on Somali Culture," *Ethnos* 4 (1947): 161; Drake-Brockman, *British Somaliland*, p. 220.

40. Rigby, "On the Origins of the Somali Race," p. 93.

41. Carleton, "Notes on a Part of the Somali Country," p. 162.

42. See Heather Marie Akou, "More than Costume History," pp. 16–22.

43. *Yebir* crafting described in J. W. C. Kirk, "The Yebirs and Midgans of Somaliland, Their Traditions and Dialects," *Journal of the Royal African Society* 4, no. 13 (1904): 95; ritual performance in Drake-Brockman, *British Somaliland*, p. 307; Burton's evaluation is from *First Footsteps in East Africa*, p. 24.

44. Kirk, "The Yebirs and Midgans of Somaliland," p. 95.

45. Drake-Brockman, *British Somaliland*, p. 216.

46. Kirk, "The Yebirs and Midgans of Somaliland," p. 92.

47. D'Haem, *The Last Camel*, pp. 163–165.

48. Women's practice described in Lewis, *Peoples of the Horn of Africa*, p. 132; quote from Carleton, "Notes on a Part of the Somali Country," p. 165.

49. Ruta Saliklis (1999), "The Dynamic Relationship Between Lithuanian National Costumes and Folk Dress," in *Folk Dress in Europe and Anatolia: Beliefs about Protection and Fertility*, ed. Linda Welters (Oxford: Berg, 1999), pp. 211–234.

3. A Clash of Civilizations—1800 to 1945

The epigraph is from Douglas Jardine, "Somaliland: The Cinderella of the Empire," *Journal of the Royal African Society* 22, no. 94 (1925): 105–106.

1. Although not well known in the West, this trade started much earlier than the Atlantic slave trade (ninth century, compared to fifteenth) and involved greater numbers of slaves. The peak of the trade occurred in the 1800s, but also shifted north (drawing in Somali middlemen) as European abolitionists tried to disrupt the trade around the island of Zanzibar. For more, see Patrick Manning, *Slavery and African*

Life: Occidental, Oriental, and African Slave Trades (Cambridge: Cambridge University Press, 1990).

2. G. D. Carleton, "Notes on a Part of the Somali Country," p. 170. The Maria-Theresa thaler was named after an empress of the Austro-Hungarian Empire and was first minted in 1741. Within fifteen years it was circulating in the Horn of Africa, valued for the coin's high silver content: see Pankhurst, *Economic History of Ethiopia,* p. 468. The practice of using standardized lengths of cotton cloth as currency occurred simultaneously in other parts of Africa. For more on this practice, see Marion Johnson, "Cotton Imperialism in West Africa," *African Affairs* 73, no. 291 (1974): 178–187; also, D. C. Dorward, "Precolonial Tiv Trade and Cloth Currency," *The International Journal of African Historical Studies* 9, no. 4 (1976): 576–591.

3. Burton's account is recorded in *First Footsteps in East Africa.* For an overview of Burton and his influence on European exploration in the Horn of Africa, see Richard E. Bohlander, ed., *World Explorers and Discoverers* (New York: Macmillan, 1992). Wayne Durrill discusses Somali history of stripping shipwrecks in "Atrocious Misery: The African Origins of Famine in Northern Somalia, 1839–1884," *The American Historical Review* 91, no. 2 (1986): 287–306.

4. David D. Laitin and Said S. Samatar, *Somalia: Nation in Search of a State* (Boulder, Colo.: Westview Press, 1987), p. 2.

5. Abdi Ismail Samatar, *The State and Rural Transformation in Northern Somalia, 1884–1986* (Madison: University of Wisconsin Press, 1989), p. 27.

6. Burton, *First Footsteps in East Africa,* p. 65.

7. Virginia Luling, *Somali Sultanate: The Geledi City-State Over 150 Years* (Piscataway, N.J.: Transaction Publishers, 2003).

8. Esmond B. Martin and T. C. I. Ryan, "The Slave Trade of the Bajun and Benadir Coasts," *Transafrican Journal of History* 9, no. 1 (1980): 104.

9. Besteman, *Unraveling Somalia,* pp. 49–51.

10. Cassanelli, *The Shaping of Somali Society,* p. 153; Mohamed Haji Mukhtar, *Historical Dictionary of Somalia,* rev. ed. (Lanham, Md.: Scarecrow Press, 2003 [1975]), p. 267.

11. Instead of returning the slaves to Central Africa, British abolitionists simply released them in the nearest "neutral" territory. Martin and Ryan, "The Slave Trade of the Bajun and Benadir Coasts," p. 119.

12. Ruth Hawley, *Omani Silver* (London: Longman Group, 1978). See also: Walter Raunig, "Yemen and Ethiopia—Ancient Cultural Links between Two Neighboring Countries on the Red Sea," in *Yemen: 3000 Years of Art and Civilisation in Arabia Felix,* ed. Werner Daum (Innsbruck, Austria: Pinguin-Verlag, 1988), pp. 409–418.

13. Burton, *First Footsteps in East Africa,* p. 61.

14. Alessandra Cardelli Antinori, "Ornamenti della Persona," in *Aspetti dell'Espression Artistica in Somalia,* ed. Annarita Pullieli (Rome: Baggatto Libri, 1988), pp. 91–109.

15. Burton, *First Footsteps in East Africa,* 61.

16. Ibid.

17. J. S. King, "Notes on the Folk-Lore and Some Social Customs of the Western Somali Tribes (Continued)," in *The Folk-Lore Journal* 6, no. 2 (1888): 120–121.

18. Révoil, *Voyage aux Pays Çomalis;* Luigi Bricchetti, *Somalia e Benadir: Viaggio di Esplorazione nell'Africa Orientale* (Milan: Societa Editrice La Poligrafica, 1902).

19. The list of metals used is from Richard W. Beachey, "The East African Ivory Trade in the Nineteenth Century," *Journal of African History* 8, no. 2 (1967): 269–290.

20. Although these photographs were taken by Europeans, it does seem likely that if Somalis had such an "exotic" practice as wearing stacks of wire that it would have shown up in some of these images. For more discussion about European photography of Somalis, see Heather Marie Akou, "Documenting the Origins of Somali Folk Dress: Evidence from the Bonaparte Collection," *Dress* 33 (2008): 7–19. This type of jewelry is still worn in the twenty-first century among groups like the Maasai and Pokot.

21. Burton, *First Footsteps in East Africa,* p. 61.

22. Drake-Brockman, *British Somaliland,* p. 257.

23. Antinori, "Ornamenti della Persona," p. 107.

24. Beachey, "The East African Ivory Trade," p. 273.

25. Bricchetti, *Somalia e Benadir,* pp. 615–16. "Grey shirting," also known as "greige goods," refers to unfinished (undyed, unprinted) cotton cloth, which was most likely plain weave (the simplest and cheapest to produce). "Drill" is a slightly more complicated twill weave, but was probably also unfinished.

26. Luling describes Somali weaving in *Somali Sultanate,* p. 66. See also Cassanelli, *The Shaping of Somali Society,* p. 167. Unlike weavers in West Africa who are famous for their narrow-band "strip" looms (the type of loom used to produce *kente* and *bogolanfini*), weavers in East Africa use much wider looms. Folklorist John Johnson recounted to me that during his fieldwork in the 1960s and '70s weavers in Afgoy were still known for adding colorful borders to cloth, but the work had to be commissioned. For images of Somalis weaving Benadir cloth, see Katheryne S. Loughran et al., *Somalia in Word and Image* (Washington, D.C.: Foundation for Cross Cultural Understanding, 1986).

27. Puccioni, *Anthropology and Ethnography,* p. 17. Luling's photograph from a few decades later was included in Loughran, et al., *Somalia in Word and Image,* p. 78.

28. Puccioni, *Anthropology and Ethnography,* p. 44. The total length was approximately three meters. See Luling, *Somali Sultanate,* p. 66.

29. Drake-Brockman, *British Somaliland,* pp. 120–121.

30. Luling, *Somali Sultanate,* p. 66.

31. Yedida Kalfon Stillman, *Arab Dress: A Short History from the Dawn of Islam to Modern Times,* ed. Norman A. Stillman (Leiden: Brill, 2000), p. 8.

32. Puccioni, *Anthropology and Ethnography,* p. 17.

33. Luling, *Somali Sultanate,* p. 67.

34. Conversation with Lidwien Kapteijns, November 2003.

35. Révoil, *Voyage aux Pays Çomalis,* pp. 38, 162. In Pakistan, camel dung is also used as a bleaching agent during the production of *ajrak* cloth: see Noorjehan Bilgrami, *The Traditional Fabric of Pakistan: Sindh Jo Ajrak* (Lahore: OUP Pakistan, 1998).

36. Swayne, *Seventeen Trips.*

37. Ibid.

38. Ibid., p. 5.

39. Laura Fair, "Dressing Up: Clothing, Class and Gender in Post-abolition Zanzibar," *Journal of African History* 39 (1998): 63–94.

40. These two images can be found in Luigi Bricchetti, *Somalia e Benadir*, pp. 163 and 229, respectively.

41. Margaret Laurence (1963), *The Prophet's Camel Bell* (London: Macmillan, 1963), pp. 203–204.

42. Besteman, *Unraveling Somalia*, p. 55.

43. Martin and Ryan, "The Slave Trade of the Bajun and Benadir Coasts," p. 119.

44. Martin and Ryan, "The Slave Trade of the Bajun and Benadir Coasts," pp. 52, 115.

45. Drake-Brockman, *British Somaliland*, p. 139.

46. Besteman, *Unraveling Somalia*, p. 82.

47. Prints and Photographs Division, U.S. Library of Congress.

48. Drake-Brockman, *British Somaliland*, p. 270.

49. Hazel Summerfield, "Patterns of Adaptation: Somali and Bangladeshi Women in Britain," in *Migrant Women: Crossing Boundaries and Changing Identities,* ed. Gina Buijs (Oxford: Berg, 1993), p. 89.

50. I. M. Lewis, "Visible and Invisible Differences: The Somali Paradox," *Africa: Journal of the International African Institute* 74, no. 4 (2004): 496.

51. Nello Puccioni, "Nord-Somali," in *Archiv für Rassenbilder*, vol. 14 (Munich: J. F. Lehmanns Verlag, 1926). Smithsonian National Museum of Natural History, National Anthropological Archives, DPA: Negritos, box 40, folder 14.

52. Hersi, "The Arab Factor in Somali History," p. 281.

53. Ibid.

54. Ibid., pp. 282–283.

55. Ibid., p. 247. *Tariqa* literally translated means "way" or "path." Sufi orders are also referred to as "schools" and "brotherhoods."

56. Mohamed M. Kassim (1995), "Aspects of the Benadir Cultural History: The Case of the Bravan Ulama," in *The Invention of Somalia,* ed. Ali Jimale Ahmed (Lawrenceville, N.J.: Red Sea Press, 1995), pp. 36–37.

57. Hersi, "The Arab Factor in Somali History," pp. 250–52.

58. Swayne, *Seventeen Trips*, p. 7.

59. Cassanelli, *The Shaping of Somali Society,* pp. 196–97.

60. Francesca Declich, "Identity, Dance, and Islam Among People with Bantu Origins in Riverine Areas of Somalia," in *The Invention of Somalia,* ed. Ali Jimale Ahmed (Lawrenceville, N.J.: Red Sea Press, 1995), p. 195.

61. The "clan system"—which has been the subject of much debate among Somalis as well as academics—revolves around six major clans (Hawiye, Isaaq, Darood, Rahanwein, Dir, and Digil) as well as numerous sub-clans, the *Saab* caste, and the "Somali Bantu" (former slaves captured in Central Africa). Historically, this system was responsible for keeping order and governing the distribution of resources in the Horn of Africa. For more, see I. M. Lewis, *Blood and Bone: The Call of Kinship in Somali Society* (Trenton, N.J.: Red Sea Press, 1994).

62. Besteman, *Unraveling Somalia*, p. 164.

63. Declich, "Identity, Dance and Islam," pp. 194–95.

64. Luigi Bricchetti, *Dal Benadir* (Milan: Società Antischiavista d'Italia, 1904), pp. 68–69.

65. Swayne, *Seventeen Trips,* p. 123; I. M. Lewis, *A Modern History of the Somali: Nation and State in the Horn of Africa,* 4th edition (Oxford: James Currey, 2002), pp. 68–69.

66. Abdi Sheik-Abdi, *Divine Madness: Mohammed Abdulle Hassan (1856–1920)* (London: Zed, 1993), p. 48.

67. One belief within Shi'ite Islam is that the last true caliph (called the Mahdi) will someday return to restore an Islamic kingdom on earth; Mahdism was derived from this idea.

68. Sheik-Abdi, *Divine Madness,* pp. 58–59.

69. Mukhtar, *Historical Dictionary of Somalia,* p. 196.

70. Oral poetry is a highly respected art form in Somali culture. Mukhtar, *Historical Dictionary of Somalia,* pp. 207, 221.

71. Samatar, *The State and Rural Transformations,* p. 38.

72. Sheik-Abdi, *Divine Madness,* p. 197.

73. This would be an excellent topic for future research, since other soldiers in Sudan wore the *fez* and *gallabiya* (tunic), sometimes mixed with versions of British colonial uniforms.

74. Drake-Brockman, *British Somaliland,* pp. 183–85.

75. Mary-Jane Fox, "Political Culture in Somalia: Tracing Paths to Peace and Conflict" (unpublished Ph.D. dissertation, Uppsala University [Sweden], 2000), p. 100.

76. Ibid., p. 101.

77. Ibid., p. 118.

78. Guido Corni, *Somalia Italiana,* vol. 2 (Milan: Editoriale Arte e Storia, 1937), pp. 590–591.

79. Ibid., pp. 586–87.

80. Lidwien Kapteijns, "Gender Relations and the Transformation of the Northern Somali Pastoral Tradition," *International Journal of African Historical Studies* 28, no. 2 (1995): 241–259.

81. Axmed Naaji, Gaarida Baarida Haween (For Competent, Excellent Women). Song translated by Lidwien Kapteijns in *Women's Voices in a Man's World: Women and the Pastoral Tradition in Northern Somali Orature, c. 1899–1980* (Portsmouth, N.H.: Heinemann, 1999), p. 208.

82. Ibid., pp. 15.

4. Dressing the Nation—1945 to 1991

The epigraph is from Maxammed Jaamac Jaaf and Mariam Mursal, Beri Hore Waxaa Jiray (In the Old Days), song from the late 1960s translated by Lidwien Kapteijns in *Women's Voices in a Man's World,* p. 202.

1. Islamism is a broad term for a political movement that seeks to establish governance based on the Qur'an and Islamic law (sharia).

2. Özlem Sandıkcı and Guliz Ger, "Aesthetics, Ethics and Politics of the Turkish Headscarf," in *Clothing as Material Culture,* ed. Suzanne Küchler and Daniel Miller (Oxford: Berg, 2005), pp. 75–76.

3. Petr Bogatyrev, *The Functions of Folk Costume in Moravian Slovakia* (The Hague: Mouton, 1971), pp. 55–56. (Originally published in 1937, translated from Slovak by Richard G. Crum.)

4. Wrigley, *The Politics of Appearances,* p. 13.

5. Lou Taylor, *The Study of Dress History* (Manchester, U.K.: Manchester University Press), p. 218.

6. Mina Roces, "Trans-national Flows and the Politics of Dress in Asia and the Americas," in *The Politics of Dress in Asia and the Americas,* ed. Mina Roces and Louise Edwards (Brighton, U.K.: Sussex Academic Press, 2007), p. 13. For more, see Irene Guenther, *Nazi Chic? Fashioning Women in the Third Reich* (Oxford: Berg, 2004).

7. Carla Jones and Ann Marie Leshkowich, "Introduction: The Globalization of Asian Dress: Re-Orienting Fashion or Re-Orientalizing Asia?" in *Re-Orienting Fashion: The Globalization of Asian Dress,* ed. Sandra Niessen, Ann Marie Leshkowich, and Carla Jones (Oxford: Berg, 2004), p. 26.

8. Franz Fanon, *Studies in a Dying Colonialism* (New York: Grove Press, 1965).

9. Parkins, "(Ad)dressing Citizens," p. 9.

10. I. M. Lewis started working in northern Somalia in the 1950s, but his books and articles have few illustrations. Catherine Bestemen did fieldwork in the 1980s for *Unraveling Somalia,* which includes discussions on "beauty" and race, but her book does not have many images (and the ones that do exist are rather small, dim, and difficult to interpret). Scholars interested in Somali artistic expression have focused on poetry and woodcarving—forms that do not require images of people. *Somalia in Word and Image* contains fieldwork photographs taken by Lee Cassanelli, Virginia Luling, and Phoebe Ferguson, but almost all of them show rural areas (with the exception of a few showing urban architecture). In fact, this book has only two images of people in Mogadishu—one of a man driving a donkey cart and one of a dance troupe taken by an American officer of the USS *Vreeland.*

11. John A. Hunt (1951), *A General Survey of the Somaliland Protectorate, 1944–1950* (Hargeisa, Somalia: Somaliland Protectorate and the Crown Agents for the Colonies, 1951), D.484, p. 437.

12. I. M. Lewis, *A Modern History of the Somali: Nation and State in the Horn of Africa,* 4th edition (Oxford: James Currey, 2002), p. 265.

13. Mukhtar, *Historical Dictionary of Somalia.*

14. Ibid., p. xxxv.

15. Virginia Lee Barnes and Janice Boddy, *Aman: The Story of a Somali Girl* (New York: Vintage, 1994), pp. 155–56.

16. Heather Marie Akou, "Nationalism Without a Nation: Understanding the Dress of Somali Women in Minnesota," in *Fashioning Africa: Power and the Politics of Dress,* ed. Jean Allman (Bloomington: Indiana University Press, 2004), pp. 78–79.

17. Doran Ross, ed., *Wrapped in Pride: Ghanaian Kente and African American Identity* (Los Angeles, Calif.: UCLA Fowler Museum of Cultural History, 1998). The pattern of men wearing Western dress and women wearing "ethnic" dress has been observed in many cultures around the world. For more on this phenomenon, see Ruth Barnes and Joanne Bubolz Eicher, *Dress and Gender: Making and Meaning in Cultural Contexts* (Oxford: Berg, 1993).

18. Besteman, *Unraveling Somalia*, p. 197.

19. Laitin and Samatar, *Somalia*, p. 62.

20. Lewis, *A Modern History of the Somali*, pp. 205–206.

21. Kapteijns, *Women's Voices in a Man's World*, p. 144.

22. Ibid., p. 137.

23. Both quotes from Lewis, "Visible and Invisible Differences."

24. Amina H. Adan, "Somalia: An Illusory Political Nation-State," *South Asia Bulletin* 14, no. 1 (1994): 102.

25. Ali A. Warsame, "How a Strong Government Backed an African Language: The Lessons of Somalia," *International Review of Education* 47, nos. 3/4 (2001): 341–360.

26. Adan, "Somalia: An Illusory Political Nation-State," p. 4.

27. Lewis, "Visible and Invisible Differences," p. 501.

28. Mohamed Diriye Abdullahi, *Culture and Customs of Somalia* (Westport, Conn.: Greenwood Press, 2001), p. 32.

29. Adan, "Somalia: An Illusory Political Nation-State," p. 5.

30. Abdullahi, *Culture and Customs of Somalia*, p. 32.

31. Ibid., p. 34.

32. Adan, "Somalia: An Illusory Political Nation-State," p. 5.

33. Lewis, "Visible and Invisible Differences," p. 502.

34. Ahmed Omer Al-Azhari, *Somalia's Arab, African and International Role* (Mogadishu, Somalia: Ministry of Information and National Guidance, 1980).

35. Cawo Mohamed Abdi, "Convergence of Civil War and the Religious Right: Reimagining Somali Women," *Signs: Journal of Women in Culture and Society* 33, no. 1 (2007): 189.

36. Mukhtar, *Historical Dictionary of Somalia*, pp. 49–50.

37. Joakim Gundel, "The Migration-Development Nexus: Somalia Case Study," *International Migration* 40, no. 5 (2002): 270.

38. Adan, "Somalia: An Illusory Political Nation-State," p. 189.

39. Abdullahi, *Culture and Customs of Somalia*, p. 118.

40. Abdi, "Convergence," p. 189.

41. The Maasai (pastoralists who live in neighboring Kenya and Tanzania) also use the word *shuka* to describe the blankets they wear as simple body coverings.

42. Barnes and Boddy, *Aman*, pp. 37–38.

43. Faegheh Shirazi, "Islamic Religion and Women's Dress Code: The Islamic Republic of Iran," in *Undressing Religion: Commitment and Conversion from a Cross-Cultural Perspective*, ed. Linda B. Arthur (Oxford: Berg, 2000), p. 120.

44. Muhammad Marmaduke Pickthall, *The Meaning of the Glorious Qur'ān: Text and Explanatory Translation* (Mecca: Muslim World League, 1979), p. 449.

45. Fair, "Dressing Up," pp. 69–70.

46. Nayereh Tohidi, "International Connections of the Iranian Women's Movement," in *Iran and the Surrounding World: Interactions in Culture and Cultural Politics*, ed. Nikke R. Keddie and Rudi Matthee (Seattle: University of Washington Press, 2002), p. 210.

47. See, for example, two books by Fazal Sheikh: *A Camel for the Son* and *Ramadan Moon* (both Winterthur, Switzerland: the Volkart Foundation, 2001).

48. Michael Maren, *The Road to Hell: The Ravaging Effects of Foreign Aid and International Charity* (New York: Free Press, 1997), p. 38.

49. Field notes, September 2002.

50. Barnes and Boddy, *Aman*, p. 215.

51. Field notes, December 2002, October 2003.

52. Abdi, "Convergence," p. 189.

53. Kapteijns, *Women's Voices in a Man's World*, p. 138.

54. Ibid.

55. Mukhtar, *Historical Dictionary of Somalia*, pp. 209–210.

56. Abdullahi, *Culture and Customs of Somalia*, p. 42.

57. Mukhtar, *Historical Dictionary of Somalia*, p. 240.

58. U.S. Department of State (2001), "Somalia: Report on Female Genital Mutilation (FGM) or Female Genital Cutting (FGC)," 2001, http://www.state.gov/g/wi/rls/rep/crfgm/10109.htm.

59. Mukhtar, *Historical Dictionary of Somalia*, p. 240.

60. Loughran et al., *Somalia in Word and Image*, p. 126.

61. Field notes, November 2003.

62. Elizabeth Warnock Fernea and Robert A. Fernea, *The Arab World: Forty Years of Change*, rev. ed. (New York: Anchor Books, 1997), p. xix.

63. André Martineau, *Djibouti*, 2nd edition (Boulogne-Billancourt, France: Delroisse, 1977), p. 19. This book shows a man wearing a *macawis*, short-sleeve shirt, *kufi*, and *imamad*, along with plastic flip-flop sandals.

64. Abdi, "Convergence," p. 187.

65. More examples of *kanga* prints can be seen in John Picton, *The Art of African Textiles: Technology, Tradition and Lurex* (London: Barbican Art Gallery, 1999 [1995]).

66. *Export Statistics of Silk & Man-made Fibre Textiles, 1981–82* (Bombay: The Silk & Rayon Textiles Export Promotion Council, 1982).

67. Field notes, October 2003. See chapter 5 for more about Benadir cloth.

68. Field notes, October 2003.

69. Laurence, *The Prophet's Camel Bell*, p. 198.

70. See images of women wearing *dirac* in: Martineau, *Djibouti*.

71. It seems likely that the term *gorgorad* comes from the Indian word *ghaghra*, a pre-shaped skirt worn with a blouse (*choli*). I discovered the elastic waistband when I had a set of *dirac, garbasaar,* and *gorgorad* made for myself at the African International Marketplace in Saint Paul, Minn., in October 2003. For examples of the West African *boubou* (*bubu*), see Salah M. Hassan, *The Art of African Fashion* (Trenton, N.J.: Africa World Press, 1998); also, Ilsemargret Luttman, ed., *Mode in Afrika: Mode als Mittel der Selbstinszenierung und Ausdruck der Moderne* (Hamburg, Germany: Museum für Völkerkunde, 2005).

72. Kapteijns, *Women's Voices in a Man's World*, p. 139.

73. Keith Jeffery, "Crown, Communication and the Colonial Post: Stamps, the Monarchy and the British Empire," *The Journal of Imperial and Commonwealth History* 34, no. 1 (2006): 46.

74. Phil Deans and Hugo Dobson, "Introduction: East Asian Postage Stamps as Socio-Political Artefacts," *East Asia* 22, no. 2 (2005): 3.

75. Frederick Lauritzen, "Propaganda Art in the Postage Stamps of the Third Reich," *The Journal of Decorative Arts* 10 (1988): 62–79.

76. Carlos Stoetzer, *Postage Stamps as Propaganda* (Washington, D.C.: Public Affairs Press, 1953), p. 1.

77. See Hjorleifur R. Jonsson and Nora A. Taylor, "National Colors: Ethnic Minorities in Vietnamese Public Imagery," in *Re-Orienting Fashion: The Globalization of Asian Dress*, ed. Sandra Niessen, Ann Marie Leshkowich, and Carla Jones (Oxford: Berg, 2003), pp. 162–163.

78. Incidentally, there were just three sets of stamps issued during that year. The third set was for World Women's Day and did not contain any images of people.

79. Abdullahi, *Culture and Customs of Somalia*, p. 177.

80. Lewis, "Visible and Invisible Differences," p. 502.

81. Barre's dismissal of Ethiopian claims about his intentions is recorded in Abdullahi Mohamed Hassan, *Jaale Siyad's OAU Chairmanship, June 1974–1975* (Mogadishu, Somalia: Ministry of Information and National Guidance, 1975), p. 41; the latter quote is cited in Al-Azhari, *Somalia's Arab, African and International Role*, p. 24. Ironically, Barre had served as chairman of the OAU from June 1974 to July 1975.

82. Mukhtar, *Historical Dictionary of Somalia*, p. 159.

83. This fact and previous block quote from Adan, p. 6.

84. Mukhtar, *Historical Dictionary of Somalia*, pp. 232–33, 238.

85. Abdullahi, *Culture and Customs of Somalia*, p. 33.

86. Maren, *The Road to Hell*, pp. 70–71.

87. Abdi "Convergence," p. 189.

88. Arlene Elowe Macleod, *Accommodating Protest: Working Women, the New Veiling, and Change in Cairo* (New York: Columbia University Press, 1993).

89. Mukhtar, *Historical Dictionary of Somalia*, p. vii.

90. Maren, *The Road to Hell*, p. 283.

91. Marvin D. Raines, "Gaining Cooperation from a Multi-cultural Society of Respondents: A Review of the U.S. Census Bureau's Efforts to Count the Newly Immigrated Population," *Statistical Journal of the United Nations* 18 (2001): 217–226.

5. Dress in a Time of Extreme Change—1991 to 2010

The epigraph is from Sadia Ahmed, "Islam and Development: Opportunities and Constraints for Somali Women," *Gender and Development* 7, no. 1 (1999): 71.

1. Information in this paragraph comes from Mary-Jane Fox, "Political Culture in Somalia," p. 55; International Committee of the Red Cross, "The People on War Report: ICRC Worldwide Consultation on the Rules of War," pp. vii–viii (1999, http://www.icrc.org/Web/Eng/siteengo.nsf/htmlall/p0758/$File/ICRC_002_0758.PDF!Open); and UNHCR, "Refugees by Numbers 2006 Edition," 2006 http://www.unhcr.org/basics/BASICS/3b028097c.html#Numbers.

2. Abdi M. Kusow and Stephanie R. Bjork, "The Somali Diaspora in a Global Context," in *From Mogadishu to Dixon: The Somali Diaspora in a Global Context*, ed. Abdi M. Kusow and Stephanie R. Bjork (Trenton, N.J.: Red Sea Press, 2007), p. 5.

3. Hunt, *A General Survey*.

4. Field notes, January 2004.

5. Nuruddin Farah, *Yesterday, Tomorrow: Voices from the Somali Diaspora* (London, Cassell, 2000), p. v.

6. These interviews were conducted in 2002 as part of a research project on Somali dress and employment issues headed by Dr. Joanne Eicher at the University of Minnesota. Information on the total numbers of refugees is from Cindy Horst, "Transnational Nomads: How Somalis Cope with Refugee Life in the Dadaab Camps of Kenya," unpublished Ph.D. dissertation, University of Amsterdam, 2003, p. 82.

7. Horst, "Transnational Nomads," p. 64.

8. Sheikh, *A Camel for the Son*, p. 72.

9. By the late 1990s, all of the camps in Kenya had been consolidated into two large camps, Kakuma and Dadaab (Horst, "Transnational Nomads," p. 83).

10. Cawo Abdi, "Refugees, Gender-based Violence, and Resistance: A Case Study of Somali Refugee Women in Kenya," in *Women, Migration and Citizenship: Making Local, National, and Transnational Connections,* ed. Evangelia Tastsoglu and Alexandria Dobrowolski (London: Ashgate Press, 2006), pp. 231–251.

11. In 1993, Fowzia Musse interviewed 192 Somali survivors of rape in the Kenyan refugee camps. "War Crimes against Women and Girls," in *Somalia—The Untold Story: The War Through the Eyes of Somali Women,* ed. Judith Gardner and Judy El-Bushra (London: Pluto Press, 2004), pp. 69–96.

12. Musse, "War Crimes," pp. 105–106. Definitely not all Somalis would feel this way; however, there is a strong history in Somali culture of preserving virginity for marriage through female circumcision (FGM), which might explain this woman's point of view.

13. Ibid., p. 140.

14. See n8, above; Sheikh, *Ramadan Moon.* Selected images from the books can also be viewed at www.fazalsheikh.org.

15. For an extensive discussion, see Peter D. Little, *Somalia: Economy Without a State* (Bloomington: Indiana University Press, 2003).

16. Sadia Ahmed, "Islam and Development," p. 70.

17. Randy James, "A Brief History of Al-Shabab," *TIME Magazine,* 12/7/2009, http://www.time.com/time/world/article/0,8599,1945855,00.html. See also: Andrew Harding, "Meeting Somalia's Al-Shabab," BBC News, 7/3/2009, http://news.bbc .co.uk/2/hi/africa/8133127.stm.

18. Abdi, "Convergence," p. 192.

19. Abdi, "Refugees, Gender-based Violence, and Resistance."

20. Rima Berns McGown (2003), "Redefining Social Roles: The Extraordinary Strength of Somali Women," in *Women & Environments* 58–59: 13–14.

21. The goal of Operation Restore Hope, which was started by President Bush and ended by President Clinton, was initially to establish order in Somalia and protect aid workers who were trying to deliver food to the hundreds of thousands of Somalis in danger of starvation after warring factions destroyed crops and food supplies. These plans fell by the wayside, however, as soldiers became involved in a direct confrontation with Mohamed Farah Aydiid, leader of the USC and one of the most heavily armed warlords. After the famous incident in October 1993 (see chapter 1, n9)

President Clinton ordered the Marines to retreat for the next six months; in March 1994, the last of the U.S. forces pulled out of Somalia.

22. Julian Emerson, "Somalis Try to Fit In, Hold Onto Tradition," *Eau Claire (Wisconsin) Leader Telegram* (4/6/2003), 1A, p. 1.

23. The town of International Falls, for example, which sits along the Canadian border and is officially registered as the "icebox" of the United States, has a climate colder than some parts of Alaska. The Twin Cities are in southern Minnesota, but still experience at least six months of below-freezing temperatures each year.

24. These were some examples relayed to me by people in Minnesota who worked with refugees in the 1980s and '90s. More than one person confessed that these misunderstandings with Somalis led them to end their volunteer work with refugees. In contrast to Somalis, a fair number of Hmong and Vietnamese refugees were willing to attend church or convert to Christianity (at least in name), performing their own rituals at home.

25. Jessica Schaid and Zoltán Grossman, "The Somali Diaspora in Small Midwestern Communities: The Case of Barron, Wisconsin," in *From Mogadishu to Dixon: The Somali Diaspora in a Global Context,* ed. Abdi M. Kusow and Stephanie R. Bjork (Trenton, N.J.: Red Sea Press, 2007), pp. 295–319.

26. Burt Gilyard, "Street Fighting Man," *Minneapolis City Pages* (5/16/2001), p. 15.

27. Schaid and Grossman, "The Somali Diaspora," p. 308.

28. Ibid., p. 309. Economic development in northern Wisconsin has always lagged behind the southern half of the state. The cold climate and rocky terrain is not well suited to farming, and traditional industries such as logging and mining did not attract large numbers of permanent settlers to the area. In 2007, the average household income in Wisconsin was $50,578, but the average income in Barron was just $37,443. Even with the influx of Somalis, between 2000 and 2007 the town's population declined by 3.2% (http://www.city-data.com/city/Barron-Wisconsin.html).

29. Heather Marie Akou, "Building a New 'World Fashion': Islamic Dress in the 21st Century," *Fashion Theory* 11, no. 4 (2007): 403–421.

30. On issues of dress and respectability for women in an Islamic context see Macleod, *Accommodating Protest;* and Ladan Affi, "Domestic Conflict in the Diaspora: Somali Women Asylum Seekers and Refugees in Canada," in *Somalia—The Untold Story: The War Through the Eyes of Somali Women,* ed. Judith Gardner and Judy El-Bushra (London: Pluto Press, 2004), pp. 107–115.

31. Franklin Goza, "The Somali Presence in the United States: A Socio-Economic and Demographic Profile," in *From Mogadishu to Dixon: The Somali Diaspora in a Global Context,* ed. Abdi M. Kusow and Stephanie R. Bjork (Trenton, N.J.: Red Sea Press, 2007), p. 266.

32. Affi, "Domestic Conflict in the Diaspora," p. 108.

33. See n6, above.

34. Erin Carlyle, "Minneapolis Somali Community Facing Dark Web of Murders: They Came to Escape Civil War, So Why Are They Killing Each Other in the Streets?" *City Pages* (11/12/2008, http://www.citypages.com/2008-11-12/news/minneapolis-somali-community-facing-dark-web-of-murders/). The most famous example of dress-based gang symbolism might be the Bloods (red clothing) versus the Crips

(blue clothing), two gangs that emerged in southern California in the 1980s and spread throughout the United States. More recently, members of MS13 have become known for their highly visible tattoos and extremely violent tactics.

35. Art Hughes, "Somalis Outraged by Police Shooting, Minnesota Public Radio," 3/11/2002, http://news.minnesota.publicradio.org/features/200203/11_hughesa_mplsshooting/.

36. Personal communication with Dr. Catherine Daly, who wrote an expert testimony affidavit on the woman's behalf.

37. Shira Kantor, "Wardere Focuses on Trust, Police-community Relations," *The Minnesota Daily*, 8/15/2001, p. 1. Wardere received 160 votes in the primary election, putting him in 11th place out of 22 candidates.

38. See Molly Priesmeyer, "Witnesses Claim Somali Polling Place Translator Was Telling People to Vote for Coleman," *The Minnesota Independent*, 11/4/2008 (http://minnesotaindependent.com/16268/witnesses-claim-somali-translator-in-minneapolis-encouraged-voting-for-coleman).

39. The agency initially responsible for this was the INS, but after the Department of Homeland Security was created that agency was moved and renamed the Bureau of Citizenship and Immigration Services (BCIS).

40. Heather Marie Akou, "Hate Crimes and Profiling," in *September 11 in Popular Culture: A Guide,* ed. Sara E. Quay and Amy M. Damico (Santa Barbara, Calif.: ABC–CLIO, forthcoming). See also "Looking Like a Terrorist."

41. McGown, *Muslims in the Diaspora.*

42. Horst, "Transnational Nomads," p. 221.

43. Unfortunately, in Western high-rises—especially during the winter when residents cannot open their windows for any significant length of time—the smoke from frankincense tends to create a haze, setting off smoke detectors and causing a general smell throughout the building that is not necessarily appealing to non-Somalis. Even for Somalis who have become highly acculturated to the West and wear Western dress, the use of frankincense signals that they have not forgotten traditional culture.

44. I. Neri, et al., "Childhood Allergic Contact Dermatitis from Henna Tattoo," *Pediatric Dermatology* 19, no. 6 (2002): 503–505.

45. Pinky, "Welcome to Fashion Henna: Offering Beautiful Henna Designs All Over NJ Area," 2008, http://www.freewebs.com/fashionhenna/.

46. Ritva Koskennurmi-Sivonen, Jaana Koivula, and Seija Mailjala, "United Fashions: Making a Muslim Appearance in Finland," in *Fashion Theory* 8, no. 4 (2004): 446.

47. Picton, *The Art of African Textiles.*

48. Wahabbism was developed in the eighteenth century during European colonization and is the official doctrine of Saudi Arabia. This branch of Islam—which followers often claim to be the only true form of Islam—is based on rejection of innovation (especially foreign influences) as well as strict adherence to the Qur'an and the "five pillars" of Islam. The five daily prayers, for example, are a legally mandated part of everyday life in Saudi Arabia.

49. Citizenship laws vary tremendously from country to country and depend on a myriad of factors. Circumstances that increase an immigrant's chances of being

accepted for resettlement or citizenship include having a "credible fear" (a legal term indicating that a refugee's life would be in danger if he or she returned home), being educated, speaking the local language, and having relatives who are already legal immigrants or citizens. Chances of being accepted are reduced for people with criminal records, lack of education, and no ties to the country of resettlement. Some countries (like Germany, for example) have extremely strict citizenship laws that prevent even second- and third-generation immigrants from becoming citizens. Switzerland is another country known for isolating asylum-seekers in resettlements camps—sometimes for years—while their cases are pending.

50. Joanne B. Eicher and Barbara Sumberg (1995), "World Fashion, Ethnic, and National Dress," in *Dress and Ethnicity,* ed. Joanne B. Eicher (Oxford: Berg), pp. 295–306.

51. Heather Akou (2004), "Islamic Dress," in *Encyclopedia of Clothing and Fashion,* ed. Valerie Steele (New York: Charles Scribner's Sons), pp. 250–254.

52. Joanne Eicher, "Dress, Gender and the Public Display of Skin," in *Body Dressing,* ed. Joanne Entwistle and Elizabeth Wilson (Oxford: Berg, 2001), pp. 233–252; Fred Davis, *Fashion, Culture, and Identity* (Chicago: University of Chicago Press, 1994).

53. Abdi, "Convergence," p. 191; Akou, "Islamic Dress," p. 251.

54. Anu Isotalo, "'Did You See Her Standing at the Marketplace?' Gender, Gossip, and Socio-Spatial Behavior of Somali Girls in Finland," in *From Mogadishu to Dixon: The Somali Diaspora in a Global Context,* ed. Abdi M. Kusow and Stephanie R. Bjork (Trenton, N.J.: Red Sea Press, 2007), p. 186.

55. Koskennurmi-Sivonen et al., "United Fashions," p. 449.

56. Akou, "Nationalism Without a Nation," p. 91.

57. Abdi, "Convergence," p. 203.

58. The *chaadaree,* which was mandated for all Afghan women under the Taliban, covers the entire body from head to toe, leaving the wearer to view the world through a screen over her face. For more, see M. Catherine Daly, "The Afghan Woman's *Chaadaree:* An Evocative Religious Expression?"; and Linda B. Arthur, "School Uniforms as a Symbolic Metaphor for Competing Ideologies in Indonesia"; both in *Undressing Religion: Commitment and Conversion from a Cross-Cultural Perspective,* ed. Linda B. Arthur (Oxford: Berg, 2000), respectively pp. 131–146 and pp. 201–216.

59. Goza, "The Somali Presence in the United States," pp. 269–270.

60. Parminder Bhachu mentions the *salwar kamiz,* a fascinating garment, in *Dangerous Designs: Asian Women Fashion the Diaspora Economies* (New York: Routledge, 2004).

61. Goza, "The Somali Presence in the United States," p. 266.

62. Equal Employment Statement (http://www.brinkshofer.com/careers_equal_employment.cfm).

6. The Relevance of History

Geeta Anand and John W. Miller, "Hijacked on the High Seas," *Wall Street Journal* (1/31/2009), p. A1.

1. Catherine Philp, "Somali Pirates Hijack Saudi Oil Tanker With Britons on Board," *The Times* (London) (11/18/2008, http://www.timesonline.co.uk/tol/news /world/africa/article5172770.ece).

2. "End Piracy as a Business Model," *Seattle Times* (4/14/2009, http://seattletimes .nwsource.com/html/editorialsopinion/2009033602_edita14pirate.html).

3. The interviewer, Dave Davies, expressed surprised that the pirates were dressed "so casually." "Surviving a Somali Pirate Attack on the High Seas," NPR, "Fresh Air," 4/6/2010, http://www.npr.org/templates/story/story.php?storyId=125507354 &sc=emaf.

4. Ali Hersi, for example, conducted research for his dissertation, "The Arab Factor in Somali History" (University of California, Los Angeles, 1977), using Arab- and Farsi-language archives in the Middle East.

5. The only person I know of currently studying dress in Ethiopia is an art historian, Peri Klemm. See "Shaping the Future, Wearing the Past: Dress and the Decorated Female Body among the Afran Qallo Oromo in Eastern Hararghe, Ethiopia" (unpublished Ph.D. dissertation, Emory University, 2002). The only person doing research on dress in Yemen is Annelies Moors. See "Fashionable Muslims: Notions of Self, Religion, and Society in Sanà," in *Fashion Theory,* 11, nos. 2/3 (2007): 319–346. I do not know of anyone currently studying dress in Sudan or Djibouti.

6. I am grateful to Hazel for not only visiting Rajsi Brothers, but bringing back fabrics and information about this manufacturer. Hazel A. Lutz, "Design and Tradition in an India–West Africa Trade Textile: Zari Embroidered Velvets" (unpublished Ph.D. dissertation, University of Minnesota, 2003).

7. "Discourse on Moral Womanhood in Somali Popular Songs, 1960–1990," *Journal of African History* 50: 121–122.

8. Eric Hobsbawm and Terence Ranger, eds., *The Invention of Tradition* (Cambridge: Cambridge University Press, 1983).

9. "Janna," 6/26/2006, www.somaliaonline.com.

10. In academic conferences I have heard this lamentation expressed many times by Somali men, that things would be better if they (the men) could just sit down under a tree and talk in the traditional way. The Somali women I know are not so convinced, having been left out of the political process in the "good old days."

Bibliography

Abdi, Cawo Mohamed. "Convergence of Civil War and the Religious Right: Reimagining Somali Women." *Signs: Journal of Women in Culture and Society* 33, no. 1 (2007): 183–207.

———. "Refugees, Gender-based Violence, and Resistance: A Case Study of Somali Refugee Women in Kenya." In *Women, Migration, and Citizenship: Making Local, National, and Transnational Connections,* ed. Evangelia Tastsoglu and Alexandria Dobrowolski, 231–251. London: Ashgate Press, 2006.

Abdullahi, Mohamed Diriye. *Culture and Customs of Somalia.* Westport, Connecticut: Greenwood Press, 2001.

Adan, Amina H. "Somalia: An Illusory Political Nation-State." *South Asia Bulletin* 14, no. 1 (1994): 99–109.

Affi, Ladan. "Domestic Conflict in the Diaspora: Somali Women Asylum Seekers and Refugees in Canada." In *Somalia—The Untold Story: The War Through the Eyes of Somali Women,* ed. Judith Gardner and Judy El-Bushra, 107–115. London: Pluto Press, 2004.

Ahmed, Ali Jimale, ed. *The Invention of Somalia.* Lawrenceville, N.J.: Red Sea Press, 1995.

Ahmed, Sadia. "Islam and Development: Opportunities and Constraints for Somali Women." *Gender and Development* 7, no. 1 (1999): 69–72.

Akou, Heather Marie. "Building a New 'World Fashion': Islamic Dress in the 21st Century." *Fashion Theory* 11, no. 4 (2007): 403–421.

———. "Documenting the Origins of Somali Folk Dress: Evidence from the Bonaparte Collection." *Dress* 33 (2008): 7–19.

———. "Hate Crimes and Profiling." In *September 11 in Popular Culture: A Guide,* ed. Sara E. Quay and Amy M. Damico. Santa Barbara, Calif.: ABC–CLIO, 2010.

———. "Islamic Dress." In *Encyclopedia of Clothing and Fashion,* ed. Valerie Steele, 250–254. New York: Charles Scribner's Sons, 2004.

———. "Looking Like a Terrorist." In *September 11 in Popular Culture: A Guide,* ed. Sara E. Quay and Amy M. Damico. Santa Barbara, Calif.: ABC–CLIO, 2010.

———. "Macrocultures, Migration and Somali Malls: A Social History of Somali Dress and Aesthetics." Unpublished Ph.D. dissertation, University of Minnesota, 2005.

———. "More than Costume History: Dress in Somali Culture." In *Dress Sense: Emotional and Sensory Experiences of the Body and Clothes,* ed. Donald Clay Johnson and Helen Bradley Foster, 16–22. Oxford: Berg, 2007.

———. "Nationalism without a Nation: Understanding the Dress of Somali Women in Minnesota." In *Fashioning Africa: Power and the Politics of Dress,* ed. Jean Allman, 50–63. Bloomington: Indiana University Press, 2004.

Al-Azhari, Ahmed Omer. *Somalia's Arab, African and International Role.* Mogadishu, Somalia: Ministry of Information and National Guidance, 1980.

Ali, Ismail Mohamed. *Beautiful Somalia.* Mogadishu, Somalia: Ministry of Information and National Guidance, 1971.

Allman, Jean, ed. *Fashioning Africa: Power and the Politics of Dress.* Bloomington: Indiana University Press, 2004.

Al-Maamiry, Ahmed Hamoud. *Oman and East Africa.* New Delhi: Lancers Publishers, 1979.

Antinori, Alessandra Cardelli. "Ornamenti della Persona." In *Apetti dell'Espression Artistica in Somalia,* ed. Annarita Pullieli, 91–109. Rome: Baggatto Libri, 1988.

Arthur, Linda B. "School Uniforms as a Symbolic Metaphor for Competing Ideologies in Indonesia." In *Undressing Religion: Commitment and Conversion from a Cross-Cultural Perspective,* ed. Linda B. Arthur, 201–216. Oxford: Berg, 2000.

Barbosa, Duarte. *A Description of the Coasts of East Africa and Malabar in the Beginning of the Sixteenth Century.* London: Hakluyt Society, 1866. English translation from a Spanish translation of the original Portuguese.

Barnes, Ruth, and Joanne B. Eicher, eds. *Dress and Gender: Making and Meaning in Cultural Contexts.* Oxford: Berg Publishers, 1992.

Barnes, Virginia Lee, and Janice Boddy. *Aman: The Story of a Somali Girl.* New York: Vintage, 1994.

Beachey, Richard W. "The East African Ivory Trade in the Nineteenth Century." *Journal of African History* 8, no. 2 (1967): 269–290.

Benitez-Johannot, Purissima, and Jean Paul Barbier. *Shields: Africa, Southeast Asia and Oceania, from the Collections of the Barbier-Mueller Museum.* Munich: Prestel, 2000.

Berns McGown, Rima. *Muslims in the Diaspora: The Somali Communities of London and Toronto.* Toronto: University of Toronto Press, 1999.

———. "Redefining Social Roles: The Extraordinary Strength of Somali Women." *Women & Environments* 58–59 (2003): 13–14.

Besteman, Catherine. *Unraveling Somalia: Race, Violence and the Legacy of Slavery.* Philadelphia: University of Pennsylvania Press, 1999.

Bhachu, Parminder. *Dangerous Designs: Asian Women Fashion the Diaspora Economies.* New York: Routledge, 2004.

Bilgrami, Noorjehan. *The Traditional Fabric of Pakistan: Sindh Jo Ajrak.* Lahore: OUP Pakistan, 1998.

Bogatyrev, Petr. *The Functions of Folk Costume in Moravian Slovakia.* Translated from Slovak by Richard G. Crum. The Hague: Mouton, 1971 [1937].

Bohlander, Richard E., ed. *World Explorers and Discoverers.* New York: Macmillan, 1992.

Bowden, Mark. *Black Hawk Down: A Story of Modern War.* New York: Atlantic Monthly Press, 1999.

Bowen, John R. *Why the French Don't Like Headscarves: Islam, the State, and Public Space.* Princeton, N.J.: Princeton University Press, 2007.

Bricchetti, Luigi. *Somalia e Benadir: Viaggio di Esplorazione nell'Africa Orientale.* Milan: Societa Editrice La Poligrafica, 1902.

Bridges, Roy. "The Visit of Frederick Forbes to the Somali Coast in 1833." *The International Journal of African Historical Studies* 19, no. 4 1986: 679–691.

Burton, Richard F. *First Footsteps in East Africa or, An Exploration of Harar.* Mineola, N.Y.: Dover Publications, 1987. Originally published by Tylston and Edwards, London, 1856.

Carleton, G. D. "Notes on a Part of the Somali Country." *The Journal of the Anthropological Institute of Great Britain and Ireland* 21 (1892): 160–172.

Cassanelli, Lee V. *The Shaping of Somali Society: Reconstructing the History of a Pastoral People, 1600–1900.* Philadelphia: University of Pennsylvania Press, 1982.

Chavez, Leo R. "Immigration and Medical Anthropology." In *American Arrivals: Anthropology Engages the New Immigration,* ed. Nancy Foner, 197–228. Santa Fe, N.M.: School of American Research Press, 2003.

Corni, Guido. *Somalia Italiana,* vol. 2. Milan: Editoriale Arte e Storia, 1937.

Daly, M. Catherine. "The Afghan Woman's *Chaadaree:* An Evocative Religious Expression?" In *Undressing Religion: Commitment and Conversion from a Cross-Cultural Perspective,* ed. Linda B. Arthur, 131–146. Oxford: Berg, 2000.

Davis, Fred. *Fashion, Culture, and Identity.* Chicago: University of Chicago Press, 1994.

Deans, Phil, and Hugo Dobson. "Introduction: East Asian Postage Stamps as Socio-Political Artefacts." *East Asia* 22, no. 2 (2005): 3–7.

Declich, Francesca. "Identity, Dance and Islam Among People with Bantu origins in Riverine Areas of Somalia." In *The Invention of Somalia,* ed. Ali Jimale Ahmed, 191–222. Lawrenceville, N.J.: Red Sea Press, 1995.

D'Haem, Jeanne. *The Last Camel: True Stories of Somalia.* Lawrenceville, N.J.: Red Sea Press, 1997.

Dirie, Waris, and Cathleen Miller. *Desert Flower: The Extraordinary Journey of a Desert Nomad.* New York: Quill, 1998.

Dorward, D. C. "Precolonial Tiv Trade and Cloth Currency." In *The International Journal of African Historical Studies* 9, no. 4 (1976): 576–591.

Drake-Brockman, Ralph E. *British Somaliland.* London: Hurst & Blackett, 1912.

Durrill, Wayne. "Atrocious Misery: The African Origins of Famine in Northern Somalia, 1839–1884." *The American Historical Review* 91, no. 2 (1976): 287–306.

Eicher, Joanne B. "Dress." In *Routledge International Encyclopedia of Women: Global Women's Issues and Knowledge,* ed. Cheris Kramarae and Dale Spender, 422–423. New York: Routledge, 2000.

———. "Dress, Gender and the Public Display of Skin." In *Body Dressing,* ed. Joanne Entwistle and Elizabeth Wilson, 233–252. Oxford: Berg, 2001.

Eicher, Joanne B., and Barbara Sumberg. "World Fashion, Ethnic and National Dress." In *Dress and Ethnicity: Change Across Space and Time,* ed. Joanne B. Eicher, 295–306. Oxford: Berg, 1995.

Export Statistics of Silk & Man-made Fibre Textiles, 1981–82. Bombay: The Silk & Rayon Textiles Export Promotion Council, 1982.

Fair, Laura. "Dressing Up: Clothing, Class and Gender in Post-abolition Zanzibar." *Journal of African History* 39 (1998): 63–94.

Fanon, Franz. *Studies in a Dying Colonialism.* New York: Grove Press, 1965. Originally published in 1959 in France as *L'An Cinq de la Révolution Algérienne.*

Farah, Nuruddin. *Yesterday, Tomorrow: Voices from the Somali Diaspora.* London, Cassell, 2000.

Fernea, Elizabeth Warnock, and Robert A. Fernea. *The Arab World: Forty Years of Change,* revised edition. New York: Anchor Books, 1997 [1985].

Fox, Lilla M. *Folk Costume of Western Europe.* Boston: Plays, Inc., 1969.

Fox, Mary-Jane. "Political Culture in Somalia: Tracing Paths to Peace and Conflict." Unpublished Ph.D. dissertation, Uppsala University (Sweden), 2000.

Gervase, Matthew. "Chinese Porcelain in East Africa and on the Coast of South Arabia." *Oriental Art* 2 (1961): pp. 50–55.

Godbeer, Deardre. *Somalia.* New York: Chelsea House, 1988.

Goodrum, Alison L. *National Fabric: Fashion, Britishness, Globalization.* Oxford: Berg, 2005.

Goza, Franklin. "The Somali Presence in the United States: A Socio-economic and Demographic Profile." In *From Mogadishu to Dixon: The Somali Diaspora in a Global Context,* ed. Abdi M. Kusow and Stephanie R. Bjork, 255–274. Trenton, N.J.: Red Sea Press, 2007.

Grottanelli, Vinigi L. "Asiatic Influences on Somali Culture." *Ethnos* 4 (1947): 153–181.

Guenther, Irene. *Nazi Chic? Fashioning Women in the Third Reich.* Oxford: Berg, 2004.

Gundel, Joakim. "The Migration-Development Nexus: Somalia Case Study." *International Migration* 40, no. 5 (2002): 255–279.

Hamdun, Said, and Noël King. *Ibn Battuta in Black Africa,* revised ed. Princeton, N.J.: Marcus Wiener, 1998.

Hassan, Abdullahi Mohamed. *Jaale Siyad's OAU Chairmanship, June 1974–1975.* Mogadishu, Somalia: Ministry of Information and National Guidance, 1975.

Hassan, Salah M. *The Art of African Fashion.* Trenton, N.J.: Africa World Press, 1998.

Hawley, Ruth. *Omani Silver.* London: Longman Group, 1978.

Hendrickson, Hildi. "Bodies and Flags: The Representation of Herero Identity in Colonial Namibia." In *Clothing and Difference: Embodied Identities in Colonial and Post-Colonial Africa,* ed. Hildi Hendrickson, 213–244. Durham, N.C.: Duke University Press, 1996.

Hersi, Ali Abdirahman. "The Arab Factor in Somali History: The Origins and the Development of Arab Enterprise and Cultural Influences in the Somali Peninsula." Unpublished Ph.D. dissertation, University of California, Los Angeles, 1977.

Hobsbawm, Eric, and Terence Ranger, eds. *The Invention of Tradition.* Cambridge: Cambridge University Press, 1983.

Horst, Cindy. "Transnational Nomads: How Somalis Cope with Refugee Life in the Dadaab Camps of Kenya." Unpublished Ph.D. dissertation, University of Amsterdam, 2003.

Hunt, John A. *A General Survey of the Somaliland Protectorate, 1944–1950.* Hargeisa, Somalia: Somaliland Protectorate and the Crown Agents for the Colonies, 1951.

Isotalo, Anu. "'Did You See Her Standing at the Marketplace?' Gender, Gossip, and Socio-Spatial Behavior of Somali Girls in Finland." In *From Mogadishu to Dixon: The Somali Diaspora in a Global Context,* ed. Abdi M. Kusow and Stephanie R. Bjork, 181–206. Trenton, N.J.: Red Sea Press, 2007.

Jardine, Douglas. "Somaliland: The Cinderella of the Empire." *Journal of the Royal African Society* 22, no. 94 (1925): 105–106.

Jeffrey, Keith. "Crown, Communication and the Colonial Post: Stamps, the Monarchy and the British Empire." *The Journal of Imperial and Commonwealth History* 34, no. 1 (March 2006): 45–70.

Johnson, Marion. "Cotton Imperialism in West Africa." *African Affairs* 73, no. 291 (1974): 178–187.

Jones, Carla, and Ann Marie Leshkowich. "Introduction: The Globalization of Asian Dress: Re-Orienting Fashion or Re-Orientalizing Asia?" In *Re-Orienting Fashion: The Globalization of Asian Dress,* ed. Sandra Niessen, Ann Marie Leshkowich, and Carla Jones, 1–48. Oxford: Berg, 2004.

Jonsson, Hjorleifur R., and Nora A. Taylor. "National Colors: Ethnic Minorities in Vietnamese Public Imagery." In *Re-Orienting Fashion: The Globalization of Asian Dress,* ed. Sandra Niessen, Ann Marie Leshkowich, and Carla Jones, 159–184. Oxford: Berg, 2003.

Kapteijns, Lidwien. "Discourse on Moral Womanhood in Somali Popular Songs, 1960–1990." *Journal of African History* 50 (2009): 101–122.

———. *Women's Voices in a Man's World: Women and the Pastoral Tradition in Northern Somali Orature, c. 1899–1980.* Portsmouth, N.H.: Heinemann, 1999.

Kassim, Mohamed M. "Aspects of the Benadir Cultural History: The Case of the Bravan Ulama." In *The Invention of Somalia,* ed. Ali Jimale Ahmed, 29–42. Lawrenceville, N.J.: Red Sea Press, 1995.

King, J. S. "Notes on the Folk-Lore and Some Social Customs of the Western Somali Tribes (Continued)." *The Folk-Lore Journal* 6, no. 2 (1888): 119–125.

Kirk, J. W. C. "The Yebirs and Midgans of Somaliland, Their Traditions and Dialects." *Journal of the Royal African Society* 4, no. 13 (1904): 91–108.

Klemm, Peri Marka. "Shaping the Future, Wearing the Past: Dress and the Decorated Female Body among the Afran Qallo Oromo in Eastern Hararghe, Ethiopia." Unpublished Ph.D. dissertation, Emory University, 2000.

Koskennurmi-Sivonen, Ritva, Jaana Koivula, and Seija Mailjala. "United Fashions: Making a Muslim Appearance in Finland." In *Fashion Theory* 8, no. 4 (2004): 443–460.

Kusow, Abdi M., and Stephanie R. Bjork. "The Somali Diaspora in a Global Context." In *From Mogadishu to Dixon: The Somali Diaspora in a Global Context,* ed. Abdi M. Kusow and Stephanie R. Bjork, 1–44. Trenton, N.J.: Red Sea Press, 2007.

Laitin, David D., and Said S. Samatar. *Somalia: Nation in Search of a State.* Boulder, Colo.: Westview Press, 1987.

Laurence, Margaret. *The Prophet's Camel Bell.* London: Macmillan, 1963.

Lauritzen, Frederick. "Propaganda Art in the Postage Stamps of the Third Reich." *The Journal of Decorative Arts* 10 (1988): 62–79.

Lennon, Alexander T. J. *The Battle for Hearts and Minds: Using Soft Power to Undermine Terrorist Networks.* Cambridge, Mass.: MIT Press, 2003.

Lewis, I. M. *Blood and Bone: The Call of Kinship in Somali Society,* Trenton, N.J.: Red Sea Press, 1994.

———. *A Modern History of the Somali: Nation and State in the Horn of Africa,* 4th edition. Oxford: James Currey, 2002.

———. *Peoples of the Horn of Africa: Somalis, Afar and Saho.* London: International African Institute, 1955.

———. "Visible and Invisible Differences: The Somali Paradox." In *Africa: Journal of the International African Institute* 74, no. 4 (2004): 489–515.

Little, Peter D. *Somalia: Economy Without a State.* Bloomington: Indiana University Press, 2003.

Loughran, Katheryne S., John L. Loughran, John William Johnson, and Said Sheikh Samatar. *Somalia in Word and Image.* Washington, D.C.: Foundation for Cross Cultural Understanding, 1986.

Luling, Virginia. *Somali Sultanate: The Geledi City-State Over 150 Years.* Piscataway, N.J.: Transaction Publishers, 2003.

Luttman, Ilsemargret, ed. *Mode in Afrika: Mode als Mittel der Selbstinszenierung und Ausdruck der Moderne.* Hamburg, Germany: Museum für Völkerkunde, 2005.

Lutz, Hazel A. "Design and Tradition in an India–West Africa Trade Textile: Zari Embroidered Velvets." Unpublished Ph.D. dissertation, University of Minnesota, 2003.

Macleod, Arlene Elowe. *Accommodating Protest: Working Women, the New Veiling, and Change in Cairo.* New York: Columbia University Press, 1993.

Manning, Patrick. *Slavery and African Life: Occidental, Oriental, and African Slave Trades.* Cambridge: Cambridge University Press, 1990.

Maren, Michael. *The Road to Hell: The Ravaging Effects of Foreign Aid and International Charity.* New York: Free Press, 1997.

Martin, Esmond B., and T. C. I. Ryan. "The Slave Trade of the Bajun and Benadir Coasts." *Transafrican Journal of History* 9, no. 1 (1980): 103–132.

Martineau, André. *Djibouti,* 2nd edition. Boulogne-Billancourt, France: Delroisse, 1977.

McMahon, Kathryn. "The Former Museums of Somalia." Unpublished report collected by the Smithsonian National Museum of African Art, 1991.

Miles, S. B. "On the Somali Country." *Proceedings of the Royal Geographical Society of London* 16, no. 3 (1871–1872): 149–158.

Moors, Annelies. "Fashionable Muslims: Notions of Self, Religion, and Society in Sanà." *Fashion Theory* 11, nos. 2/3 (2007): 319–346.

Mukhtar, Mohamed Haji. *Historical Dictionary of Somalia,* rev. ed. Lanham, Md.: Scarecrow Press, 2003 [1975].

Musse, Fowzia. "War Crimes against Women and Girls." In *Somalia—The Untold Story: The War Through the Eyes of Somali Women,* ed. Judith Gardner and Judy El-Bushra, 69–96. London: Pluto Press, 2004.

Myers, Fred R. (2001). "Introduction: The Empire of Things." In *The Empire of Things: Regimes of Value and Material Culture*, ed. Fred R. Myers, 3–64. Santa Fe, N.M.: School of American Research Press, 2001.

Neri, I., E. Guareschi, F. Savoia, and A. Patrizi. "Childhood Allergic Contact Dermatitis from Henna Tattoo." *Pediatric Dermatology* 19, no. 6 (2002): 503–505.

Nicholson, G. Edward. "The Production, History, Uses and Relationships of Cotton (*Gossypium* spp.) in Ethiopia." *Economic Botany* 14, no. 1 (1960): 3–36.

Pankhurst, Richard. *Economic History of Ethiopia*. Addis Ababa, Ethiopia: Haile Selassie I University, 1968.

———. *An Introduction to the Economic History of Ethiopia from Early Times to 1800*. London: Sidgwick and Jackson, Ltd., 1961.

Parkins, Wendy. "Introduction: (Ad)dressing Citizens." In *Fashioning the Body Politic: Dress, Citizenship, Gender*, ed. Wendy Parkins, 1–18. Oxford: Berg, 2002.

Paulitschke, Phillip. *Ethnographie Nordost-Afrikas: Die Materielle Cultur der Danâkil, Galla und Somâl*. Berlin: Geographische Verlagshandlung Dietrich Reimer, 1893.

Pickthall, Muhammad Marmaduke. *The Meaning of the Glorious Qur'ān: Text and Explanatory Translation*. Mecca: Muslim World League, 1979.

Picton, John. *The Art of African Textiles: Technology, Tradition and Lurex*. London: Barbican Art Gallery, 1999.

Prussin, Labelle. *Nomadic Architecture: Space, Place, Gender*. Washington, D.C.: Smithsonian Institution Press, 1995.

Puccioni, Nello. *Anthropology and Ethnography of the People of Somalia*. Trans. Kathryn A. Looney. Human Relations Area Files, 1960. Originally published by Reale Società Geografica Italiana, Bologna, Italy, 1936.

Raines, Marvin D. "Gaining Cooperation from a Multi-cultural Society of Respondents: A Review of the U.S. Census Bureau's Efforts to Count the Newly Immigrated Population." *Statistical Journal of the United Nations* 18 (2001): 217–226.

Raunig, Walter. "Yemen and Ethiopia—Ancient Cultural Links between Two Neighboring Countries on the Red Sea." In *Yemen: 3000 Years of Art and Civilisation in Arabia Felix*, ed. Werner Daum, 409–418. Innsbruck, Austria: Pinguin-Verlag, 1988.

Révoil, Georges. *Voyage aux Pays Çomalis: Dix Mois a la Côte Orientale d'Afrique*. Paris: Challamel et Cie, Éditeurs, 1889.

Rigby, C. P. "On the Origins of the Somali Race, Which Inhabits the North-eastern Portion of Africa." *Transactions of the Ethnological Society of London* 5 (1867): 91–95.

Robecchi-Bricchetti, Luigi. *Dal Benadir*. Milan: Società Antischiavista d'Italia, 1904.

Roces, Mina. "Trans-National Flows and the Politics of Dress in Asia and the Americas." In *The Politics of Dress in Asia and the Americas*, ed. Mina Roces and Louise Edwards, 1–18. Brighton, U.K.: Sussex Academic Press, 2007.

Roces, Mina, and Louise Edwards, eds. *The Politics of Dress in Asia and the Americas*. Brighton, U.K.: Sussex Academic Press, 2007.

Ross, Doran, ed. *Wrapped in Pride: Ghanaian Kente and African American Identity*. Los Angeles: UCLA Fowler Museum of Cultural History, 1998.

Ruhlen, Rebecca N. "Korean Alterations: Nationalism, Social Consciousness, and 'Traditional' Clothing." In *Re-Orienting Fashion: The Globalization of Asian Dress*, ed. Sandra Niessen, Ann Marie Leshkowich, and Carla Jones, 117–137. Oxford: Berg, 2003.

Saliklis, Ruta. "The Dynamic Relationship Between Lithuanian National Costumes and Folk Dress." In *Folk Dress in Europe and Anatolia: Beliefs about Protection and Fertility*, ed. Linda Welters, 211–234. Oxford: Berg, 1999.

Samatar, Abdi Ismail. *The State and Rural Transformation in Northern Somalia, 1884–1986*. Madison: University of Wisconsin Press, 1989.

Sandıkcı, Özlem, and Guliz Ger. "Aesthetics, Ethics and Politics of the Turkish Headscarf." In *Clothing as Material Culture*, ed. Suzanne Küchler and Daniel Miller, 61–82. Oxford: Berg, 2005.

Schaid, Jessica, and Zoltán Grossman (2007). "The Somali Diaspora in Small Midwestern Communities: The Case of Barron, Wisconsin." In *From Mogadishu to Dixon: The Somali Diaspora in a Global Context*, ed. Abdi M. Kusow and Stephanie R. Bjork, 295–319. Trenton, N.J.: Red Sea Press, 2007.

Schoff, William H. (1912). *The Periplus of the Erythraean Sea: Travel and Trade in the Indian Ocean by a Merchant of the First Century*. Annotated translation from Greek. New York: Longmans, Green, and Co., 1912.

Scott, Joan Wallach. *The Politics of the Veil*. Princeton, N.J.: Princeton University Press, 2007.

Sheikh, Fazal. *A Camel for the Son*. Winterthur, Switzerland: Volkart Foundation, 2001.

———. *Ramadan Moon*. Winterthur, Switzerland: Volkart Foundation, 2001.

Sheik-Abdi, Abdi. *Divine Madness: Mohammed Abdulle Hassan (1856–1920)*. London: Zed, 1993.

Shirazi, Faegheh. "Islamic Religion and Women's Dress Code: The Islamic Republic of Iran." In *Undressing Religion: Commitment and Conversion from a Cross-Cultural Perspective*, ed. Linda B. Arthur, 113–130. Oxford: Berg, 2000.

Slinkard, Petra. "Dreadlocks in Babylon: Techniques and Motivations for Wearing Dreadlocked Hair in Southern Indiana." Unpublished M.S. thesis, Indiana University, 2008.

Stillman, Yedida Kalfon. *Arab Dress: A Short History from the Dawn of Islam to Modern Times*, ed. Norman A. Stillman. Leiden, the Netherlands: Brill, 2000.

Stitziel, Judd. *Fashioning Socialism: Clothing, Politics, and Consumer Culture in East Germany*. Oxford: Berg, 2005.

Stoetzer, Carlos. *Postage Stamps as Propaganda*. Washington, D.C.: Public Affairs Press, 1953.

Summerfield, Hazel. "Patterns of Adaptation: Somali and Bangladeshi Women in Britain." In *Migrant Women: Crossing Boundaries and Changing Identities*, ed. Gina Buijs, 83–98. Oxford: Berg, 1993.

Swayne, Harald G. C. *Seventeen Trips through Somaliland and a Visit to Abyssinia*, 3rd edition. London: Rowland Ward, 1903.

Tarlo, Emma. *Visibly Muslim: Fashion, Politics, Faith*. Oxford: Berg, 2010.

Taylor, Lou. *The Study of Dress History*. Manchester, U.K.: Manchester University Press, 2002.

Tohidi, Nayereh. "International Connections of the Iranian Women's Movement." In *Iran and the Surrounding World: Interactions in Culture and Cultural Politics,* ed. Nikke R. Keddie and Rudi Matthee, 205–231. Seattle: University of Washington Press, 2002.

Warsame, Ali A. "How a Strong Government Backed an African Language: The Lessons of Somalia." *International Review of Education* 47, nos. 3/4 (2001): 341–360.

Welters, Linda. "Women's Folk Costume in Attica, Greece." In *Traditional Folk Textiles and Dress,* ed. Barbara K. Nordquist, E. Jean Mettam, and Kathy Jansen. Dubuque, Iowa: Kendall/Hunt, 1986.

White, Shane, and Graham White. *Stylin': African American Expressive Culture, from Its Beginnings to the Zoot Suit.* Ithaca, N.Y.: Cornell University Press, 1999.

Wickramasinghe, Nira. *Dressing the Colonised Body: Politics, Clothing, and Identity in Colonial Sri Lanka.* New Delhi, India: Orient Longman, 2003.

Wrigley, Richard. *The Politics of Appearances: Representations of Dress in Revolutionary France.* Oxford: Berg, 2002.

Index

Heather Marie Akou

is Assistant Professor of Dress Studies
and Fashion Design at Indiana University–
Bloomington. Her work appears in
Contemporary African Fashion
(IUP, 2010) and *Fashioning
Africa* (IUP, 2004).

www.ingramcontent.com/pod-product-compliance
Lightning Source LLC
Chambersburg PA
CBHW071425180526
45170CB00001B/228